The BED -and- BREAKFAST Traveler

"From Victoria to Vancouver in the north to San Francisco in the south, *The Bed and Breakfast Traveler* covers the B&B scene like a blanket. Make this book your B&B bible."
—Joseph Kula, travel editor, *The Vancouver Province*

"Lewis Green has created a high-quality, useful guide . . . by combining the three most essential elements of good travel writing: selectivity, practicality, and sound judgment."
—Knute Berger, executive editor, *Washington* magazine

"The Bed and Breakfast Traveler is a departure from the usual bed-and-breakfast fare—which generally are just lists of inns often subsidized by the inns themselves. It's a more selective book, and not merely a directory."
—Cary Ordway, *Bellevue Journal-American*

"Green is a seasoned travel writer and draws from his first-hand knowledge and unyielding standards for quality and excellence."
—*Arizona Senior's World*

"If bed-and-breakfasts are your idea of fine vacationing, *The Bed and Breakfast Traveler* is your season ticket to a wonderful season on the West Coast."
—*Northwest Briefs*

The BED -and- BREAKFAST Traveler

Touring the West Coast

by Lewis Green

A Voyager Book

The Globe Pequot Press

Chester, Connecticut 06412

Cover: The Gaslight Inn, Seattle. Illustration by Jerome Fellrath.
Back-cover map: Steven Fisher
Book design: Judy Petry

Previously published by Pacific Search Press.

LIBRARY OF CONGRESS CATALOGING-IN-PUBLICATION DATA

Green, Lewis.
     The Bed and breakfast traveler.

     Includes indexes.
     1. Northwest, Pacific—Description and travel—
1981–   —Guide-books. 2. Bed and breakfast
accommodations—Northwest, Pacific—Guide-books.
I. Title.
F852.3.G74   1987   917.95'04   86-25591
ISBN 0-931397-18-9

Manufactured in the United States of America
First Edition/Second Printing, November 1987

First Globe Pequot Press edition

Contents

INTRODUCTION   7
CALIFORNIA   8
    San Francisco   11
    The Wine Country   41
    The Gold Country   73
    The Interstate 5 Corridor   91
    The North Coast   102
OREGON   123
    Portland   125
    The Oregon Coast   133
    Oregon's Heartland   155
WASHINGTON   177
    Seattle   179
    Washington's Islands   198
    The Olympic Peninsula   225
    Inland Washington   239
BRITISH COLUMBIA   259
    Victoria   261
    Vancouver   273
INDEX TO PLACES   284
INDEX TO BED-AND-BREAKFAST INNS   285

Introduction

*G*enerally, travel books come in two styles—the directory or encyclopedia of listings, or the guidebook, which describes a geographic region. For the traveler, this has often meant buying two books. With this effort, I hope that problem has been solved, at least for the reader whose first choice of lodging is bed and breakfast.

While the recommended lodgings are bed-and-breakfast inns, this is not another bed-and-breakfast book. Enough of those already weigh down bookstore shelves. Instead, this is a guidebook to a region that includes Northern California, Oregon, Washington, and the British Columbian cities of Vancouver and Victoria.

This book is designed both to assist you in creating a customized vacation and to offer you insight into this diverse region. It offers suggestions of things to see and do, as well as dining recommendations. In addition, it describes in some detail most of this area's finest bed-and-breakfast inns.

All of the information offered here comes from my personal experiences or from interviews with hundreds of insiders, including frequent travelers, innkeepers, restaurateurs, and travel writers. At the time of publication, all information is accurate. But keep in mind that the travel industry is always in a state of change, places come and go, and prices fluctuate. For those reasons, as well as others, it is inevitable that inaccuracies will creep onto these pages. I welcome letters from readers concerning changes and offering suggestions.

For your convenience, lodging rates are for two people. In the section on British Columbia, prices are given in Canadian currency.

If you would like to correspond, send your letters to: Lewis Green, P.O. Box 20744, Seattle, WA 98102.

ANGWIN
    Forest Manor
CALISTOGA
    Foothill House
CHICO
    Bullard House
EUREKA
    Carter House
FERNDALE
    The Gingerbread Mansion
FORT BRAGG
    The Grey Whale Inn
GEORGETOWN
    American River Inn
GEYSERVILLE
    Hope-Merrill House
GRASS VALLEY
    Murphy's Inn
HEALDSBURG
    Camellia Inn
    Grape Leaf Inn
    Haydon House
IONE
    The Heirloom
JACKSON
    Gate House Inn
LITTLE RIVER
    Glendeven
    The Victorian Farmhouse

MENDOCINO
    The Headlands Inn
    Joshua Grindle Inn
    Whitegate Inn
MURPHYS
    Dunbar House
NAPA
    Beazley House
    Coombs Residence
    The Old World Inn
NEVADA CITY
    Red Castle Inn
POINT REYES STATION
    Holly Tree Inn
RED BLUFF
    The Faulkner House
SACRAMENTO
    Amber House
    The Briggs House
SANTA ROSA
    Melitta Station Inn
ST. HELENA
    The Ambrose Bierce House
    Bartels Ranch
    Chestelson House
    Cinnamon Bear
    The Ink House
    Villa St. Helena
SUTTER CREEK
    The Foxes

California

OREGON

N

PACIFIC OCEAN

NEVADA

Eureka

Ferndale

Red Bluff

101

5

Chico

Fort Bragg
Mendocino
Little River

Nevada City
Grass Valley

Georgetown

1

29

Geyserville

80

Healdsburg
128

Calistoga
Angwin
St. Helena

Sacramento

Sutter Creek
Jackson

Santa
Rosa

Napa

Ione

49

Murphys

Point Reyes
Station

San Francisco

Sonora

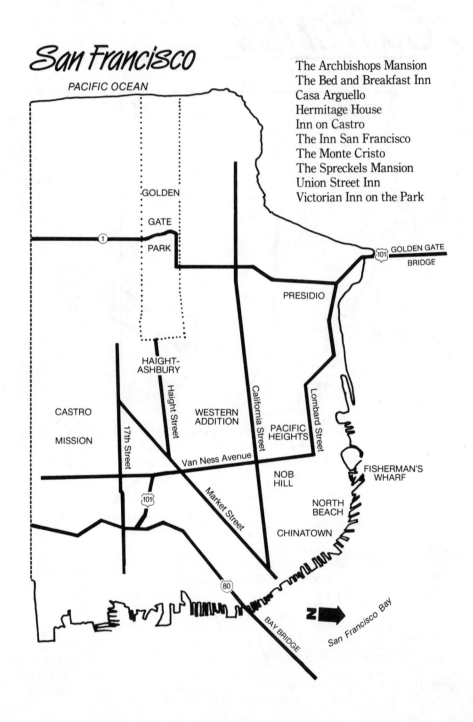

San Francisco

PACIFIC OCEAN

The Archbishops Mansion
The Bed and Breakfast Inn
Casa Arguello
Hermitage House
Inn on Castro
The Inn San Francisco
The Monte Cristo
The Spreckels Mansion
Union Street Inn
Victorian Inn on the Park

GOLDEN

GATE

PARK

1

GOLDEN GATE
101
BRIDGE

PRESIDIO

HAIGHT-
ASHBURY

CASTRO

MISSION

17th Street

Haight Street

WESTERN
ADDITION

California Street

Lombard Street

PACIFIC
HEIGHTS

Van Ness Avenue

NOB
HILL

FISHERMAN'S
WHARF

101

Market Street

NORTH
BEACH

CHINATOWN

80

N

BAY BRIDGE

San Francisco Bay

San Francisco

*T*o music lovers, it is home to the heart. To former President Taft, it was "The city that knows how." Local columnist and punster Herb Caen describes it as "The city that knows chow." To Californians, it is known simply as "The City."

San Francisco—a city of hills, restaurants, and neighborhoods. There is no denying its natural charms. Surrounded on three sides by water, the city's skyscrapers, Victorians, and greenbelts rise out of the waters and roll across a compact landscape that measures a mere forty-nine square miles. From atop nearly every one of San Francisco's forty-three hills, visitors can view the city spreading out to meet the sea.

As it reaches out to touch green-gray waters, San Francisco calls attention to itself in myriad ways. World-renowned museums such as the De Young and the Museum of Modern Art meld with the architectural wonders of the Palace of Fine Arts and the Transamerica Pyramid. Nowhere are the performing arts more alive and well. The War Memorial Opera House hosts both the San Francisco Opera and the San Francisco Ballet, while the Louise M. Davies Symphony Hall is home to the San Francisco Symphony. Internationally acclaimed, the American Conservatory Theatre presents a year-round schedule of classical and modern drama at the Geary Theatre. And nightclubs and discos are scattered throughout San Francisco, with the greatest concentration found downtown in the North Beach district.

Above all else, San Francisco is a Mecca for shoppers and diners. In the heart of "Shoppers' World" sprawls Union Square. Here Macy's, Neiman-Marcus, I. Magnin, and Saks spread their fashionable and pricey wares. But smart shoppers do not stop here: they let their plastic travel around the city, from the nearby Embarcadero Center, to the waterfront's Ghirardelli Square and the Cannery, to trendy and expensive Union Street.

Like the smart shopper, wise and wary gastronomes select their eateries carefully. With more than forty-three hundred restaurants to choose from, one for every 158 residents, diners should watch out for tourist traps, where food is mediocre and overpriced. Do not assume that the best in seafood is to be found at Fisherman's Wharf or that Chinatown boasts all of the city's finest Chinese restaurants. Life exists beyond the borders of downtown.

That brings me to my San Francisco—the neighborhoods. Within these polyglot enclaves you discover both the energy of New York and the easy style of Seattle. So after you have donned your tweeds and discovered downtown, get into something comfortable and explore its soul—the neighborhoods.

Of the city's 720,000 people, one out of every three comes from a home where English is a second language. San Francisco boasts a rich ethnic heritage, which is the result of more than 120,000 citizens of Chinese ancestry, some 100,000 Italians, and some 84,000 Hispanics. This cultural diversity has spawned a city of variety, one that is both worldly and accepting.

Adrenalin pulses through my veins when I walk down Haight among aging hippies, brash punks, and stylish New Wavers. My taste buds water within the confines of Japantown and Chinatown. Sophistication taps my spirit as I stroll with the chic hip down Union Street. An appreciation for alternative lifestyles opens my mind in The Castro. I love the rhythm of San Francisco's working and family people in the Mission. And seeing South of Market rise from the ashes of decline to one of residences, cafés, and clubs gives me a sense of the city's courage and life force.

The boundaries of San Francisco's communities merge and meld. Sometimes it is hard to tell where one ends and another begins. Yet each district has a heart that beats to its own drummer, from the steady syncopations of blue collar Mission to the up-tempo hums of Pacific Heights.

GETTING TO KNOW SAN FRANCISCO

DOWNTOWN

San Francisco's hub is bordered by Market Street to the south, Van Ness Avenue to the west, and San Francisco Bay to the north and east. Two trendy neighborhoods, Nob Hill and Russian Hill; two cities within a city, North Beach and Chinatown; a tourist haven, the northern waterfront; the Wall Street of the West, Montgomery Street; the city's public sense, the Civic Center; and its shopping hub, Union Square, join hands to make up downtown.

Nob Hill, whose name derives from the rich, or nabobs, who settled this lofty retreat in the 1870s, was once called "the hill of palaces" by Robert Louis Stevenson. That was in the days when cable cars, which were born on the hill, clattered up the 376-foot slopes to the mansions of C. P. Huntington, Mark Hopkins, and James Flood.

Today's cable cars, which recently resumed operation after a two-year forced retirement, still climb up and over the hill. However, the 1906 earthquake left most of the mansions in ruins. Out of their ashes rose palaces of another sort—world-class hotels. The rich and famous now grace the glitter of The Stanford Court, built on the site of railroad magnate Leland Stanford's mansion; The Fairmont Hotel, the setting for the television series "Hotel;" and the Mark Hopkins Hotel, home to the Top of the Mark.

Like Nob Hill, nearby Russian Hill still welcomes the clanging of cable cars. The Powell-Hyde line, which can be caught at the corner of Powell and Market streets, ascends both Nob and Russian hills.

It remains unclear as to how or precisely when Russian Hill earned its name. However, it gained its reputation as a haven for bohemians, intellectuals, and the rich and famous as early as the turn of the century. Such notables as George Sterling, Ambrose Bierce, and Maynard Dixon once called Russian Hill home. Not much has changed. Its bay-view high-rise apartments, with rents equaling their lofty heights, still welcome people of distinction.

Stretching in the shadows of Nob and Russian hills, Grant Avenue represents San Francisco's Marco Polo connection: it is where the Italians bid the Chinese ciao and dim sum wafts toward chicken polenta.

North Beach, stretching from Columbus Avenue to the waterfront, wears the label of Little Italy. In recent years, its identity has become somewhat muddled by the emigration of neighbors from Chinatown, the takeover of Fisherman's Wharf by the tourists, the bump and grind of Broadway, the infusion of wanderlust left over from Jack Kerouac's beat generation, and the not-so-subtle evictions caused by skyrocketing rents.

Nevertheless, you can still sip Original Ambrosia at Enrico's sidewalk café at 504 Broadway, North Beach's most popular pew for people watching; ride the elevator to the top of the Coit Tower crowning Telegraph Hill; explore the pasta-panettone belt along Columbus Avenue for salami and provolone; picnic in Washington Square, the piazza of North Beach; and visit the Church of St. Peter and St. Paul for a spiritual boost.

Chinatown, which is best avoided between mid-January and March during Chinese New Year, makes up a twenty-four block area that borders North Beach, Nob Hill, Union Square, and the Financial District. Entrance onto the main thoroughfare, Grant Avenue, should be made at the dragon gate on Bush Street.

Be warned: like an army of wishful Southern soldiers, tourists have conquered Grant, and now the real heart of Chinatown beats down back alleys and one block west on Stockton Street. Except for those of you addicted to souvenir shopping, skip Grant. Most of the curios are worthless and too expensive at half the price.

On the other hand, Stockton offers visitors a trip through time and space to Hong Kong. Surrounded by throngs of Chinese, Korean, Vietnamese, and Filipino residents, you can weave your way in and out of exotic shops, food markets, tea rooms, and temples.

Dim sum, Chinese lunch, is usually served between 11 A.M. and 3 P.M. It is a tasty introduction to Chinese culture. In Chinatown, Tung Fong at 808 Pacific Street offers an authentic experience. Here, the tiny portions of steamed, baked, and deep-fried pastries come around on trays. You point to the dishes you want, then at the end of your meal the waitress adds up your choices to determine the bill. A word of caution: small neighborhood restaurants, such as this one, may become impatient with questions. But the quality of the food and the low prices usually make the adventure worth the experience.

Fisherman's Wharf, Golden Gate Bridge, The Cannery, Ghirardelli Square, and Pier 39, all located on or near the northern waterfront, rank in San Francisco's top ten tourist attractions. All first-time visitors should join the crowds at these sites, where shopping, eating, and picture-taking capture the imaginations of hordes of tourists each year. Nevertheless, to fully appreciate the waterfront and San Francisco Bay, climb aboard a boat traveling to one of the Bay's islands.

Morbid fascination with The Rock and its hardened antiheroes such as Al Capone and Machine Gun Kelly, draw thousands of people each year to Alcatraz Island. Ferries for the two-hour tour depart every forty-five minutes from Pier 41. A more secluded isle-away, Angel Island, lures hikers, bicyclists, and picnickers to its steep slopes and sandy beaches. The island can be reached by boarding a carrier of the Red and White Fleet (415-546-2805) or the Angel Island State Ferry (415-435-2131).

The gold rush of 1849, the discovery of the Comstock silver lode in 1859, and the completion of the transcontinental railroad in 1869 sparked San Francisco's genesis as the financial center of the West. Today, Montgomery Street carries on this tradition of high finance. The canyons echo with the sounds of bankers and brokers wheeling and dealing.

About a dozen blocks away, on the western edges of downtown, more mellow sounds create a different song of San Francisco.

Recognized as the best example of Beaux Arts architecture in America, San Francisco's Civic Center clusters around formal gardens and fountains. It represents the city's hub of government and culture. Besides the granite and marble City Hall, the center boasts the San Francisco Museum of Modern Art, the War Memorial Opera House, and the Louise M. Davies Symphony Hall.

Next to eating, America's favorite pastime is extolling the fruits of capitalism. We are bewitched by the shelves and racks of shopping centers. The lure is unrelenting. Beckoning not far from the civic center, Union Square sings a siren's song that seduces even the strongest among us.

It is all here, from curb flower stands to chic boutiques. Panhandlers and street musicians rub shoulders with royalty and jet setters. There are the exclusive shops of Sutter Street, quilted jackets from Jeanne Marc, designer garments from Wilkes Bashford, jade from Gump's, woolen sportswear from Jaeger, and pipes from Alfred Dunhill of London. Conducting this symphony of consumerism are Saks, Macy's, I. Magnin, and Neiman-Marcus.

BEYOND DOWNTOWN

While much is written and ballyhooed about downtown, the soul of San Francisco shines elsewhere. Beyond the glass-and-steel towers of commerce exists a city of parks and schools, corner stores and cafés, apartments and mansions and nary a tourist. Restaurants prepare food for neighbors, not strangers, and boutiques price clothes for regular customers, not one-time shoppers.

HAIGHT-ASHBURY

Framed by Golden Gate Park on the west and Buena Vista Park to the southeast, the Haight is the quintessential prototype of The City. It is inhabited by subcultures ranging from punks to gentry, while culture runs from street musicians to the nearby De Young Memorial Museum. The neighborhood is safe and excellent for walking, although to those used to suburban living, the street-smart appearance of some of the younger people may appear threatening. But they are not.

The best way to see the neighborhood is to walk along Haight, between Ashbury and Stanyan. Cafés, bookstores, boutiques, bakeries, and clubs line the sidewalks. Stop in at the Achilles Heel for a drink and friendly conversation or into All You Knead for excellent pizza and creative sandwiches.

It is not quite as hot (or as funky) as it was in the 1960s, but the Haight still knows how to tap its toes and snap its fingers. The Other Cafe at 100 Carl Street presents the best in local comedy, while Rockin' Robins on Haight keeps rock and roll alive and well.

Some of the city's most beautiful homes, including many restored Victorians, dot the edges of Haight-Ashbury, particularly on Buena Vista Hill, which considers itself a neighborhood in itself. To see the homes, walk or drive up the hill on Ashbury, then wend your way over toward Buena Vista Avenue.

GOLDEN GATE PARK

This three-mile-long, one-half-mile-wide urban wonder actually makes up both the northern and western borders of the Haight. Stretching eight blocks between Fell and Oak streets and blending the smells of eucalyptus with the voices of park-goers, a grassy promenade known as the Panhandle welcomes walkers, runners, cyclists, and motorists to Golden Gate Park.

Although the best way, by far, to enjoy the park is either on foot or astride a bicycle, its sprawling dimensions suggest that an automobile may be more practical. To enter the park, take Fell Street to Kennedy Drive. This wide boulevard traverses the length of the park. At the ocean, Kennedy meets the Great Highway, which parallels the Pacific. There is parking here for walks along the beach, or drive north to Cliff House for views, soups, and sandwiches, or head south to the zoo and zoological gardens.

Inside Golden Gate there are gardens to stroll, museums to explore, lakes to ply, and sports to play. The stars of the park, present man's achievements in art and science. Located in an area no larger than a city block and sandwiched around the Music Concourse sit the California Academy of Sciences (home to a museum of natural history, Steinhart Aquarium, and the Morrison Planetarium), the Asian Art Museum (beneficiary of Avery Brundage's world-famous collection), and the M. H. De Young Museum (the city's most diversified gallery).

A few notes about the park: the eastern section, which includes the museums, is closed to vehicles on Sundays; the De Young is closed Mondays and Tuesdays.

THE CASTRO

This small neighborhood makes up an area that runs south of Market and includes several blocks of Castro, Hartford, and 18th streets. It embraces San Francisco's gay community, yet many straights live here, and the feeling is one of a small, close-knit town. When you pack your bags for San Francisco, leave your prejudices hanging in the closet. To miss Castro would be to miss one of this city's finest neighborhoods and to forego the opportunity to gain a better understanding of a fast-growing segment of our population.

There are fashionable bars, tasteful boutiques, excellent small restaurants, florists, bookstores, Victorian homes, and lively street parties. The neighborhood is safe and excellent for walking and shopping.

Do not miss the Castro Theatre at 429 Castro. This 1930s movie house shows revival films to enthusiastic audiences. For lunch visit Mediterranee at 288 Noe Street. It features good Mediterranean food in a comfortable setting. Dinner should be taken at Snow Peas, located at 4072 18th Street. This lively restaurant combines French and Chinese cooking styles.

MISSION

Most guidebooks skip past this neighborhood because it is not in tourist country. Instead, it represents San Francisco's most self-contained community, where residents live, work, and play. The working-class environment is inhabited mainly by Latinos, Filipinos, Asians, Samoans, and Irish. The neighborhood is safe and an education in urban living.

Evidence of community spirit adorns the walls of many neighborhood buildings located between Mission and York streets and 14th and Army streets. The murals are a result of resident artists.

History buffs should visit Mission Dolores on Dolores and 16th streets. This California mission is recognized as San Francisco's oldest building. Then stop at nearby Dolores Park for a picnic lunch on manicured lawns with great city views.

A walk on the wild side will take you to Hamburger Mary's at 1582 Folsom Street. Besides loud music, great burgers, and loads of fun, this is a hangout for San Francisco's free spirits. Only the most adventurous need apply.

Two of the city's finest Italian restaurants call the Mission home. With pictures of opera stars lining the walls of La Traviata, you might just find yourself seeing double as one of those well-known faces may be seated next to you. Located at 2854 Mission Street, this candle-lit restaurant is famous for milk-fed veal and calamari. A few blocks away, at 2389 Mission Street, Bruno's sells an old-world ambience and homemade pasta to neighborhood families.

SOUTH OF MARKET

A brief note here about the neighborhood known by locals as SOMA, which is quickly being transformed from urban drab to trendy sparkle. Much of the credit for this metamorphosis lies at the doorsteps of the 1981 construction of the Moscone Center, part of the Yerba Buena Center between Third and Fourth streets, and affordable rents, rarities in San Francisco. Spurred by renewal and economics, SOMA is becoming the "in place" for singles, artists, and urban professionals. Tagging along behind the leather ties and creative energies are boutiques, restaurants, clubs, galleries, theaters, and unfortunately, escalating rents. For the latest information on "where it's at," go to the Billboard Cafe at Folsom and Ninth streets.

WESTERN ADDITION

Because of gentrification, revitalization, and the emergence of new neighborhoods, this community can only be loosely defined. But for the purpose of this discussion, we shall call it the neighborhood bordered by Hayes and California to the south and north, and Masonic and Gough to the west and east. Within these boundaries lies a neighborhood in transition—one fighting to overcome a reputation for crime and poverty. Visitors should avoid both long waits at bus stops and walking the streets at night.

With those warnings firmly in mind, I must tell you that I thoroughly enjoyed my visit here and found the people warm and friendly. Two places account primarily for my good experiences: Nohonmachi, or Japantown, and Alamo Square.

While Japantown is home to fewer than 5 percent of San Francisco's Japanese-Americans, it serves as their center for shopping, culture, and socializing. Located in a five-acre commercial and cultural district that extends north of Geary between Laguna and Fillmore, Japan Center offers an eight hundred-car parking garage and easy access to shops, restaurants, and galleries.

Like most of San Francisco, eating heads the list of things to do. Kushi Tsuru at 1737 Post Street in the Center is an excellent place to have lunch, while Ino Sushi at 1620 Webster Street features one of the city's best sushi bars. Check out Fuki-Ya at 22 Peace Plaza for dinner.

Nearby, on Steiner between Fulton and Hayes, climbs Postcard Hill. From a bench in Alamo Square, a cozy park, you can enjoy the beauty of Victorian houses, known as the Painted Ladies of Alamo Square. In the background rise the spires of downtown. This is a small park that allows visitors time to sit and ponder the city. It is not a place full of revelry.

PACIFIC HEIGHTS

If you have wealth, enjoy wealth, or even just like watching it pass by, Pacific Heights is the place for you. San Francisco's finest mansions meld with exclusive shops and restaurants along the tree-lined streets climbing these heights. Bounded by Lombard Street to the north and California on the south, with Presidio and Van Ness making up its silky sleeves, Pacific Heights boasts more college diplomas and silver spoons than the Ivy League and the world's royal palaces combined. Modest homes here start at $225,000. But do not start saving yet. There are very few of these bungalows around.

The best way to view the opulence is to walk along the Broadway Bluff between Webster and Lyon streets. One gets the feeling that if just half these mansions were donated to the government, the Feds could finance the deficit and have enough left over to give themselves a raise. Should your eyes tire of these diamonds, however, stop at Broderick and Broadway for magnificent vistas of some nearby pearls—the Marina, Palace of Fine Arts, Golden Gate Bridge, and the hills of Marin County.

Like the cherries and whipped cream atop a hot fudge sundae, you cannot have an exclusive neighborhood without the toppings. Pacific Heights surrounds itself with chic shops and special restaurants. Nearby Cow Hollow, a most ungenteel label left over from the days when this was dairy farming territory, serves as the Heights' icing. Along Union Street, from Gough to Steiner, you will find blocks of Victorians and Edwardians housing art galleries, antique stores, small bakeries, cozy cafés, and fashionable boutiques.

Within recent years, tweedy young professionals have found their way down the other side of the Heights to Fillmore between Jackson and Bush. Now this street is experiencing a boom in trendy shops and eateries. The difference between Fillmore and Union is that the tourists have not discovered Fillmore yet.

RICHMOND

This residential neighborhood is made up primarily of neat single-family homes and small apartment buildings. Just east of Richmond climbs well-heeled Presidio Heights, while just north sprawls the Presidio. Drive through and around the fifteen hundred-acre army base for a taste of pastoral serendipity in the heart of the city. Also to be explored in this area are the specialty shops and antique stores along Sacramento Street and the emerging Chinatown on Clement Street.

A PRACTICAL GUIDE TO SAN FRANCISCO

THE CLIMATE

San Francisco's charms may be hot, but its weather is not. In summer, expect daytime temperatures between 60 degrees and 65 degrees, while winter highs range from 55 degrees to 60 degrees. San Francisco's infamous fog rolls in during much of the summer but usually burns off by noon of each day. Fall features San Francisco's warmest weather.

YOUR CLOTHES

Most people will feel comfortable in light wools and worsteds. Occasionally a suit and tie or evening dress will be required for theater or dining. Do not forget a light jacket and a topcoat. Downtown attire tends to be more formal, except in the tourist districts, than in the neighborhoods.

DRIVING AND PARKING

Despite the hills, which are conveniently controlled by four-way stops, San Francisco is a very easy city to drive in. Be sure to obtain a good street map. I recommend the ones published by either the H. M. Gousha Company, Box 6227, San Jose, CA 95150 or Topaz Maps, 1707 Market Street, Suite 200, San Francisco, CA 94103. The inns featured here will be able to provide you with a free copy of one of these maps.

Parking may be a problem. First, avoid driving downtown—parking lots are expensive and busy, meters are limited-time. In the neighborhoods, patience will deliver free on-street parking. But do not park alongside colored curbings and read those street-cleaning signs carefully. Finally, curb your wheels.

PUBLIC TRANSPORTATION

Buses, cable cars, and light rail vehicles serve the city. Call 415-673-MUNI for more information.

VISITOR INFORMATION

Your first source of information is the San Francisco Convention & Visitors Bureau, 201 Third Street, Suite 900, San Francisco, CA 94103 (415-974-6900) or visit their center in the lower level of Hallidie Plaza at 900 Market Street.

POINTS OF INTEREST

GOLDEN GATE PARK. A 1,017-acre park bounded by Fulton, Lincoln, Stanyan, and the Great Highway. Museums, gardens, lakes, walking, jogging, bicycling, tennis, golf, and lawn bowling.

JAPANTOWN. North of Geary between Laguna and Fillmore. Japanese cultural and shopping center.

CHINATOWN. Dragon gate entrance at Grant and Bush streets. Called the Hong Kong of the West.

NORTH BEACH. Extends north and east along Columbus Avenue. Synonymous with Little Italy.

UNION SQUARE. Bounded by Powell, Stockton, Post, and Geary. Downtown's most exclusive shopping.

JACKSON SQUARE. The city's only downtown business buildings to survive the 1906 earthquake. Once known as the lusty Barbary Coast. It became San Francisco's first Historic District. The square makes up an area bounded by Montgomery, Pacific, Washington, and Kearny streets.

PIER 39. A two-level restaurant-shopping complex near Fisherman's Wharf that resembles a turn-of-the-century San Francisco street scene.

FISHERMAN'S WHARF. Once the center of the city's commercial fishing fleet, today a hub for souvenir hunters.

GHIRARDELLI SQUARE. A former woolen mill and once a chocolate factory, it has been converted into downtown's most attractive and appealing tourist restaurant-shopping center.

THE CANNERY. Another tourist shopping center located near Fisherman's Wharf.

ALCATRAZ ISLAND. Tours to The Rock leave every forty-five minutes from Pier 41 (415-546-2806). Good views. Dress warmly.

GOLDEN GATE NATIONAL RECREATION AREA. Fort Mason is the most developed section of this park, which encompasses more than sixty-eight square miles of land and sea. Fort Mason, headquarters for the area, is located along the northern waterfront and can be approached via Van Ness Street, Franklin Street, or Marina Boulevard.

THE EXPLORATORIUM. Located in the Palace of Fine Arts along the waterfront at 3601 Lyon Street (415-563-7337). Recognized as one of the world's best science museums, this is a hands-on experience.

PRESIDIO. Located on the northernmost point of the San Francisco peninsula, this military outpost offers scenery and views. A must-do driving tour.

TWIN PEAKS. Outstanding panoramas of the city.

ASIAN ART MUSEUM. Located in Golden Gate Park (415-558-2993). Exhibits the Avery Brundage collection.

M. H. DE YOUNG MEMORIAL MUSEUM. Located in Golden Gate Park (415-221-4811). Wide range of art exhibits.

MUSEUM OF MODERN ART. Civic Center (415-863-8800).

CABLE CAR MUSEUM. Washington and Mason streets (415-474-1887).

NATIONAL MARITIME MUSEUM. Located in Aquatic Park near Ghirardelli Square (415-556-8177).

OLD MINT. Fifth and Mission streets (415-974-0788). Four million dollars in gold bars displayed within this Federal classical revival building.

BAY CRUISES. Blue and Gold Fleet, departs from Pier 39 (415-781-7877); Red and White Fleet, departs from Pier 41 (415-546-2810).

SAN FRANCISCO SIGHT-SEEING. The Gray Line (415-771-4000); Dolphin Tours (415-441-6853).

RESTAURANTS OF NOTE

The list below contains a small select group of restaurants, ranging from cafés to sophisticated dining. My recommendations are based both upon my own good fortunes and those of San Franciscans who have shared their favorite dining spots with me. Generally, you can expect good food in a relaxed setting. There is little pretension with regards to service or dress. If there are questions concerning attire, call ahead to ask. In any case, it is always a good idea to make reservations for dinner well in advance.

ALFRED'S. 886 Broadway, North Beach (415-781-7058). Best steaks in town.

ASIA GARDEN. 772 Pacific, Chinatown (415-398-5112). Good dim sum in a noisy setting.

BRUNO'S. 2389 Mission, Mission (415-824-2258). Large servings of good Italian food.

CAFFE SPORT. 574 Green, North Beach (415-981-1251). Perhaps the best Italian restaurant in "The City."

FOURNOU'S OVENS. 905 California, Nob Hill (415-989-1910). Elegant setting in the Stanford Court Hotel.

FUKI-YA. 22 Peace Plaza, Japantown (415-929-0127). Charcoal-grilled foods plus a sushi bar.

THE GARDEN HOUSE. 133 Clement, Richmond (415-221-3655). Family owned. Fresh Chinese food.

GOLDEN EAGLE. Embarcadero 4, Financial District (415-982-8831). Excellent traditional American food.

HAMBURGER MARY'S. 1582 Folsom, SOMA (415-626-5767). Good burgers, but the atmosphere is the thing here.

HAYES STREET GRILL. 324 Hayes, Civic Center (415-863-5545). One of San Francisco's finest. Grilled fresh fish.

INO SUSHI. 1620 Webster, Japantown (415-922-3121). One of San Francisco's best sushi bars.

IRONWOOD CAFE. 901 Cole, Haight (415-664-0224). Fresh seafood, good wine list.

KUSHI TSURU. 1737 Post, Japantown (415-922-9902). Excellent lunches.

LA POSADA. 2298 Fillmore, Pacific Heights (415-922-1722). Traditional Mexican food.

LA RONDALLA. 901 Valencia, Mission (415-647-7474). Simple setting, good Mexican food.

LA TRAVIATA. 2854 Mission, Mission (415-282-0500). Competes favorably with Caffe Sport for great Italian food.

LE CASTEL. 3235 Sacramento, Presidio Heights (415-921-7115). May be the best French restaurant in "The City."

L'ENTRECÔTE DE PARIS. 2032 Union, Cow Hollow (415-931-5006). Known for its sauces.

MACARTHUR PARK. 607 Front, Financial District (415-398-5700). Mesquite grilled ribs and chicken.

MAMA'S. Several locations; favorite one in North Beach at 1701 Stockton (415-362-6421). Good brunches and sandwiches.

MANDARIN DELIGHT. 941 Kearny, Chinatown (415-362-8299). Excellent spicy Northern Chinese food.

MEDITERRANEE. 288 Noe, Castro (415-861-7210). Charming neighborhood restaurant. Good lunches.

THE MING PALACE. 933 Clement, Richmond (415-668-3988). Superb cuisine.

PACIFIC HEIGHTS BAR & GRILL. 2001 Fillmore, Pacific Heights (415-567-3337). Excellent oyster bar.

PANOS'. 4000 24th, Noe Valley (415-824-8000). Good Greek food.

PREGO. 2000 Union, Cow Hollow (415-563-3305). Trendy and informal. Italian cuisine.

TUNG FONG. 808 Pacific, Chinatown (415-362-7115). Authentic food and setting. Excellent dim sum.

ZUNI CAFE. 1658 Market, Civic Center (415-552-2522). Mesquite grilled fish.

WHERE TO STAY

THE ARCHBISHOPS MANSION

The Archbishops Mansion is the most elegant, most spectacular, bed-and-breakfast inn I have yet to visit. Its accommodations rival those of the finest hotels both in ambience and price, and its small staff reflects the utmost in professionalism.

Located on the edge of Alamo Square, in the shadows of restored Victorians lining Postcard Hill, the mansion was built in 1904 to serve as the residence and diocesan entertainment center for San Francisco's archbishop. It fell from grace in 1955, then went through some twenty-five years of indignities before being rescued by current owners, Jonathan Shannon and Jeffrey Ross, who purchased it in the early 1980s. Their idea was to transform the mansion into a small luxury-class hostelry. Restoration, as opposed to renovation, began almost immediately.

They restored the three-story mansion, distinguished by a mansard roof, to its original Second Empire French styling. Inside, the antique patina of the redwood woodworking, which marks the coffered ceilings, walls, and columns, found new life. Adding embellishment to the grand surroundings, the parlor's triple-arch ceiling was stenciled and hand-painted in the design motif of a nineteenth-century Aubusson carpet, and the sixteen-foot, stained-glass dome crowning the open staircase was saved. Statuary, paintings, and bronze chandeliers were brought in to adorn the Great Hall and the public rooms.

The Archbishops Mansion (Russell Abraham)

Each of the fifteen guest rooms, named for nineteenth-century operas in praise of romance and in honor of the nearby opera house, carries on the feeling of a French manor house. The rooms are large, ranging in size from fifteen by twelve feet to twenty by twenty-five feet, and furnishings consist of antiques and reproductions reminiscent of La Belle Epoch. Carpets adorn the floors, while Chinese lace coverlets grace the beds. Many of the accommodations have fireplaces, all have private baths.

To keep the mansion from smothering itself in formal air, Jonathan has introduced bits of whimsy. In the evenings, piano melodies dance up the stairway beckoning guests to wine in the parlor. Nothing startling in itself, except that the 1884 ebony Bechstein, which once belonged to Noel Coward, needs no pianist—it has been completely computerized. Even more fanciful are the rubber ducks that wait to join guests in their evening baths.

The Archbishops Mansion sits in a class by itself at the pinnacle of the bed-and-breakfast industry, which is precisely why I recommend it only to those who feel comfortable in sophisticated surroundings. Every detail is attended to: there are hand-embroidered linens, elaborate canopy beds, French-milled soaps, and even wine lists in each of the guest rooms. This is bed and breakfast served on a silver platter.

*　　　*　　　*

The Archibishops Mansion, 1000 Fulton Street, San Francisco, CA 94117 (415-563-7872). Fifteen guest rooms, all with private baths and queen-size beds. Several two-room suites. Rates range from $95 to $300 (subject to change). VISA/MasterCard/American Express. Children with prior approval; no pets; smoking in drawing room only. Some off-street parking available. Small meetings, conferences, dinner parties, weddings, and business lunches welcome. The mansion is located across the street from Alamo Square, six blocks west of the Civic Center.

THE BED AND BREAKFAST INN

In 1976, Bob and Marily Kavanaugh purchased Four Charlton Court, a one hundred-year-old Victorian row house located in a mews off trendy Union Street. At the time, Bob and Marily, whose children had grown, hoped that running a bed-and-breakfast inn would offer some of the same challenges and excitement that raising a family had provided.

Four Charlton Court was an experiment of sorts: it was the first bed and breakfast in San Francisco and one of the first on the West Coast, so the Kavanaughs had no way of knowing how consuming their new business venture would become.

Today, The Bed and Breakfast Inn has grown far beyond the four guest rooms in the original house. Now Bob and Marily also offer The

The Bed and Breakfast Inn (Courtesy The Bed and Breakfast Inn)

Mayfair, a penthouse suite in the original house, which once served as their living quarters; four guest rooms at Two Charlton Court next door; one accommodation at Five Charlton Court across the street, and the original four accommodations.

Unlike most of San Francisco's finer bed and breakfasts, this is not an inn of grand proportions nor one of elegant design. Except for The Mayfair, the rooms are small and modestly adorned. In addition, their thin walls make the accommodations seem even smaller than they are.

Despite these drawbacks, however, The Bed and Breakfast Inn reigns as one of San Francisco's most popular. The reasons are simple: great location, superb hospitality, and myriad personal touches. Generally, these same characteristics have always been the trademarks of the industry, the things that have caused bed and breakfasts to grow in numbers and to prosper.

Each of the rooms here displays a personality of its own, a result of the Kavanaughs' caring. Such extras as the Oriental window garden in Autumn Sun; the private garden deck that splashes breaths of color onto Garden Park, Kensington Gardens, and the Willows; the arbor sitting alcove of Covent Gardens; and the sunken bathtub of Celebration, make the rooms feel cozy instead of cramped. Bob and Marily have also employed amenities to ensure guest comfort. All rooms boast fresh fruit, flowers, books, magazines, and clock radios, while the six accommodations with private baths also feature decanters of sherry as well as telephones and televisions.

The Bed and Breakfast Inn is typical of the traditional bed and breakfast in that its main selling point is its homey and friendly atmosphere. In fact, there is no other San Francisco inn that offers more of this at-home feeling.

*   *   *

The Bed and Breakfast Inn, Four Charlton Court, San Francisco, CA 94123 (415-921-9784). Ten guest rooms, six with private baths. The Mayfair is a private flat. Rates range from $63 to $174 (subject to change). No credit cards. Children with prior approval; no pets; smoking permitted. On-street and garage parking. Located off Union Street between Laguna and Buchanan.

CASA ARGUELLO

Emma Baires is one of those people who has managed to find their niche in this world: she is the perfect bed-and-breakfast innkeeper. As Emma sits in her living room, telling me why she loves having guests in her home, a smile creases her face and her eyes sparkle with enthusiasm.

Casa Arguello (Courtesy Casa Arguello)

"I love to see my guests so happy," she says in a thick Spanish accent. "When they so happy, I happy. When they don't sleep so good, I tired too."

I do not imagine that sleepless nights plague Emma. Most guests will feel right at home here. Casa Arguello is a comfortable turn-of-the-century townhouse, located on a tree-lined residential street between Richmond and Presidio Heights. The neighborhood is made up of single-family homes, manicured gardens, neighborhood schools, and churches.

Each of Emma's five guest rooms is large and sunny. Furnishings such as brass beds, overstuffed chairs, and televisions create a homey atmosphere. Two of the rooms, numbers one and three, overlook rooftops toward Lincoln Park and offer unique views of the city's residential areas. And room number five is a two-room suite with a private bath.

Emma serves breakfast between 8 A.M. and 10 A.M. in the main floor dining room. It usually includes orange juice, tea, coffee, cereal and bananas, and pastry from a local bakery. Unlike many of San Francisco's inns, which deliver breakfast to the room, the morning meal here presents an opportunity for guests to socialize.

"In the morning, the communication is beautiful," Emma says. "All my guests make friends."

That is what Casa Arguello is all about, making friends. Emma emigrated from El Salvador in the early 1940s because she loves the United States, particularly San Francisco. With Casa Arguello, she has the chance to share her love of this city with visitors.

*   *   *

Casa Arguello, 225 Arguello Boulevard, San Francisco, CA 94118 (415-752-

9482). Five guest rooms, two with private baths. Rates range from $43 to $58 (subject to change). No credit cards. Children over seven; no pets; no smoking. On-street parking. Located one block north of California, several blocks south of the Presidio.

HERMITAGE HOUSE

Hermitage House reflects the elegance of its surroundings—posh Pacific Heights. Inside the four-story Greek Revival building, high ceilings, inlaid hardwood floors and carved heart redwood detailing in the pillars, beams, and stairway scrolls place guests in a setting typical of this exclusive neighborhood.

The house was originally built at the turn of the century by architect William Blaisdell for Judge Charles Slack. It remained a private residence until the 1970s, when it was turned into a halfway house for drug abusers. Not terribly concerned with decor or ambience, the directors of the center permitted painting of the redwood interiors and the tacking of gaudy carpeting with four-inch-long nails.

Today, the seventeen-room house shows no evidence of its traumatic past. In 1978, Marian and Frederick Binkley purchased the home to convert it into a bed-and-breakfast inn. Making it a family effort, the

Hermitage House (Courtesy Hermitage House)

restoration of the house took two and a half years to complete.

Once again the redwood's patina glistens, and the hardwood floors display their inlaid edgings. Antique furnishings blend well with the Laura Ashley papers and fabrics, while crystal chandeliers and tile fireplaces distinguish several rooms.

Each of the five guest rooms mirrors elegance. Most of the accommodations—like The Master Bedroom with its cream and green color scheme, ruffled curtains and bedspread, and cozy sitting area in front of the tile fireplace—promote a soft, light air. Hermitage House, however, has not neglected the masculine feeling. Judge Slack's Study boasts beams, redwood shake paneling, walls lined with books, and a stone fireplace. Still, a soft beige comforter, frilly shams, and embroidered pillows maintain a balance, preventing the room from being too hard.

A balance is also maintained between the inn's formal looks and its informal atmosphere. Fresh flowers, candies, and baskets of designer toiletries brighten each room, while an open-door policy in the kitchen welcomes guests to use the refrigerator and other facilities.

"We want people to feel very much at home," Jane Selzer, manager, says. "We encourage our guests to feel free to use the entire home."

To further help guests feel at home, the inn provides both telephones and televisions on request and keeps clocks and radios in the rooms. Breakfast is also kept leisurely by serving it buffet-style in the downstairs breakfast room.

Although many of Hermitage House's guests are well-heeled, the inn's location likely presents most of us with our best chance of staying in Pacific Heights. And the inn's informal attitude prevents our shirts from becoming overstuffed.

*   *   *

Hermitage House, 2224 Sacramento Street, San Francisco, CA 94115 (415-921-5515). Five guest rooms, all with private baths. Rates range from $75 to $105 (subject to change). VISA/MasterCard/American Express. Children with prior approval; no pets; smoking permitted. Small group gatherings and weddings welcome. Off-street parking available for a small fee. Located two blocks east of Fillmore and five blocks north of Japantown.

INN ON CASTRO

As I sat at the oval, white pedestal table, it never once occurred to me that I was in an inn. While Patrick, the manager, and I sipped coffee, discussed the neighborhood, and waited for the spin cycle to finish with my clothes, neighbors popped by to say "hi," and the phone rang with messages from well-wishers.

In the meantime, my eyes danced back and forth between the dining and living rooms, which, like the guest rooms downstairs, stand in stark contrast to the inn's painted Victorian facade. Inside, Joel Roman—painter, designer, and co-owner—has accomplished what nearly every innkeeper aims for: gracious hospitality. Perhaps this is partly because Joel and his partner, Sam, call the inn home.

The living room invites guests to sink down into plump chocolate brown Italian modules that wrap around a kilim rug. Lush plants, crystal and glass pieces, throw pillows, and Joel's paintings add rich color and tone.

Flowers and plants carry on the exotic, classic contemporary theme in the dining room. Atop modular wicker storage units sit more of Joel's collectables—mercury glass objects, soft sculptures, and an assortment of heart-shaped boxes. In a way, these delicate boxes tell the inn's complete story. They represent gifts from guests who have fallen in love with the place. It is easy to do.

First, Joel and Patrick are lovable innkeepers: they exude cheeriness, friendliness, and enthusiasm. Second, the inn's location in the heart of San Francisco's gay neighborhood places guests in an exciting environment, rich in restaurants and shops. Finally, Joel's talents as a designer and artist create an atmosphere that is both refreshing and relaxing.

Each of the four guest rooms, sporting Italian names because both Joel and Sam lived in Italy, breathes atmosphere and reflects a unique personality. Green colors, wicker, and suspended paper umbrellas set the tone in Il Camino; papier-mâché birds and white lacquer chests blend with the yellows in La Gabbia; deep browns, colorful throw pillows, coolie hats on the ceiling, and a bay window view of Mission Dolores make up Lo Studio; while fiery reds, rattan furniture, and a private greenhouse welcome guests to La Serra.

Personal touches are not something just talked about here, they are real. All the bathrooms boast lighted make-up mirrors; the rooms feature track lighting with dimmers; fabrics are rich and colorful; morning juice is freshly squeezed and coffee is a special house blend; all of the paintings are Joel's; the inn houses a wealth of fine books and magazines; and on rainy days, guests are provided with umbrellas that color-coordinate with their attire.

Patrick sums up this caring attitude best: "All the things you would have at home for yourself, we have here for your use. And we don't have anything here that we wouldn't want for ourselves."

*   *   *

Inn on Castro, 321 Castro Street, San Francisco, CA 94114 (415-861-0321). Four guest rooms, all with private baths. Rates are $85 for a double (subject to change). VISA/MasterCard/American Express. Children with

Inn on Castro (CeccaRomanelli)

prior approval; no pets; smoking permitted. On-street parking. Located just north of the intersection of Market and Castro.

THE INN SAN FRANCISCO

Joel Daily is a bright and cheerful young man, who quite frankly, is a pleasure to be around. It comes as no surprise that he's a popular

The Inn San Francisco (James Stedman)

innkeeper. But to completely appreciate Joel's success, you have to understand his inn's history and the roadblocks he has had to overcome.

Built in 1872 by John English, a former city commissioner, the mansion was just one of several estates that occupied a neighborhood of elegance and wealth. In fact, San Franciscans called South Van Ness, which was Howard Street prior to 1900, Mansion Row. Even in its youth, English's home stood like a grande dame, its impressive attributes boasting twenty-four rooms, including butler's and servant's quarters.

But as so often happens in American cities, the character of neighborhoods changes with the times, leaving even great ladies wrinkled with age. By 1900, the area was in transition from landed gentry to working class. The mansion lost its owner and its status. It soon became a fifteen-room boardinghouse. Then in the 1930s, the house suffered even greater indignities as all of the original trim and ornament—the portico, window hoods, decorative railings, metal capitals, classic columns, and carved decorations—were removed so the facade could be stuccoed. In 1977, Joel, an artist-designer, and a partner bought the place as a "fixer-upper."

"After about a year, we realized what a jewel this was," Joel says. "We had a hotel license, had heard about inns, knew lots of people who loved coming to the city but hated staying downtown, so we thought we would convert it into a small tourist hotel."

By researching the mansion's history and studying its "scars," Joel and a team of architects breathed new life into the house. In May of 1980, The Inn San Francisco, its Victorian facade nearly restored and its redwood interior glistening, welcomed its first guests.

Despite the mansion's elegance and its historical significance, Joel still faced an obstacle in attracting guests—the neighborhood. Located in the Mission District, the inn is surrounded by a look of industry. The homes are modest, some in varying states of decay or renovation; the shops are simple and geared toward serving their middle-class neighbors, not tourists; and the streets echo with voices speaking in foreign accents.

"I've had guests drive up who won't get out of their car," Joel says. "But after I talk to them a few minutes, they are ready to check in, and most return time and time again."

That is understandable. This is a safe, family-oriented neighborhood. It is close to downtown and features excellent restaurants. And the inn is an elegant retreat in the city.

Besides fifteen comfortable guest rooms, most with private baths, the inn has a hot tub tucked into a garden setting, a roof garden with panoramas of the city, a magnificent breakfast of fresh fruits and pastries, and extremely reasonable rates. And, of course, there is Joel.

*　　*　　*

The Inn San Francisco, 943 South Van Ness Avenue, San Francisco, CA 94110 (415-641-0188). Fifteen guest rooms, fourteen baths. At this writing, plans call for an additional four rooms in the house next door plus a lap pool. Rates range from $49 to $128 (subject to change). VISA/MasterCard/American Express/Diners Club. Children with prior approval; no pets; smoking permitted. Limited off-street parking. Located south of Market between 20th and 21st streets.

THE MONTE CRISTO

From the outside, this two-story salmon-colored building looks more like an apartment complex or a small urban hotel than a bed-and-breakfast

The Monte Cristo (James Stedman)

inn. However, once you pass through the iron door-gate into the embrace of The Monte Cristo and the warm welcome of Frances Allan, there is little doubt that bed and breakfast is served in ample doses here.

The 1875 building inherited its design, including the long hallways, from its checkered past, when it served alternately as a hotel, saloon, and bordello. It inherits its charm from Frances.

"I was living in Marin," Frances says, "and becoming extremely bored with the suburbs. I found myself spending three to four days a week in San Francisco. An inn seemed like an ideal way to live in the city and run my own business at the same time."

So, with partner Kathleen Hughes, Frances purchased the building in

1980. They decorated the rooms with antiques, used color to create a soft mood, graced each room with silk flowers, and fashioned a comfortable, informal setting in both the parlor and the breakfast rooms.

"Above all else, I want my guests to feel comfortable," Frances says.

I suspect most do. Although the inn does not boast the opulence found in most San Francisco hostelries, every room here is unique and special.

The most unusual, and I think the most romantic, is the Chinese Wedding Room. Adorned with an ornate 250-year-old Chinese wedding bed, textured grass wall cloth, and a deep, tiled sunken tub, one can imagine all sorts of marvelous things happening here to a couple in love.

Other rooms of particular note are not to be overlooked, however. There are the Bordello Room, blushing with pink satin bedspread and pillows; the Gooseberry Room, featuring soft green gooseberry paper and a four-poster lace canopy bed; the Rose Suite, with its brass queen bed, separate sitting area, and claw-footed tub; and the Gothic Room, dominated by a hand-carved antique bed and matching armoire.

Breakfast at The Monte Cristo is both delicious and sociable. It is one of the few places in San Francisco where the setting encourages conversation with other guests.

Served buffet-style, in a room furnished with cozy tables set with fine china and silver, breakfast runs for several leisurely hours. It features fresh-ground French roast coffee, a variety of tea, fresh-squeezed orange juice, cereals, muffins, and seasonal fruit.

Like most things, the elegance of bed and breakfast is relative. When compared to many of its San Francisco peers, The Monte Cristo offers a modest environment. But its comfort level, unique decorating style, reasonable rates, and friendly service prompt me to recommend it strongly.

*   *   *

The Monte Cristo, 600 Presidio Avenue, San Francisco, CA 94115 (415-931-1875). Fourteen guest rooms, ten baths. Rates range from $50 to $95 (subject to change). VISA/MasterCard/American Express/Diners Club/Discover. Children with prior approval; no pets; no smoking in breakfast room. On-street parking. Located one block south of California, at the corner of Pine and Presidio.

THE SPRECKELS MANSION

As a travel writer, one whose first responsibility remains tied to a diverse readership with varied tastes, I try to keep from becoming emotionally involved with my subjects. In other words, stay aloof, keep a safe arm's distance, and look for the flaws, surely some must exist.

The Spreckels Mansion (Courtesy The Spreckels Mansion)

Still, my defenses sometimes fail me, and such was the case at The Spreckels Mansion. I fell completely in love with the place (or, I should say, places, since today two neighboring houses make up the inn). Everything about it—its location, history, design, decor, staff, clientele—makes me wish I were the owner. I would revel in my good fortune and become a recluse in my "heaven on earth."

However, Jonathan Shannon and Jeffrey Ross (also of Archbishops) found Spreckels first and in 1979 saved it from the evils of short-sighted developers. With great care and attention to detail, they converted the house into an inn. Permitting the architecture to set the mood, Jonathan and Jeffrey restored rather than renovated. They upgraded the wiring and plumbing, installed bathrooms, added sound proofing, refinished the parquet flooring, selected comfortable antique furnishings, and garnished with new fabrics and wall coverings.

Spreckels, an 1887 Colonial Revival mansion with dashes of Victorian, was named for its builder, sugar baron Richard Spreckels. It stands on Buena Vista Hill facing a park. Street traffic is light so the inn is always quiet. Its hilltop perch offers splendid views of the city, and such noted personalities as Jack London and Ambrose Bierce once lived here.

Five guest rooms make up the mansion. On the main floor are The

Garden Room and The Morning Room. The former is a two-room suite that was originally a sun porch. The latter is an enormous double room graced with two chandeliers, two brass beds, and fan windows. Its off-hall location may not be desirable to those who relish privacy. On the second floor are The Dreamer's Room, distinguished by a large window alcove, and the Sugar Baron Suite, where the size of the bathroom, with its free-standing tub and fireplace, equals most standard guest rooms. The San Francisco Suite takes up the entire third floor, which was originally a ballroom.

Recently, the inn expanded to ten rooms with the addition of the 1897 house next door. Formerly the abode of a famous rock star, this house features an elegant country look as compared to the more formal feel of the mansion. Natural wood paneling, skylights, vaulted ceilings, and eclectic decor establish a more relaxed, yet still comfortable posh tone in this part of the inn, known as The Guest House.

The Gypsy Hideaway, highlighted by a queen bed swathed in garnet and amber hangings, represents one of the inn's most popular accommodations. However, my tastes prefer The Star-Gazer Suite, so named for the skylight above the bed but memorable because of the Japanese-style bath and the room's sunset views.

*   *   *

The Spreckels Mansion, 737 Buena Vista West, San Francisco, CA 94117 (415-861-3008). Ten guest rooms, eight with private baths. Rates range from $88 to $290 (subject to change). VISA/MasterCard/American Express. Children with prior approval; no pets; no cigars. On-street parking. Small group gatherings and catered dinners welcome. Located several blocks south of Haight.

UNION STREET INN

I was reaching a point of desperation. The waters were rising in the Napa River, and I was but a few blocks away and a thousand miles from home. Fate and bad timing had placed me in the middle of the worst floods California had ever experienced. What to do? I called Helen Stewart. Without hesitation, she told me to drift back to San Francisco, where I was welcome as her guest.

That is Helen—gracious and caring. And that is the Union Street Inn, Helen's bed and breakfast located on Union Street.

Helen, a tall, attractive woman who exudes graciousness, is a former school teacher who fell victim to Proposition 13. But, inspired by a book entitled "The Joy of Money" and her own visits to English bed-and-breakfast inns, Helen decided to buy a house and become an innkeeper.

Union Street Inn (Courtesy Union Street Inn)

In 1978, she purchased this turn-of-the-century two-story Edwardian home. She immediately began the task of remodeling. She had the floors refinished and carpets laid. She blended antiques with more contemporary pieces, hung new draperies, and set green plants and flowers about the house. The refurbishing resulted in an inn that looks and feels like a home.

The two downstairs guest rooms, New Yorker and English Garden, represent the house's most expensive fare. New Yorker features a canopy queen brass bed, decorative fireplace, and bay-window view of Union, while English Garden opens through a Dutch door to the deck in Helen's courtyard garden.

Here, the inn's essence flourishes and tranquility prospers. Rich with the blossoms of camellias and scented with the fruity fragrance of lemon trees, the garden welcomes guests to take leisurely breakfasts or enjoy breaks from shopping and sight-seeing.

Beyond the garden stands the inn's newest accommodation, the Carriage House. Ideal for romance, its rattan furnishings and potted palms create an exotic atmosphere, while a skylit Jacuzzi tub in the center of the house invites indulgence.

Still, it is Helen Stewart's presence that makes Union Street Inn special. She knows how to make guests feel right a home, and she cares enough to make the effort.

*   *   *

Union Street Inn, 2229 Union Street, San Francisco, CA 94123 (415-346-0424). Five guest rooms, two with private bathrooms, and a carriage house with private bath. Rates range from $75 to $175 (subject to change). VISA/MasterCard/American Express. Children with prior approval; no pets; smoking permitted. On-street or garage parking. Located at the end of Union Street's magic mile between Fillmore and Steiner.

VICTORIAN INN ON THE PARK

San Francisco's "painted ladies," those ornate Victorian homes that once housed gold kings, silver barons, and railroad magnates, have in recent years been making a comeback. The Victorian Inn on the Park represents just such a place.

Located on the northern border of Haight-Ashbury, within the shade and fragrance of the panhandle's ubiquitous eucalyptus trees, the mansion was built in 1897 by Thomas Jefferson Clunie. He was a prominent lawyer and legislator who wanted a home worthy of his stature and in keeping with those of his wealthy neighbors. Clunie commissioned architect William Curlett to design and construct his dream palace.

Curlett's efforts resulted in a grand three-story Victorian. Its most distinguishing characteristic is a belvedere tower that hosts a porch and is topped by a curved roof and finial. Inside, Curlett used mahogany, oak, and redwood paneling to give the walls their rich quality, and inlaid oak to enhance the floors.

Following Clunie's death in 1903, the mansion remained a private residence until 1945. Then it rode the waves of change that seem to capture the spirit of Haight-Ashbury.

During World War II it functioned as a nursing home, then later became an apartment house. Flower children and rock bands communed there in the 1960s, and guru Leonard Orr carried out "rebirthing" in his Theta Seminars during the 1970s. Finally, in 1980, current owners Shirley and Paul Weber purchased the tired mansion to convert it into an inn. Renovation became the first order of business.

Wherever possible, existing mouldings and woodwork were saved, while new matching trim and mouldings were added where necessary. Entire floors, walls, and ceilings were taken down to accommodate new heating, wiring, and plumbing. Bruce Bradbury created hand silk-screened nineteenth-century art wallpapers especially for the inn. Fireplaces were refurbished, and antique appointments, many of them Victorian, were brought in to furnish the rooms. Finally, and most

Victorian Inn on the Park (Shirley Weber)

important, daughter Lisa and son-in-law Willie became the innkeepers.

Anyone can put a four-poster canopy bed in a room or recapture the patina of antique wood. However, it takes special qualities to excel as innkeepers. Lisa and Willie have these characteristics.

This young hard-working couple are vibrant and interesting hosts. Lisa, who bubbles with enthusiasm, creates a cheery and friendly atmosphere, while Willie displays an efficient, professional *modus operandi* that keeps the inn on a steady course. A third member of the family, daughter Cassandra, packs enough charm in her tiny frame to melt the hearts of a dozen Simon Legrees.

*   *   *

Victorian Inn on the Park, 301 Lyon Street, San Francisco, CA 94117 (415-931-1830). Twelve rooms, all with private bathrooms. Rates range from $75 to $120 (subject to change). VISA/MasterCard/American Express. Children with prior approval; no pets; no smoking in dining room. Exceptional breakfast of seasonal fruits, cheese, muffins, home-baked bread, croissants, fresh-squeezed orange juice, and French roast coffee. On-street parking. Located seven blocks east of Golden Gate Park, three blocks north of Haight, on the corner of Fell and Lyon.

The Wine Country

*T*his much rain had not fallen since Noah set sail. For six days and nights, the skies wept. By the time it ended, some thirty inches of rain had fallen on the hills, valleys, and towns of California's wine country. Bloated rivers consumed their banks and swallowed entire towns. Byways, and highways became paved waterways and vineyards disappeared beneath newly formed lakes. It was March 1986, and California was experiencing some of its worst flooding in history.

But this is wine country, and in the land of the grape a little water does not keep the people from doing what comes naturally. So while the waters ran rampant outside, wine continued to flow inside. True, there were times—usually lasting a few hours—when parking lots became inaccessible to all but those with boats. Nevertheless, when the deluge took a breather, becoming only a downpour, tourists returned and vintners' doors opened. That is the way things are here.

The business of Napa Valley and parts of Sonoma County is grapes and wine. And these days business is good. So good that it lures more than one million tourists each year to the wine country's rolling hills and nutrient-rich valleys. To meet the needs of these visitors, a thriving hospitality business sprouts alongside the vineyards, which includes shopping complexes, first-class restaurants, and a variety of bed and breakfasts.

The seeds of viticulture, the art of growing grapes, were first planted in Northern California by Franciscan missionaries. In 1823, Father José Altimara visited this region in search of a mission site. He chose Sonoma and established the Mission San Francisco de Solano.

In order to make sacramental wine, the padres planted European seedlings. The vines flourished and produced grapes of high quality. However, instead of vineyards, the white settlers opted to cover the valley floor with sheep and cattle. So it was not until the 1860s, when European winemakers arrived, that grapes began to make their mark. By 1880, some six hundred vineyards dotted Napa Valley, and its alluvial fans wore a carpet of vines.

Today, more than three hundred wineries call Napa and Sonoma counties home: nearly half of them welcome the public to tour and taste. Some intrepid—and, one might say, foolish—travelers attempt to sip their way into oblivion by visiting all of these wineries on a long weekend. That is a mistake!

First, if you have seen one winery, basically you have seen them all, although there are variations on a theme. Second, why dull your senses? This country produces world-class wine: it should be savored, not guzzled. And finally, there are other things to experience here, including some of the finest food in America, so do not spend all your time rushing from winery to winery in order to ogle more stainless steel fermenting tanks.

As evidenced by the people who sloshed through California's 1986 rains, tourists take their visits to the wine country seriously. They come year-round to test the grape. Each season offers a different experience.

The popular summer season is a time of waiting, when bunch-heavy vines soak up 90-degree sun, soil turns to dust, and the hills burn dun dry. Then, as the valleys begin to cool and August greets September, the vines blush red and glint golden as pickers invade to harvest the grapes. It is the season of "The Crush," and the hills burst with Autumn colors, while the sweet fragrance of fermenting wine wafts across the countryside. Winter's rain and fog put the vines to rest in their gray hides until spring arrives. Then, like breaths of new life, the vines turn a soft green, almond trees sprout white blossoms, and mustard weed blankets the vineyards in gold.

Of course, summer means vacation for most people, so during the heat of June, July, and August, the highways crawl with traffic and restaurants resemble feeding bins. And because of its accessibility to the heavily populated Bay Area, the wine country remains crowded during "The Crush," especially on weekends. Throughout the remainder of the year, the pace slows and crowds diminish so that visiting the towns and vineyards that dot the region becomes a more leisurely experience.

GETTING TO KNOW THE NAPA VALLEY

When people think of California's wine country, Napa Valley usually comes to mind. The valley begins as a wide plane that shoulders San Pablo Bay, some forty miles north of the Golden Gate Bridge. Slowly, as it cuts its way north through the towns of Napa, Yountville, St. Helena, and Calistoga, the valley narrows and surrenders its flatness to rolling hills.

It is beginning in Napa that the valley dedicates itself to viticulture. From Napa to Calistoga, some 140 wineries lie along State Route 29, the Silverado Trail, and the byways that branch from them. Napa Valley's towns cling to State Route 29 like a string of pearls, inviting tourists to headquarter there while exploring the valley.

NAPA

Napa's fifty-four thousand residents make up more than half of the valley's population, which partly accounts for the town's Rodney Danger-field image. In a rural valley, where small and quaint are beautiful, Napa's blue-collar, small-city appearance garners up-valley prejudice. In addition, Napa's south-valley location leaves it on the edge of the vineyards and wineries. But in a valley the size of a thimble, where you can drive from one end to the other in thirty minutes, this criticism hardly seems fair.

In truth, Napa mirrors the typical small American city, with a compact downtown and a number of small neighborhoods. The town is quiet and the people are friendly, making it an excellent overnight home for travelers.

ST. HELENA

St. Helena (pronounced Ha-lee-na) is the kind of quaint town that the valley likes to call its own. Squeezed by rolling hills and embraced by acres of vineyards, the town's main street (State Route 29) is home to cozy cafés and unique shops. It is the kind of place where locals gather at Palmer's for excellent food, then take in a double feature at the Liberty Theater, where the owner gets up on stage to personally welcome those in attendance.

CALISTOGA

This is the one town in Napa Valley that would continue to attract tourists even if the wine dried up. In fact, the community was founded as a resort town in the mid-1800s long before the call of the grape echoed from the valley floor.

Located in the shadow of Mount St. Helena, Calistoga was the vision of entrepreneur and rascal Sam Brannan. He saw money flowing from the thermal hot springs that course from the base of the mountain and the white volcanic ash that abounds in Calistoga, which, when mixed with the water, makes a warm mud bath. And so spas came to the valley and prospered. Today, they still represent Calistoga's main tourist attraction.

GETTING TO KNOW SONOMA COUNTY

Sonoma County stretches inland from the Pacific, over rolling hills and across valleys, to Napa County. It is blessed with fishing villages, rocky headlands, redwood forests, country towns, and of course, vine-yards. It is country that quietly stirs the imagination, not needing neon lights to advertise its wares. Individuals are left alone to be themselves.

With this environment as a backdrop, creative people have found sanctuary here. Jack London found inspiration in Glen Ellen; Charles Schulz brings Snoopy and Charlie Brown to life in Santa Rosa; and an art community of painters, weavers, and potters thrives in Bodega Bay.

As well as being beautiful to look at, the countryside is fertile. Grapes grow particularly well in the Russian River, Alexander, and Dry Creek valleys to the north, and Sonoma Valley in the southeast. More than one hundred wineries dot the county.

Nevertheless, wine touring in Sonoma County does not reflect the same feeling of frenzied enthusiasm that affects the burgeoning Napa Valley industry. Perhaps it is because the county's varied landscape offers the tourist other alternatives, or maybe the reasons revolve around the absence of a central highway that connects the wineries like a drawing of dots.

Whatever the cause or causes, wine touring and tasting are a more casual affair in Sonoma County. The atmosphere is unhurried, tours are sometimes self-guided, and tastings can often be arranged without a tour or an appointment. Still, the wise and courteous traveler always calls ahead to inquire about each winery's schedule of tours and tastings.

SANTA ROSA

Santa Rosa is located in the heart of the county, where U.S. 101 meets State Route 12. Its central location, just fifty miles north of the Golden Gate Bridge, makes it ideal for exploring the vineyards. The drawback, however, is that Santa Rosa is a city of ninety thousand. The pastoral essence of the county remains in hiding here. On the other hand, there are restaurants, shopping centers, museums, theaters, a symphony orchestra, ballet, and opera within the city's doors.

HEALDSBURG

Located seventy miles north of San Francisco, along U.S. 101, Healdsburg is the kind of quaint community tourists expect of the wine country. Its seventy-eight hundred people live in friendly neighborhoods made up of a mix of wood-frame houses and historic homes that stretch out behind the town's tiny plaza.

GEYSERVILLE

Resting beneath the gaze of Geyser Peak, Geyserville barely gives the appearance of a town at all, being little more than a few restaurants, a gas station, and a post office, with a few stores thrown in for good measure. Its homes are mostly modest, the people are sociable, and the atmosphere is best described as sleepy. For those who really want to get away, this is the place.

A Practical Guide to the Wine Country

The Climate

From May through September, daytime temperatures hover in the 80s and 90s, while the remaining months usually bring 60-degree and 70-degree weather. Rain and fog can be heavy at times from late October to March, with lots of sunny days mixed in.

Your Clothes

Dress is casual except in the region's finer restaurants. Light clothes are a must for the summer, but sweaters or light jackets are advised for nighttime cool downs.

Visitor Information

For general information, contact the Redwood Empire Association, One Market Plaza, Spear Street Tower, Suite 1001, San Francisco, CA 94105 (415-543-8334). For a free folder listing wineries, contact the Wine Institute, 165 Post Street, San Francisco, CA 94108 (415-986-0878).

Points of Interest (Napa Valley)

Bale Grist Mill State Historic Park. Located three miles north of St. Helena on State Route 29. A restored 1846 flour mill powered by a thirty-six-foot waterwheel. Open 10 A.M. to 5 P.M.

Silverado Museum. 1490 Library Lane in St. Helena (707-963-3757). Features memorabilia and personal belongings of Robert Louis Stevenson. Open noon to 4 P.M.

Charles Krug Winery. 2800 St. Helena Highway, St. Helena (707-963-2761). Oldest operating winery in Napa Valley.

Calistoga Soaring Center. 1546 Lincoln Avenue, Calistoga (707-942-5592). Gliders available for rides and instruction.

International Spa. 1300 Washington Street, Calistoga (707-942-6122). Mud baths, herbal facials, and therapeutic massages. Make reservations two to four weeks in advance.

Old Faithful Geyser. One mile north of Calistoga on Tubbs Lane (707-942-

6463). Erupts about every forty-five minutes.

SHARPSTEEN MUSEUM. 1311 Washington Street, Calistoga (707-942-5911). Historical museum depicting Calistoga's pioneer past.

ROBERT LOUIS STEVENSON STATE PARK. Five miles north of Calistoga on State Route 29. Undeveloped park with nature trails. Hike to the top of Mount St. Helena for vistas that sweep across Northern California.

VINTAGE 1870. Washington Street in Yountville. A century-old winery that has been converted into a shopping complex.

WILD HORSE VALLEY RANCH. Wild Horse Valley Road, Napa (707-224-0727). Trail rides.

BALLOONING. One-hour flights range from $100 to $125 per person. For more information, call: Adventures Aloft, Yountville (707-255-8688); Balloon Aviation, Napa (707-252-7067); Great Balloon Escape, Napa (707-253-0860); Napa Valley Balloons, Yountville (707-253-2224); or Once in a Lifetime, Calistoga (707-942-6541).

RESTAURANTS OF NOTE (NAPA VALLEY)

Napa Valley is blessed with some of the West Coast's finest restaurants. The following cover a broad spectrum of taste, style, and price, but each promises good food. Therefore, be sure to book reservations well in advance. I have listed the restaurants by location, beginning in Napa and working north through the valley.

BOMBARD'S. 4050 Byway East, Napa (707-224-8717). The best Cajun-Creole food I have had since leaving New Orleans.

THE RED HEN CANTINA. 5091 St. Helena Highway, Napa (707-255-8125). Excellent Mexican food with views of the vineyards.

THE FRENCH LAUNDRY. Creek and Washington, Yountville (707-944-2380). Saturday dinner reservations for this gourmet French restaurant are often booked two to three months in advance.

MAMA NINA'S. 6772 Washington Street, Yountville (707-944-2112). Excellent northern Italian food featuring fresh homemade pasta and rich desserts.

YOUNTVILLE STATION. 6480 Washington Street, Yountville (707-944-2070). Cuisine revolves around the unlikely combination of French, Polish, and Chinese. Decor melds brass chandeliers and Victorian antiques.

LE RHONE. 1234 Main Street, St. Helena (707-963-0240). Artful French cooking. *Gourmet* magazine says, "the kind of chef-owned treasure that wayfarers in France discover and always remember."

STARMONT. 900 Meadowood Lane, St. Helena (707-963-3646). Located at Meadowood Resort, this restaurant serves California country cuisine in a clubhouse setting.

CALISTOGA INN. 1250 Lincoln Avenue, Calistoga (707-942-4101). This quaint inn is renowned for its seafood.

POINTS OF INTEREST (SONOMA COUNTY)

LUTHER BURBANK HOME AND MEMORIAL GARDENS. Corner of Santa Rosa and Sonoma avenues, Santa Rosa (707-576-5115). Historic home of renowned naturalist.

MISSION SAN FRANCISCO DE SOLANO. Corner of First Street East and East Spain Street in Sonoma. Built in 1823, this was the northernmost of California's missions.

BUENA VISTA WINERY. 18000 Old Winery Road, Sonoma (707-938-1266). Historic winery founded in 1857.

JACK LONDON STATE HISTORIC PARK. Located one and a half miles west of Glen Ellen (707-938-5216). Features the cottage where he lived and London memorabilia. Museum open 10 A.M. to 5 P.M.

RUSSIAN RIVER. Excellent canoeing, swimming, and fishing.

ARMSTRONG REDWOOD STATE RESERVE. Major redwood groves two miles north of Guerneville off of State Route 116.

FORT ROSS STATE HISTORIC PARK. Located eleven miles north of Jenner on State Route 1 (707-847-3286). Restored and reconstructed 1812 trading outpost founded by Russian seal and fur hunters.

SALT POINT STATE PARK. Located north of Fort Ross off State Route 1 (707-847-3221). Tide pools, undersea caves, and good diving.

RESTAURANTS OF NOTE (SONOMA COUNTY)

Fine cuisine is a little difficult to discover in Sonoma County, but you should not be disappointed with these restaurants.

JOHN ASH & CO. 2324 Montgomery Drive, Santa Rosa (707-527-7687). An excellent wine list anchors the menu, which changes daily. Elegant fresh seasonal dishes.

THE PLAZA GRILL. 109A Plaza Street, Healdsburg (707-431-8305). California cuisine in a comfortable setting.

SOUVERAIN. 400 Souverain Road, between Healdsburg and Geyserville (707-433-3141). French fare in a prestigious winery overlooking vineyards.

CATELLI'S THE REX. 21047 Geyserville Avenue, Geyserville (707-857-9904). Family-owned Italian restaurant. Locals love the place.

CHRISTINE'S HOFFMAN HOUSE. 21712 Geyserville Avenue, Geyserville (707-857-3224). Good food. Moderate prices. Steaks sold by the ounce. Located in a historic home.

WHERE TO STAY

BEAZLEY HOUSE

This is the kind of fine old house that veteran bed-and-breakfast travelers hope to find when they are on the road. It has everything—history, style, romance, and location.

Built in 1902 by a prominent Napa surgeon, this two-story Colonial Revival stands on a neighborhood corner lot. Its shingles and awnings shade and primp themselves with trees and bushes; the lawn is deep green and neatly trimmed.

Inside, there are inlaid hardwood floors, high curved ceilings, bay windows, redwood paneling and trim, vintage rugs, large light-over-glass windows, window seats, and antique furnishings. Prisms of light radiate through a beviled half-round stained-glass window and fall across the wide stairway that leads to the four upstairs guest rooms, which feature plaster cove ceilings and more antiques.

The formal flair of the main house surrenders to a country feeling in

Beazley House (Jim Beazley)

the carriage house, which stands in the backyard. Beneath a spreading palm and looking beyond a lawn carved by gravel walkways and garnished with flowers, the carriage house offers five additional guest rooms. Fir paneling, beamed ceilings, brick fireplaces, and cedar bathrooms mark these units.

The house's character also has a human side to it. Jim and Carol Beazley are the people who make the inn a warm and welcome place to stay. Their stories have become a cliché in the bed-and-breakfast industry: scratch an innkeeper and you are likely to find corporate burnout lurking in their past.

Jim's career as a photojournalist and Carol's nursing profession finally lost their old zing in the late 1970s. They decided working for someone else left a great deal to be desired and rather than look for other jobs, they took to the road in search of a dream. In June 1981, they opened the Beazley House. They have never looked back.

"That first winter we cinched up our belts and ate lots of pasta," Jim says. "But we have always shown a profit, and we love what we do."

*   *   *

Beazley House, 1910 First Street, Napa, CA 94559 (707-257-1649). Nine guest rooms, shared baths in mansion (private baths planned), private baths in carriage house. Rates range from $70 to $105 (subject to change). VISA/MasterCard. No children under twelve; no pets; no smoking. Parking for nine cars behind carriage house. Take First Street exit off State Route 29, travel east on Second Street, then left on Warren to the Beazley House.

COOMBS RESIDENCE

Hospitality and service represent the trademarks of bed-and-breakfast inns. Most often, it is the innkeeper who makes the difference between an excellent inn and one that is just adequate. This is particularly true of Coombs Residence, where Rena Ruby takes an average-at-best setting and turns it into a comfortable homelike atmosphere. She is caring without being doting and a good conversationalist as well.

While Rena is the glow that keeps Coombs Residence warm, the house radiates a certain charm of its own. Built in 1852, this two-story brown-shingled home derives its name from politician and former ambassador Frank Coombs. He purchased the house for $10 in 1904, and his family lived here until 1977.

Bed and breakfast arrived on the scene in 1983; Rena came one year later. She liked Napa and wanted to leave Las Vegas. So when she found this place for sale, she could not resist. There was but one problem: Rena

Coombs Residence (Richard Wheeler)

did not know a thing about running a bed and breakfast.

"But I wanted to give it a try," Rena says. "I decided that what I needed to do was just treat people the way I would want to be treated."

Her philosophy works. To begin with, the home invites good feelings. The front parlor boasts a wallpapered ceiling, tile fireplace, overstuffed furniture, and an upright piano, while the four guest rooms, if not necessarily elegant, are homey and comfortable.

But Rena's touches are what make the difference: the down quilts, the his and hers terry robes, the open-door kitchen policy, the complimentary sherry and port, the home-baked breads, and the gracious manner in which Rena serves breakfast.

The ambience at Coombs Residence mirrors the best of bed and breakfast. Travelers who use this alternative form of lodging for that special experience will find it here.

*   *   *

Coombs Residence, 720 Seminary, Napa, CA 94559 (707-257-0789). Four guest rooms share two and a half baths. Rates range from $70 to $85 (subject to change). VISA/MasterCard. No children; no pets; smoking in living room only. Backyard boasts a swimming pool and Jacuzzi. On-street parking. From State Route 29, take First Street exit east, then Second Street to a right on Seminary.

THE OLD WORLD INN

The facade of this 1906 house resembles many of its brethren in the bed-and-breakfast business. Although not a specific architectural style, the blend of wood shingles, wide porches, clinker brick and columns, dormers, and leaded- and beviled-glass windows establishes the home as a member of the hospitality fraternity. But once you are inside, the home's uniqueness stands out like Spock's ears.

When you walk through the front door, the first thing that draws your attention is a painted message on the wall by the staircase: "Welcome Home. Romance Spoken Here." Then you notice that the living and morning rooms also radiate sayings to live by.

Before long, however, your eyes are seduced to venture beyond the lettering to the decor. Of course, there are the obligatory antiques and plump chairs and sofa around a fireplace, but it is the colors and fabrics that catch your imagination. Pastels—French blue, pink, peach, green, and persimmon—create a dreamworld setting, while the fabrics, courtesy of Macy's China Seas/HomePort collection, result in rich motifs that are both artistic and inviting.

The guest rooms reflect the same bold, yet comfortable, atmosphere as the common rooms. Most have either full or half-canopied beds. Antiques, some of them painted in pastels, appoint the accommodations, which boast old-fashioned baths and touches such as stenciled bows

The Old World Inn (Courtesy The Old World Inn)

rambling across pastel walls.

In addition to the distinctive decor, service here reaches beyond the norm. As well as the breakfast, afternoon tea is served from 3:30 P.M. to 5:00 P.M.; chilled wine is delivered to each room around 4:45 P.M.; then from 5:15 P.M. to 8:30 P.M., an international cheese board is offered in the morning room; while homemade sweetmeats and dessert wines are featured from 8:30 P.M. to 10:30 P.M.

I could go on to tell you about the English hospitality of innkeepers Janet and Geoffrey Villiers, or the Jacuzzi that sits in the shade of orange trees, but I think you have the idea now. The Old World Inn is indeed a distinctive bed and breakfast.

*　　*　　*

The Old World Inn, 1301 Jefferson Street, Napa, CA 94559 (707-257-0112). Eight guest rooms, all with private baths. Rates range from $75 to $100 (subject to change). VISA/MasterCard/American Express. No children; no pets; no smoking. Parking behind inn, which is located in a neighborhood on the edge of downtown. From State Route 29, take Lincoln East exit, then turn right on Jefferson to the inn.

THE AMBROSE BIERCE HOUSE

The Ambrose Bierce House has two things in common with its most famous owner—its name and its unusual disposition.

Having the look and feel of a two-flat rather than a historic residence, this post-Victorian home sits behind a white picket fence, just north of downtown St. Helena. Its unlikely architectural style arose in 1886, when Bierce purchased the fourteen-year-old structure. Feeling a need for more room, he jacked up the entire house and added a new main floor.

Today, the downstairs serves as living quarters for the owners, Tony and Sheila, while the upstairs welcomes bed-and-breakfast guests. An exterior staircase winds up to an open porch and etched-glass door, that opens into a sitting room and three guest accommodations.

Although the decor takes you back to Bierce's day, the ambience does not. Known as "Bitter Bierce" for his pessimistic attitude toward people and his biting wit, writer Ambrose Bierce would likely shun the idea of welcoming strangers into his home. That is certainly not the case with Tony and Sheila, who greet guests with ready smiles and firm hands.

The way they came to be the innkeepers here tells you quite a lot about how they feel about the place. Briefly, in October 1984, Tony and Sheila laid their heads down at Ambrose Bierce as guests. It was such a pleasurable experience that they purchased the home in September 1985.

"We've had no regret," Tony says, his words falling with a light

The Ambrose Bierce House (Courtesy The Ambrose Bierce House)

British accent. "After the first two weeks of craziness, we knew this was what we had always wanted to do."

And they do it very well. Besides a warm personable welcoming, guests are greeted by fresh-cut flowers and complimentary sherry in each of the rooms. In addition, a bit of history reaches out and touches them. Named Ambrose Bierce Suite, Lillie Langtry, and Eadweard Muybridge, each accommodation features a biography of its famous namesakes as well as memorabilia honoring their colorful pasts.

The hospitality continues in the morning with juice and coffee delivered to the sitting room before breakfast, so guests can slowly acclimate their waking bodies to a new day. Then, between 8:30 A.M. and 10 A.M. a breakfast of seasonal fruit and pastries arrives.

I doubt Ambrose Bierce would relate well to all of this, but fortunately for travelers who call this place their home on the road, his former house seems to be handling it all quite well.

*　　*　　*

The Ambrose Bierce House, 1515 Main Street, St. Helena, CA 94574 (707-963-3003). Three guest rooms, all with private baths and queen beds. The Ambrose Bierce Suite is a two-room accommodation. Rates range from $85 to $135 (subject to change). American Express. Children with prior approval; no pets; smoking in sitting room only. Parking lot in rear of house. In St. Helena, State Route 29 is also Main Street. The inn is located north of downtown on the west side of the street.

Bartels Ranch

Located three miles from St. Helena, on one hundred acres of rolling meadowland studded with clusters of oak trees, this country estate offers amenities usually found only at first-class resorts. Yet owner Jami Bartels provides the kind of personal attention available only at bed and breakfasts.

"If you come to stay here," Jami says, "you would be my guest. But I will treat you like my friend."

Being Jami's friend means luxury, comfort, and fun. A narrow country lane climbs past grazing horses, to her sprawling stone California country ranch house. In front of the covered entranceway sits a shiny Mercedes, or maybe even two.

Inside, the house opens up like a spring flower. In the center sits a kitchen Julia Child could love. It is spacious and homey with brick walls. From here, the house spans out like an open fan.

To one side is Jami's living room; to the other is the Napa Valley Room. Here, guests can either relax or play.

A fire usually crackles in the brick fireplace, while classical music cascades about the beamed vaulted ceiling. As you turn your back to the fire and the overstuffed sofa that nestles before it, the room becomes a playground for adults. There are a billiard table, ping-pong table, and jukebox. In the back courtyard, there are a pool and Jacuzzi, while in the

Bartels Ranch (Richard Wheeler)

front a wooden deck overlooks meadows to the wooded hills beyond.

Anywhere else, the three guest rooms would border on elegance. At Bartels, they pale in comparison to the common rooms. Nevertheless, each is comfortable and offers a good night's sleep and lots of privacy.

It is not surprising that Bartels Ranch caters to an up-scale clientele. Still the atmosphere here is typically bed and breakfast, so there is absolutely no aloofness.

*   *   *

Bartels Ranch, 1200 Conn Valley Road, St. Helena, CA 94574 (707-963-4001). Three guest rooms, all with private baths. The Sunset Room is easily the finest accommodation, featuring a king-size half-canopied bed, peacock wicker chairs, and private access to the pool. Rates range from $95 to $140 (subject to change). VISA/MasterCard/American Express/Discover. Children with prior approval; arrangements can be made for pets; smoking permitted. Small conferences and catered dinners welcome. Limousine and helicopter services available. From St. Helena, take Pope Street to the Silverado Trail. Jog left to a right on Howell Mountain Road, then turn right again onto Conn Valley Road.

CHESTELSON HOUSE

The American version of bed and breakfast has metamorphosed from quaint "mom-and-pop" homes, where guests sleep in what was once Junior's room, to a diverse range of accommodations, including the elegant, sophisticated, and sometimes museumlike character of many of today's inns. Among other things, these changes now make possible the melding of posh surroundings and personal attention.

However, a faint cry sounds from travelers who lament the shrinking numbers of intimate bed-and-breakfast homes, which are often now available only through reservation services. For those people, the wine country's Chestelson House is the answer.

Located just a few blocks from downtown St. Helena, this cozy bungalow, which sits behind a white picket fence, boasts no significant architectural style to set it off from its neighbors.

The house was built in 1905 and remained a private residence until 1978, when Claudia Chestelson purchased it. She opened the home to guests in 1980. Today, Jackie Sweet carries on the bed-and-breakfast tradition started by Claudia.

Jackie exhibits an easy, comfortable manner. She is soft-spoken, worldly, and intelligent. And for her, running a bed and breakfast represents a dream come true.

"I've wanted to do this for ten years," Jackie says. "I really like it. I've

Chestelson House (Courtesy Chestelson House)

met so many nice people—people who I think could be friends if they didn't live so far away."

Jackie's hospitality is the main draw here. Still, each of the three guest rooms offers charm. The front bedroom features a large bay window and is furnished in antiques; the back room boasts a private deck that looks out on the surrounding hills. The White Room is suite size and is distinguished by a raised tub nestled against a greenhouse window lush with ferns.

I would be the first to admit that staying in a grand mansion, echoing with the sounds of history, makes for treasured memories. But, at the same time, staying in a home such as Jackie Sweet's is like sitting back in my favorite easy chair, with my cat cuddled up on my lap and a cup of hot tea warming my insides.

*　　　*　　　*

Chestelson House, 1417 Kearney Street, St. Helena, CA 94574 (707-963-2238). Three guest rooms, two with private baths. Rates range from $75 to $95 (subject to change). No credit cards. Children with prior approval; no pets; no smoking. On-street parking. Full breakfast served in dining area or on veranda. From State Route 29, turn west on Adams Street to Kearney.

CINNAMON BEAR

As the name suggests, there lurks a bit of whimsy at the Cinnamon Bear. Throughout the house, a menagerie of fuzzy bears smiles and stares. They sit above the parlor hearth, lay about on rocking chairs and stretch out on beds.

The capriciousness, however, does not begin and end with the bears. This house is full of fun and silliness. There are the furry bear slippers for keeping feet cozy and a game room with an old pump organ, a 1920 maple game table, and lots of games. And, like most bed and breakfasts, there is an evening social hour—except the Cinnamon Bear's resembles a party. Beginning at 5:30 P.M., guests gather in the parlor or on the porch to meet each other, sip wine, nibble on snacks, and listen to music. There may even be live entertainment. All of this comes together under the direction of Genny Jenkins, owner and innkeeper.

"We live in such a pressure cooker," Genny says. "So occasionally we need a break. We need to be childlike once in a while. I try to create an atmosphere for that here."

Genny began offering her brand of "bed-and-breakfast therapy" in 1979 after her three children had grown and left home. At first, the business was merely a part-time experience, but Genny had such "great fun," she found herself "hooked." So in 1980, she opened three upstairs guest rooms full time.

Her two-story 1904 bungalow sits on a corner just two blocks from downtown St. Helena. It is simple, but attractive, with brown shingles,

Cinnamon Bear (Courtesy Cinnamon Bear)

light-over-glass windows, and wide columned porches.

Guests enter the parlor to discover a warm and inviting setting. There are a tile fireplace, lots of redwood trim, a blend of furniture, and Persian area rugs.

Fir floors run throughout the upstairs rooms, whose characters are defined by unique features. There are sloped ceilings, wainscoting, and a deacon's bench in Nutmeg. Laura Ashley prints and a claw-footed tub distinguish Vanilla. And Ginger boasts an unusual angular shape, which results in a cozy ambience.

Like its neighbor, Chestelson House, the Cinnamon Bear reaches deep inside itself to create a homelike experience. Yet, without overdoing "cute," it manages to have some fun in the process.

* * *

Cinnamon Bear, 1407 Kearney Street, St. Helena, CA 94574 (707-963-4653). Three guest rooms, all with private baths. The rate is $95 each (subject to change). VISA/MasterCard/American Express. No children under ten; no pets; no smoking. On-street parking. From State Route 29, turn west on Adams to Kearney.

THE INK HOUSE

Theron H. Ink, who built this two-story Italianate Victorian farm-house in 1884, was an empire builder. Ink House was his dream mansion, and an observatory was his special pride. Perched atop the house like a royal crown, this lofty spot allowed Ink to admire his holdings quietly and privately. But the inevitable allowed him only a few years of glory, and in 1893 Ink died. Some sixty years later, the badly deteriorating observatory was gone too, and his dream house was in rapid decline.

Today, the house stands renewed, and the refurbished observatory once more sits atop the roof. The rescue mission began in 1967, when new owners, Lois and George Clark, started to breathe new life into this old house. In the process, the Clarks raised both a house and a family.

In 1977, with the children grown and gone, the sounds of silence began echoing about the twelve-foot ceilings. Lois decided it was far too quiet. The solution: bring in an extended family to care for. Thus was born The Ink House Bed and Breakfast.

Because of the restoration effort, guests here experience the home of Ink's era. In the parlor, flames flicker in a tile fireplace and glitter in the crystal chandelier suspended from the plaster ceiling. Victorian furnishings grace the Persian rug that adorns the hardwood floor.

Four guest rooms sit on the second floor, at the top of steep stairs. The accommodations are dressed in antiques of iron, brass, walnut, and oak.

The Ink House (Courtesy The Ink House)

Tall windows look out on the surrounding vineyards.

Outside, stately old oak trees and tall pines shade the veranda, which wraps around the house. Chairs and swings welcome moonlit nights. Hedges and a wrought-iron fence protect the home from nearby State Route 29.

The feeling here is one of peace. It is also one that permits a long look back to the turn of the century. Except for the mechanized army of tourists passing Ink's front door and the rumble of tractors and trucks assisting in the harvest, little has changed here.

*　　*　　*

The Ink House, 1575 St. Helena Highway, St. Helena, CA 94574 (707-963-3890). Four guest rooms, all with private baths. Rates range from $70 to $90 (subject to change). No credit cards. No children; no pets; no smoking. Private parking in front of house. The inn is located between Rutherford and St. Helena on the corner of Whitehall Lane and State Route 29.

VILLA ST. HELENA

Hidden in the hills above St. Helena sprawls a grand Mediterranean-style villa, which seems more suited to entertain the whims of landed

Villa St. Helena (Richard Wheeler)

gentry than the needs of bed-and-breakfast travelers. Yet adding another page to the encyclopedia of diverse styles making up this industry, Villa St. Helena plays its role as a bed-and-breakfast host with warmth and charm.

The setting places guests in a remote pastoral environment. The villa is surrounded by twenty acres of valleys and rolling hills studded with old oaks, bays, and madronas. Built by internationally renowned architect Robert M. Carrere, the three-level brick structure represents a forerunner of California ranch house architecture.

In the heart of the mansion sits an oasis of tranquility—the courtyard. A fifty-foot swimming pool fronts a large barbecue area tucked neatly into an elliptically arched wall.

Serving as the home's focal point are the beamed living room and the adjoining solarium. A massive stone fireplace dominates the eclectic living room. Sun pours through the large windows that make up one wall of the solarium.

A rambling veranda leads to the four guest rooms, which are simply identified as A, B, 1, and 4. Room A is by far the most elegant and spacious of the accommodations. It boasts a marble fireplace, queen-size bed, parquet floor, picture-window views of Heath Canyon, and a private balcony that overlooks the pool. The other rooms are less spectacular but still appealing.

It should come as no surprise that Villa St. Helena's guests often bear the labels of success and money. Still, the environment caters to casual and informal attitudes. The mansion's large dimensions do present a drawback for those who like to socialize: chances of not seeing other guests, except at breakfast, are quite good.

Forty years ago starlets and statesmen wined and dined within the villa's elegance. Only a slight blink of the imagination readily conjures up the picture they must have painted here. Today, the villa attempts to entertain its guests in the same grand fashion of years past.

*   *   *

Villa St. Helena, 2727 Sulphur Springs Avenue, St. Helena, CA 94574 (707-963-2514). Four guest rooms, all with private baths. Rates range from $105 to $185 (subject to change). VISA/MasterCard/American Express. No children; no pets; smoking permitted. This is not an easy place to find, and reclusive neighbors are not very helpful. Be sure to ask for specific directions. Sulphur Springs Avenue turns west off of State Route 29, just south of St. Helena.

FOREST MANOR

Forest Manor is a secluded mansion in the woods.

Located on a twenty-acre estate in the hills above St. Helena, this English Tudor country house sits in a forest of fir and pine. A circular drive curves in front of the three-story timbered manor.

Inside, sunlight washes through banks of tall paned windows and brushes across rich furnishings. It highlights the dark wood trim and massive hand-carved beams that cross sweeping vaulted ceilings. A sense of power and dignity permeates the structure; however, it is strength without indifference.

Forest Manor is a human place. There are the half-read books sitting open on a table, the sweet smells of home-baked muffins, potted plants, and Oriental art adorning walls.

Guest facilities distinguish each open level of the house. The downstairs Queen Anne Suite equals the size of many urban apartments. Carved furniture from Thailand appoints the living room, which is warmed with a brick fireplace and garnished with Iranian rugs. Down a short hall awaits a breakfast room furnished in wicker. The refrigerator cools soft drinks and a coffee maker sits nearby. For snacks, there is a basket of fruit. Beyond the hall, the bedroom, which opens onto a private deck, overlooks a fifty-three-foot lap pool and a Jacuzzi.

An equally elegant accommodation, the second-floor Magnolia Suite, features overstuffed chairs, a metal fireplace, a mirrored bathroom with a mosaic-tile double Jacuzzi tub, and a windowed breakfast alcove that overlooks the landscaped yard and pool. The Burgundy Room nestles into a corner of the third floor. Two recreation rooms feature a billiard table,

Forest Manor (Richard Wheeler)

ping-pong table, color television, and video cassette recorder.

In so many ways, the setting here resembles an exclusive resort. But owners and innkeepers Harold and Corlene Lambeth provide a personal friendly ambience.

*   *   *

Forest Manor, 415 Cold Springs Road, Angwin, CA 94508 (707-965-3538).

Three guest rooms, all with private baths. (A fourth room is planned for the future.) Rates range from $100 to $150 (subject to change). VISA/ Mastercard. No children under twelve; no pets; no smoking. If there is a drawback here, it is the home's remote location. However, it is only a fifteen-minute drive from St. Helena, and the tradeoff results in a tranquil environment. From north of St. Helena on State Route 29, take Deer Park Road to a right on Cold Springs Road. Follow Cold Springs to just before it dead-ends, then turn left up a country lane to Forest Manor.

FOOTHILL HOUSE

Foothill House may be the perfect bed and breakfast, if indeed such a place actually exists. Except for the fact that Foothill House has but three guest accommodations, requiring lots of advanced planning and some good luck for reservations, the inn is flawless.

Located in the foothills just north of Calistoga, this remodeled turn-of-the-century farmhouse nestles in a country setting surrounded by trees. And being north of most of Napa Valley's wineries, it is out of the flow of heavy tourist traffic, making it even more tranquil.

Innkeepers Michael and Sue Clow set up the Foothill House based upon their own experiences from eight years of traveling to country inns and bed and breakfasts. After seeing firsthand what does and does not work, they began their search for the perfect country getaway. Foothill House is the result.

"We wanted to offer guests as much privacy and flexibility as possible," Mike says. "We wanted to anticipate their every need without being intrusive."

Lofty goals for sure, but Mike and Sue have managed to climb to the heights of the bed-and-breakfast mountain. And they have done it without sacrificing comfort, service, or hospitality.

Guest room decor and ambience are impeccable. The color schemes center around handmade quilts, which adorn queen-size four-poster beds. Wallpapers and paints soothe rather than overwhelm. The country antiques combine comfort and taste, while wood-burning fireplaces, ceiling fans, and air conditioners allow room temperatures that meet individual tastes.

Creature comforts abound here, as well. Room refrigerators hold complimentary Calistoga water and Napa Valley wine, jars of Foothill House Sweet Dreams (incredible chocolate chip cookies) beckon from bedside tables, AM-FM stereo cassette players provide music, fresh flowers add subtle fragrances, beds are turned down in the evenings, and towels are always fresh.

Foothill House (Gene Dekovic)

It is hard to imagine better accommodations at these prices or even at rates two or three times these. Nevertheless, perhaps the best testimonials for Foothill House come from the dozen or so California innkeepers who praise the inn without reservation.

*   *   *

Foothill House, 3037 Foothill Boulevard, Calistoga, CA 94515 (707-942-6933). Three guest rooms, all with private baths and private entrances. The Evergreen Suite, with its bay window view of Mount St. Helena and private garden deck, is like a cozy country house. Rates range from $70 to $95 (subject to change). VISA/MasterCard. Children with prior approval; no pets; no smoking. Private parking. Follow State Route 29 north until it becomes State Route 128. Look for Foothill House on the left, one and a half miles past Lincoln Avenue.

MELITTA STATION INN

Like most bed and breakfasts across the country, wine country inns often pay tribute to themselves: they praise their architectural styles, honor their designer fabrics and papers, and memorialize their pasts. These are often the things that attract us to them.

But, pausing for air five miles east of Santa Rosa, in Jack London's

"Valley of the Moon," sits a low redwood barnlike building known as Melitta Station Inn. While it poses as prettily as any other, this folksy inn celebrates its surroundings—the country. There are the whispers of a little creek that flows behind it and the pastures and hills that make up the surrounding landscape.

A bay tree and willows surrender their fragrances for home potpourri, and an herb garden volunteers for many country duties. Dried flowers, blossoms, wreaths, and baskets bring more of the countryside home; French doors and large windows welcome the sun and the air.

Inside the living room, oiled fir floors glisten around handwoven scatter rugs, and wicker, cane, and rattan continue the folksy atmosphere. A corner wood stove removes the chill from cool evenings, and a Welsh sideboard contains evening wine and morning repast.

Guest rooms do not shy away from the country either. Antiques, quilts, and collectables create more of the sense of rural America, which is exactly what innkeepers Diane and Jeff Jefferds sought when they came here.

It was a bed-and-breakfast trip to Europe several years ago and then a summer on the East Coast that inspired Diane's love of country—more specifically her affection for folk art, antiques, and country inns. Combined with a desire harbored by both her and husband Jeff to escape the hectic pace of the city, the Jefferds were moved to establish a country

Melitta Station Inn (Courtesy Melitta Station Inn)

inn. The result is Melitta Station Inn, a restored turn-of-the-century railroad station.

The Jefferds' creation is a breath of fresh air. It does not overwhelm you with itself but instead invites you to gain appreciation for the "Valley of the Moon."

*   *   *

Melitta Station Inn, 5850 Melita Road, Santa Rosa, CA 95405 (707-538-7712). Six guest rooms, four with private baths. Rates range from $55 to $70 (subject to change). VISA/MasterCard. Children with prior approval; no smoking; no pets. Across from the inn, two state parks offer horseback riding, hiking, and fishing. From U.S. 101, take State Route 12 towards Sonoma. Just past the Calistoga Road, turn right onto Melita Road to the inn.

CAMELLIA INN

In 1981, Ray and Del Lewand left the freeways and urban sprawl of Los Angeles behind, for the rolling hills and fertile valleys of northern California's wine country. They moved into a historic home in Healdsburg and donned the smiles of bed-and-breakfast innkeepers.

"We had wanted to move to the wine country for several years," Del says, "but first needed to figure out a way to support ourselves. Looking back on our positive experience with bed and breakfasts in Europe, we decided this was something we could do. So here we are."

The home and setting they chose is ideal for bed and breakfast. Located in a residential neighborhood on a lot blessed with some thirty varieties of camellias and ringed by majestic old trees, the Italianate Victorian home dates back to 1869.

For thirty years, it served as the home of a successful and rather colorful local merchant. Then in 1892, Dr. J. W. Seawell purchased the home and used it both as a private residence and as a small hospital for his patients. Throughout the home's lifetime, including its medical stint, this elegant residence has complemented the lifestyles of moneyed and sophisticated owners and their guests.

The double parlors downstairs set the tone for the home. Twin marble fireplaces, ceiling medallions, Palladian windows, and antique furnishings recall the rustle of silk dresses and the aroma of expensive cigars.

This historical and classical spirit carries on in each of the guest rooms. Three of the accommodations are located upstairs, while four more distinguish the adjoining wing. All boast antiques and vintage rugs. In addition, the Lewands provide a few extra touches, such as fragrant roses

Camellia Inn (Ken Veeder)

or camellias, individually gift-wrapped soaps and extra pillows, and a
backyard swimming pool.

Camellia Inn mirrors what we have come to know as a traditional
American bed and breakfast. Ray and Del have done a good job of both
bringing out the country charm of this home and providing for the more
contemporary needs of their guests.

*   *   *

Camellia Inn, 211 North Street, Healdsburg, CA 95448 (707-433-8182).

Seven guest rooms, five with private baths. Rates range from $50 to $75 (subject to change). VISA/MasterCard. Children with prior approval; no pets; smoking in parlors only. Breakfast is served buffet-style in the dining room. Small parking lot behind the inn. North Street turns east off Healdsburg Avenue, just north of the town plaza.

GRAPE LEAF INN

Healdsburg's Grape Leaf Inn does not shy away from attention. In fact, this 1902 Queen Anne first winks and then shouts at passersby.

Nestled on a corner lot, the two-story inn peeks from behind young trees before flashing its lavender, purple, blue, and white body. Grape vines cling to the curved porch that embraces the inn, while filigreed dormers poke from the roof like fancy party hats.

Inside, fragrant wines and pungent cheeses lead guests through the parlor to the living room, which is adorned with a white brick fireplace, overstuffed furniture, and hardwood floors.

Within whispering distance, the three downstairs rooms (like all seven accommodations, named for grape varietals) offer a relaxing, quiet

Grape Leaf Inn (Courtesy Grape Leaf Inn)

atmosphere. In these rooms, big beds and antique trimmings create scenes reminiscent of the turn of the century.

There are four additional guest rooms upstairs. Sunlight and fresh air stream through seventeen skylights, which dot the sloped ceilings of both bedrooms and bathrooms in Cabernet Sauvignon, Merlot, Zinfandel, and the Chardonnay Suite. Iron and brass beds commingle with vintage rugs and hardwood floors, giving the rooms an antique flavor. Stained-glass windows and cathedrallike angles produce subtle undertones of reverence. But all subtleties are stripped naked in the lavish bathrooms, where mirrors and deep tiled two-person whirlpool tubs invite pleasure.

Grape Leaf Inn opened its doors to bed and breakfast in August 1981. But the credit for remodeling and adding such trappings as skylights and whirlpools goes to current owner Terry Sweet, who purchased the home in September 1982. His innkeeper, Kathy Cookson, deserves credit for the full homemade breakfast, which is served buffet-style each morning.

Terry indeed has a sense of style. His choice of colors, the tubs and mirrors, and the extensive use of skylights might seem gaudy elsewhere. Yet, although the house begs notice, it ultimately reflects a class act.

*   *   *

Grape Leaf Inn, 539 Johnson Street, Healdsburg, CA 95448 (707-433-8140). Seven guest rooms, all with private baths. Chardonnay Suite is two rooms with a queen-size iron and brass bed plus a day bed. Rates range from $60 to $100 (subject to change). VISA/MasterCard. Children with prior approval; no pets; no smoking. Private parking available. From Healdsburg Avenue, travel east on Grant Street to Johnson.

HAYDON HOUSE

Despite painstaking research, travel writers occasionally overlook a masterpiece. I am no exception. Such was the case with Haydon House, which, without the prodding of several wine country innkeepers, would not have been part of this book. Not only did I fail to schedule a visit, I completely left it off my initial list of inquiries.

Fortunately, I redeemed myself. For, without a doubt, Haydon House is a gem of an inn.

Built in 1912, this two-story Queen Anne home sits behind a white picket fence on a tree-lined neighborhood street. A columned veranda curves around one side, drawing the roof down in a turretlike fashion. A dormer rises above the entranceway.

In nearly every way, Haydon House looks like the All-American home. It is hard to imagine that the house served a thirty-year tenure of institutional drab—first as a convent, then a boy's home, and finally a rest

Haydon House (Lenny Siegel)

home.

In 1983, Joanne and Richard Claus lived up to their name and played Santa to the tired home. Working several months of what approached twenty-four hour days, the Claus's scraped, painted, cleaned, and refurbished. Today, the patina of the fir floors gleams renewed, Laura Ashley prints dance with life, and antiqued parlors add touches of days past.

All five bedrooms occupy the second floor. French and American antiques, lace curtains, dried and silk floral arrangements, fresh flowers, custom-made quilts, vintage tubs, and gathering baskets overflowing with fluffy towels create the *Better Homes & Gardens* look.

Although all the guest rooms have charm, the Attic Suite is special. Skylights in the curving sloped ceiling, to potted plants, to the queen bed, claw-footed tub, and cane rocker meld to create a unique setting.

Haydon House has all the markings of an elegant bed-and-breakfast inn: size, carefully designed decor, professional innkeeping. Still, there is a real homelike atmosphere that prevails.

*　　*　　*

Haydon House, 321 Haydon Street, Healdsburg, CA 95448 (707-433-5228). Five rooms, one with private bath; however, each of the others has a wash basin, while three have tubs. Rates range from $60 to $75 (subject to change). VISA/MasterCard. No children under twelve; no pets; smoking in common rooms only. Full breakfast is served in dining room. From Healdsburg Avenue, turn east on Matheson, then right on Fitch, to a left on Haydon.

HOPE-MERRILL HOUSE

Conversation flowed as liberally as the wine. There were stories of trips to India, tales of Mexico, and romantic episodes in the lives of newlyweds. The Hope-Merrill House was once again in full swing, celebrating its daily evening social hour.

Located in the sleepy village of Geyserville, the inn has become famous for both its hospitality, which is most apparent during the evening parlor party and morning breakfast feast, and its authentic Victorian look. In fact, this inn reflects the ornate style of Victorianism to such a high degree that it could pass for a nineteenth-century museum.

This is not to say that the inn is stuffy, it is not. But, except for the sun room, the color and ornament of that period dominates every nook and cranny of the house.

Like so many old Victorian ladies, this home stood neglected for years before it received the primping and preening needed to restore its former charms. The rescue effort came in 1980, when Bob and Rosalie Hope purchased the house.

At the time, they were living in the Hope-Bosworth House just across the street, a home they had purchased in 1979 to enjoy semiretirement while running a small inn. But Rosalie could not take her eyes off the Merrill House. She had always wanted a large Victorian home, so when it came up for sale, the Hopes purchased it. So much for semiretirement. Today, after lots of hard work and careful restoration, Hope-Merrill House is a first-rate example of Victorian splendor.

Inside the circa 1875 Eastlake stick-style Victorian, the rooms are stuffed with antiques and collectables. The silk-screened wallpapers of designer Bruce Bradbury bring balance of light to the typically dark Victorian setting. Lace curtains and elegant drapes adorn windows, redwood trim garnishes walls, vintage rugs carpet floors, and ten-foot-high ceilings highlight bold motifs.

While breakfasts are often special events in guest houses, few offer gourmet repasts equal to those served at Hope-Merrill House. Such delicacies as strawberry bread with homemade fruit butters and jams, puff pastries wrapping tender sausage, chili egg puffs, or Drambuie-dipped French toast often make appearances on Rosalie's cranberry china.

Hope-Merrill House adds a touch of elegance to the simple and tranquil town of Geyserville. Innkeepers Bob and Rosalie Hope mix in

Hope-Merrill House (Lewis Green)

large quantities of hospitality. All in all, it is not a bad place to swap stories.

*   *   *

Hope-Merrill House, 21253 Geyserville Avenue, P.O. Box 42, Geyserville, CA 95441 (707-857-3356). Five guest rooms, two with private baths. (As of this writing, two additional rooms with private baths and fireplaces are scheduled for availability by 1987.) Rates range from $65 to $80 (subject to change). VISA/MasterCard/American Express. No children; no pets; no smoking. Private parking available. Ask about "Stage-A-Picnic," tours of the wine country by horse-drawn stage. The inn is located on Geyserville Avenue, just north of downtown.

The Gold Country

On a January morning in 1848, James Wilson Marshall turned over a boulder in the American River and changed the face and fortune of California. As his shadow danced in the waters, Marshall's mouth formed the words that carried California from wilderness into statehood: "Boys," he said, "I believe I have found a gold mine."

Before Marshall's discovery, only fourteen thousand non-Indians roamed and worked California's wilderness. The Coloma Valley, where Marshall and a few men operated Sutter's Mill, posed pristine and peaceful. San Francisco, some 160 miles west of the town of Coloma, stood knee deep in dust and sleep.

But the gold awakened this dormant giant. By 1865 hundreds of thousands of fortune seekers swarmed over the Sierra Nevada foothills. Astute entrepreneurs rushed into the fledgling towns of San Francisco and Sacramento, where they raised cities on the sweat of prospectors. Five hundred rowdy, rickety towns sprung up along the mother lode, between Mariposa and Georgetown. And before the madness ended, hundreds of millions in gold gilded the pockets of merchants, who happily unburdened the miners of their glitter.

Today, only the legends and about half of the settlements remain. But the visions of mules laden with supplies, miners' pouches filled with gold dust, and saloons echoing with gambling and drink still lure visitors to this country. Some come to pan for the elusive dream; most journey here to peek into the past and enjoy the sights of rolling hills framed by snow-clad peaks and valleys cut by icy rivers.

Winding its way from the pastures of Mariposa to the heights of Yuba Pass, State Route 49—known as the Golden Chain—snakes past ghost towns, as well as through tiny hamlets of commerce and tourism.

Although the highway skirts the foothills for some three hundred miles, the most interesting stretch bridges Sonora with Nevada City. Within this ribbon, tourists can visit historic sites; take sidetrips to caves and wilderness belts; explore lakes, rivers, and recreation areas; and, of course, discover abandoned mines. In addition, the major attractions of Yosemite National Park and Lake Tahoe sprawl within easy driving distance of the towns that link the Golden Chain.

During the past several decades a new gold has produced wealth in these foothills—wine. Climbing the western slopes of the Sierra Nevadas, vineyards flourish between Murphys and Placerville.

The growth of the gold country's wine industry actually dates back to the 1890s, when more than one hundred wineries flanked these mountains. But the combination of mine closures and prohibition left acres of vineyards untended and wineries empty.

Then in the 1960s, winemakers rediscovered the fertile foothills. At about the same time, people seeking a tranquil environment began flocking to the gold country's small towns. Today, more than twenty wineries—small and usually family run—produce premium wines, from the Zinfandel yielded by the Shenandoah Valley to the exceptional Rieslings coming out of El Dorado County.

The gold country offers travelers an opportunity to experience both the old and the new California. And the towns dotting State Route 49 provide civilized access to a land that in many ways still walks on the wild side.

GETTING TO KNOW THE GOLD COUNTRY

SONORA

During the gold rush Sonora became the gateway to the Southern Mines and home to the Big Bonanza Mine, one of California's richest gold mines. Miners prowled the streets with gamblers, outlaws, and painted ladies.

Today, the city's streets and avenues paint a much quieter scene. However, history lives on in Sonora's old buildings. California's second oldest Episcopal Church, St. James, still rings its bells at the corner of North Washington and Snell streets, while along West Bradford Avenue stand the 1860s home of pioneer merchant Josiah Hall and the Toulumne County Museum, which was built in 1857 to serve as the county jail. All in all, some fifty historic buildings still endure in Sonora.

MURPHYS

Located alongside State Route 4, ten miles from the larger community of Angels Camp, Murphys rests off the beaten path, out of the general traffic of most tourists. Only a few stores, restaurants, and frame homes make up this tiny town. Its most famous building is the Murphys Hotel, where Black Bart once propped his elbows on the bar.

Murphys is an ideal location for exploring the nearby caves, the giant sequoias of Calaveras Big Trees and Columbia Historic State parks. In addition, people here have time to be friendly and have not yet grown weary of tourists.

JACKSON

This town grew out of the gold fields and matured during the quartz mining days of the 1880s and 1890s. However, by the turn of the century, Jackson thrived on commerce, so when the last of the mines closed in 1942, its population of two thousand remained nearly stable.

Today, modern motels, gift stores, and gas stations stand beside several dozen 1860s brick buildings. The most interesting of these is the Amador County Museum on Church Street. Besides furniture, relics, and artifacts dating back to the mid- and late 1800s, a separate building houses several working scale models of mine structures.

IONE

This small farming community never celebrated fame as a gold town. Instead, it served as a supply center for the miners. It continues to wear that label today as it meets the needs of the farmers and ranchers who work the fertile Ione Valley.

Located on State Route 104, a gray line that intersects State Route 88 several miles west of Sutter Creek, Ione sees few tourists, as few venture into the valley, which just sits on the edge of gold country. That makes for quiet drives through rolling valleys, where cattle graze peacefully and distant views await atop nearly every rise.

SUTTER CREEK

Sutter Creek's historic buildings and covered sidewalks bustle with tourism. Cash registers sing a happy song along Antique Row and inside stores, studios, and saloons. Its fifteen hundred people live in neat white cottages and play eager hosts to the weekend crowds that jam Sutter Creek's meticulously clean streets. Although it seductively winks at tourists, Sutter Creek has maintained respect for itself and has shunned honky-tonk capitalism.

GEORGETOWN

North of the crossroads community of Placerville, State Route 49 twists and turns through rugged countryside. Here sits the town where the cry of "eureka!" first rang out. Today, 70 percent of Coloma makes up the Marshall Gold Discovery State Park.

Surrounding the park and reaching out into the hills, pine forests, vast valleys, and stark canyons turn this landscape into a vivid portrait. Georgetown sits high in the hills, only ten miles but a slow tortuous drive from the Golden Chain. The community survives in its past: one-story brick and frame buildings sporting covered sidewalks and a long white line of posts make up the postage-stamp-size community. You do not come here to wallow in tourist shops—there are none. Instead, you venture these back roads to experience California's history and to see its untamed landscape.

GRASS VALLEY

Once the richest of all California towns, today's Grass Valley continues to display its heritage, while bearing the look and feel of a contemporary small city.

Its early development fell under the spell of the prosperous and enduring Empire Mine, which along with several smaller operations removed some $960 million worth of gold from the area. In 1975, the state purchased 784 acres of Empire Mine properties to turn them into the Empire Mine State Historic Park.

NEVADA CITY

Nevada City is the decorative pendant that adorns the Golden Chain. Embraced by waves of forested hills, the residential streets of Nevada City showcase gingerbread homes boasting turrets and gables, while the downtown historic preservation district sparkles in the light of gas lamps.

This is the gold country's one town that has kept its past for everyone to see, yet still meets the needs of contemporary travelers: shopping opportunities abound, fine restaurants flourish, and entertainment thrives.

A PRACTICAL GUIDE TO THE GOLD COUNTRY

THE CLIMATE

Summer days can be scorchers here (90-degree range in July), while winters are relatively mild (seldom dipping below freezing). Rainfall can be heavy at times from November to April, with snow generally on the light side.

YOUR CLOTHES

Dress should be casual and sturdy. Good walking shoes are highly recommended.

PANNING FOR GOLD

Placer gold still beckons from the rivers and creeks of gold country. No one is going to get rich from the deposits, but panning, and the dreaming that goes with it, can be lots of fun. All you need is a twelve-inch steel pan and a riverbed. Some popular locations are the south fork of the Yuba River near Nevada City; the Bear River, fifteen miles south of Grass Valley on State Route 174; the Mokelumne River near Jackson; and the Stanislaus River above Sonora.

VISITOR INFORMATION

For more information, contact the following Chambers: Amador County Chamber of Commerce, P.O. Box 596, Jackson, CA 95642 (209-223-0350); Calaveras County Chamber of Commerce, P.O. Box 177, San Andreas, CA 95249 (209-754-1821); El Dorado County Chamber of Commerce, 542 Main Street, Placerville, CA 95667 (916-626-2344); Nevada County Chamber of Commerce, 248 Mill Street, Grass Valley, CA 95945 (800-752-6222, inside California or 800-521-2075, outside California); Toulumne County Visitors Bureau, P.O. Box 4020, Sonora, CA 95370 (209-984-4636 or 209-533-4420).

POINTS OF INTEREST

COLUMBIA HISTORIC STATE PARK. Located approximately five miles north of Sonora on Parrotts Ferry Road. Automobile traffic is banned from the park, but tours are available by stagecoach. This was once the gem of the Southern Mines.

CALAVERAS BIG TREES STATE PARK. Located off of State Route 4, a few miles east of Angels Camp (209-795-2334). Two groves of giant sequoias, picnicking, hiking, visitor center.

MERCER CAVERNS. Located one mile north of Murphys (209-728-2101). Thirty-minute guided tours.

MOANING CAVERN. Located on Parrotts Ferry Road between Angels Camp and Murphys (209-736-2708). Forty-five minute traditional tour, three-hour adventure tour, or rappel into the main chamber.

BEAR VALLEY NORDIC SKI AREA. Located along State Route 4, about thirty miles east of Murphys (209-753-2834).

STEVENOT. Award-winning winery located three miles north of Murphys on San Domingo Road (209-728-3436).

AMADOR COUNTY MUSEUM. (209-223-3230). A historical museum depicting nineteenth-century life and gold mining structures. Open Wednesday through Sunday in Jackson.

KENNEDY TAILING WHEELS. Located at Jackson Kennedy Wheels City Park on Jackson Gate Road north of Jackson. Large wheels used to remove tailings from mines.

INDIAN GRINDING ROCK STATE HISTORIC PARK. A forty-acre park located one and a half miles off State Route 88 on the Pine Grove-Volcano Road. Giant grinding rock on display.

DAFFODIL HILL. Open only in spring. Gorgeous display of color. Located north of Volcano.

D'AGOSTINI WINERY. Located on Shenandoah Road northeast of Plymouth (209-245-6612). State historical landmark first established in 1856.

KNIGHT'S FOUNDRY. Located on Eureka Street in Sutter Creek. Open to the public on Friday evenings. Claims to be the only water-powered foundry in the United States.

APPLE HILL. Just out of Placerville (916-644-5380). Prime apple-growing area.

LAKE TAHOE. Fifty-five miles east of Placerville. The second largest alpine lake in the world. Excellent skiing. Casino gambling on Nevada side.

MARSHALL GOLD DISCOVERY STATE HISTORIC PARK. Located in Coloma (916-622-3470). Site of Sutter's Mill and the discovery of gold. In January, a festival celebrates the discovery. Gold rush exhibits. Replica of the mill.

EMPIRE MINE STATE HISTORIC PARK. Located on East Empire Street in Grass Valley (916-273-8522). Site of the oldest and richest gold mine in California.

THE NORTH STAR MINING MUSEUM AND PELTON WHEEL EXHIBIT. Located on Allison Ranch Road in Grass Valley (916-273-9853). Displays mining equipment and artifacts from the 1880s.

THE NATIONAL HOTEL. Located in downtown Nevada City. The oldest continuously operating hotel in California.

THE AMERICAN VICTORIAN MUSEUM. 325 Spring Street, Nevada City (916-265-5804). Devoted to Victoriana.

RESTAURANTS OF NOTE

The following restaurants are listed by location, beginning at the southern end of the gold country.

CITY HOTEL. Main Street, Columbia (209-532-1479). Excellent French cuisine prepared by Columbia College students. This is fine dining and reservations are recommended.

MURPHYS HOTEL. 457 Main Street, Murphys (209-728-3454). The American-

style food here is quite average, but the nineteenth-century ambience
is superb. Fried chicken is very good. The bar is friendly.

TERESA'S. 1235 Jackson Gate Road, Jackson (209-223-1786). Authentic
Italian food. Family operated.

HARROWER'S SUTTER CREEK CAFE. State Route 49, Sutter Creek (209-267-
5114). Good home-style fresh food. Very casual. Menu changes daily.

PELARGONIUM. State Route 49, Sutter Creek (209-267-5008). Fresh seasonal
foods served in pleasant surroundings.

SUTTER CREEK PALACE. 76 Main, Sutter Creek (209-267-9852). Continental
cuisine served in historic hotel. Excellent service.

ART C. BISTRO. 423 Broad Street, Nevada City (916-265-6648). The food here
is fresh and delicious. Vegetarian dishes usually available.

SELAYA'S. 320 Broad Street, Nevada City (916-265-5697). Founded by the
late Peter Salaya, one of California's most famous chefs. Good food.

JACKS. 101 Broad, Nevada City (916-265-3405). This is elegant dining in the
home of the owners and chefs (both named Jack), who prepare the
food in their own kitchen. The menu features only one entrée, but it
changes daily. Reservations should be made several days in advance.

WHERE TO STAY

AMERICAN RIVER INN

Standing like a queen among peasants, the American River Inn is
easy to spot in the Old West community of Georgetown. With its American
flag flapping in the cool mountain breezes, the three-story ivory inn—its
trim painted a rich Wedgwood blue—rises above the plain one-story brick
and frame buildings making up downtown.

Formerly called the American Hotel, the inn was built during the gold
rush days as a boardinghouse for miners. In 1899, fire reduced the hotel to
a pile of ashes. But, refusing to die, it rose from the dust that very same
year, a clone of its former self. However, in 1945 the hotel began a steady
thirty-year decline.

In the 1980s, the inn made a comeback. After several years of total
restoration, its red fir floors sparkle once again and guests spend quiet
nights within its arms. And, since the spring of 1985, the Queen Anne
house next door has also opened its doors to guests of the American
River Inn.

No matter which building you stay in, you will find polished floors,
vintage rugs, antique appointments, and queen-size beds. Flowers and
plants freshen the setting, while warm comforters, fluffy pillows,

American River Inn (Courtesy American River Inn)

decorative quilts, and soft towels add to the creature comforts.

When days are sunny—and they frequently are—wide verandas and decks are inviting. Gardens bathe in the coos pouring from the nearby dove aviary. A natural stone swimming pool and a Jacuzzi create a resortlike atmosphere.

The elegance of the American River Inn seems out of place in this rugged environment. Armoires and claw-footed tubs do not readily come to mind in a town where pickups outnumber automobiles and first-class dining means a steak at the Ponderosa Saloon.

But that is the beauty of the inn. This is a place for getting away, for slowing down and appreciating the high country. The inn offers travelers a rare opportunity to escape to this untamed wilderness, yet at the same time relax in a luxurious climate.

*   *   *

American River Inn, Orleans Street, P.O. Box 43, Georgetown, CA 95634 (916-333-4499). Eighteen guest rooms, thirteen in the inn (four with private baths), five in the Queen Anne house. Rates range from $57 to $75 (subject to change). VISA/MasterCard/American Express. No children under ten; no pets; smoking permitted. Breakfast is superb, including such items as an egg entrée, Canadian bacon, and a variety of home-baked muffins. From State Route 49, take State Route 193 to Georgetown and turn up Main Street to the inn.

DUNBAR HOUSE

The trend in bed and breakfast today leans towards historic homes, preferably in the country, which can be preened and primped to reflect the elegance of a regal era. Although the refurbishing and restoration result in a luxurious look, the homes often lose their country appeal.

Despite the move toward the lavish period look, however, it is still possible to find a century-old home in the provinces, one that reflects the simple, tranquil life around it. Dunbar House is just such a place.

Surrounded by a white picket fence, this 1880 two-story Italianate shuns museumlike pieces for the homeyness of an eclectic blend of comfortable furnishings. There are some antiques in the guest rooms, such as the oak double bed and matching dresser in Blue Oak, the armoire in Sequoia, and the claw-footed tub in the second-floor bathroom. But, in general, the overstuffed ambience created in the living room and the casual buffet-style breakfast served in the rustic dining room provide a truer picture of Dunbar House's country comfort.

The home is named for its builder and first resident, Willis Dunbar. This former prominent citizen, who served as superintendent of the local waterworks, paid tribute to his young bride by presenting her with this fine home upon their marriage. Together they raised five boys here. The home remained a private residence until 1982, when the current owners,

Dunbar House (R. L. Baylor)

John and Barbara Carr, purchased it to convert it into a bed-and-breakfast inn.

"Our reasons for doing this were really quite simple," John says. "We owned a weekend place here, and every visit it became tougher and tougher to return home. So we decided to find something we could do here that would allow us to enjoy this country year-round."

Dunbar House represents the fruits of their search. After buying the house, they spent three and a half months painting, wallpapering, and decorating before it looked like a home again. In addition, they endured a year of separation before John could leave his old job and join Barbara in Murphys.

However, their sacrifices produced a fine, relaxing atmosphere. The place again looks like a home where a young family could raise five boys in peace and harmony with the environment.

*   *   *

Dunbar House, 271 Jones Street, P.O. Box 1375, Murphys, CA 95247 (209-728-2897). Five guest rooms share two baths. Rates range from $55 to $65 (subject to change). No credit cards. No children under ten; no pets; no smoking. On warm sunny days, breakfast is served in the yard, where guests relax around garden tables shaded by large umbrellas. From State Route 4, take the Murphys exit, which leads to Main Street. Look for Dunbar House to the left, before you enter downtown.

THE FOXES

Expansion often trips over the heels of success. In the world of bed and breakfast, however, growth finds itself limited by the size of the house. Therefore, adding space usually translates into purchasing the neighbors' home or constructing a carriage house in the backyard. So when Pete and Min Fox found themselves grappling with the problem of regularly waving their no-room-at-the-inn sign, they turned to their friendly building contractor for help.

Oddly enough, bed and breakfast never occurred to the Foxes in 1979, when they purchased this large 1857 home. Reminding me very much of the frame houses that line the streets of my New England hometown, the charm of this old house struck the Foxes as the perfect place to live their lives. Here they could reside together, while Pete conducted his real estate affairs from a spacious downstairs office and Min used one of the large rooms for an antique shop.

Then, in a town where accommodations are often at a premium, a local innkeeper asked Min if she had room for a young honeymoon couple. Both she and Pete thought "why not?" and from that one referral, the

The Foxes (Courtesy The Foxes)

Foxes grew into a three-room bed and breakfast within three years. At this writing, they are opening three more rooms in their new carriage house.
Elegance and privacy distinguish bed and breakfast at the Foxes.

Each of the rooms in the main house is suite-size and luxuriously furnished. The downstairs Honeymoon Suite compares favorably with the West Coast's finest rooms. Boasting a private entrance, the suite features a queen-size half-canopy bed, an antique armoire, a bright and cheerful breakfast nook, rich leather chairs sitting before a red brick fireplace, and an old-fashioned bathroom with brass fixtures and a claw-footed tub. The upstairs rooms are equally plush, sans fireplace, although those not fond of taxidermy may want to avoid The Anniversary Suite, also called The Game Room.

All of the rooms in the Carriage House should boast comparable amenities. Antique furnishings, sitting areas, queen-size beds, and private baths are promised.

To enhance privacy, the inn does not offer a common room. In addition, breakfast is delivered to the rooms in silver servers on silver trays.

These are the ingredients that have spelled success for the Foxes. These are the things that have made expansion necessary.

*   *   *

The Foxes, 77 Main Street, P.O. Box 159, Sutter Creek, CA 95685 (209-267-5882). Six guest rooms, all with private baths. Rates range from $70 to $115 (subject to change). VISA/MasterCard. No children; no pets; no smoking. Private covered parking behind house. Main Street is also State Route 49, and the inn is located at the north end of downtown.

GATE HOUSE INN

They came to the gold country to get away from the hectic pace of the Bay Area and ended up working eighteen-hour days. In effect, they traded stop-and-go drudgery for a never-ending labor of love—a bed-and-breakfast inn.

This is the story of innkeepers Ursel and Frank Walker. Theirs is a tale that wears the familiar face of nearly every innkeeper I know, yet very few express regrets. So far, neither do the Walkers.

Their turn-of-the-century Victorian sits behind a swinging wrought-iron gate on a spacious plot of land lush with camellias, crepe myrtle, dogwoods, and walnut trees. In addition, the yard has a swimming pool and a screened barbecue area.

The backyard also embraces the Walkers' pièce de résistance—the Summerhouse. Once the caretaker's quarters, this country cottage offers a unique contrast to the Victoriana of the main house. Warmed by a wood-burning stove that sits atop a brick pedestal, the Summerhouse is the Walkers' most popular accommodation. I suspect the fanciful bath-

Gate House Inn (Courtesy Gate House Inn)

room—with its terraced claw-footed tub, brass chandelier, and stained-glass window—entices most guests.

Elegant appointments and fine craftsmanship distinguish the main house. In the parlor, there is an Italian marble fireplace, as well as an inlaid oak parquet floor and bay-window views of wooded hills. The adjoining dining room features an Italian crystal chandelier. Furnishings throughout the house are a blend of Italian and Victorian. Some one hundred antique clocks fill nooks and crannies.

The inn's smallest accommodation is the downstairs Parlor Room. It boasts a queen-size iron bed. There are three more rooms upstairs, including the Master Suite, marked by an Italian tile fireplace, and the Woodhaven Suite, paneled with polished tongue-and-groove fir boards and decked with shiny pine floors.

Besides exceptional accommodations, breakfast here is a special event. Entrées are prepared in gourmet fashion, while muffins and pastries are home-baked.

*   *   *

Gate House Inn, 1330 Jackson Gate Road, Jackson, CA 95642 (209-223-3500). Four guest rooms in the house plus the Summerhouse in the backyard, all with private baths. Rates range from $55 to $95 (subject to change). No credit cards. No children; no pets; no smoking. Jackson Gate Road winds into the countryside north of downtown Jackson. When traveling south on State Route 49, begin looking for it on your left as soon as you pass through Martell.

THE HEIRLOOM

Ione is a town of tired, squat buildings. Their only common thread appears to be a connection to the past. The thought of finding a two-story antebellum mansion in their midst seems unimaginable. In fact, if Rhett and Scarlett had lived in Ione, the book would never have been written. On the other hand, this sleepy environment might have calmed their spirits, allowing them to live happily ever after.

By now, you have guessed where I am leading. There is a Southern mansion in Ione, and it does have a peaceful effect on its guests.

Built in 1863 by Virginian Luther Brusi, the brick mansion with its white-pillared front veranda and balcony once reigned over ten acres of rich Ione Valley earth. Then, Brusi's slaves grew crops to help feed the miners working the nearby hills. Today, the grounds have shrunk to one and a half acres, but the smell of magnolias and the cheerful blooms of wisteria still conjure up the days when plantation whites sipped sherry and black field hands sang songs of inspiration.

Since 1980, innkeepers Patricia Cross and Melisande Hubbs have welcomed guests to the mansion, now a bed-and-breakfast inn. Garbed in long-skirted period dresses and speaking in soft refinement, these gracious ladies capture the gentler moments of days past.

Towering trees, lush shrubs, and landscaped gardens surround the mansion, which sits at the end of a long tree-lined drive. When guests enter the home, they find themselves standing in a lavish yet friendly living

The Heirloom (Courtesy The Heirloom)

room. A fire crackles in the red brick fireplace; perhaps a couple plays backgammon. To one side sits a square rosewood grand piano, to another a centuries-old Italian refectory table.

A graceful staircase ascends to four upstairs guest rooms, each named for one of the four seasons. Some open onto balconies, all feature antiques, light colors, fresh flowers, baskets of fruit, and dishes of candy.

Alongside the mansion stands a rammed-earth building, which shelters two additional accommodations—Early American and Early California. Beamed ceilings, pine and cedar paneling, redwood doors, and wood stoves create a country feeling.

The Heirloom brings touches of Southern hospitality to an otherwise forgettable community. The setting is quiet and ideal for getting away.

*   *   *

The Heirloom, 214 Shakeley Lane, P.O. Box 322, Ione, CA 95640 (209-274-4468). Four guest rooms in mansion, one with private bath. Two accommodations in cottage share a connecting bath. Rates range from $45 to $65 (subject to change). No credit cards. No children under ten; no pets. This is an ideal location for weddings or parties. Breakfast is both creative and excellent. From State Route 88, take State Route 104 to Ione. Turn left on Preston Avenue to Shakeley Lane.

MURPHY'S INN

Before taking to the road, I spend months researching inns. Then, I painstakingly select the ones I wish to visit—the places I believe will offer the best value for the dollar. Despite my thoroughness, however, very often I need more than a little help from my friends, the innkeepers. That is how I came to visit Murphy's Inn.

First in Sacramento, then in quaint towns dotting the gold country, innkeepers kept telling me that Marc Murphy runs a very special inn. Naturally, I had to find out for myself. What I found put me in total agreement with those who say Murphy's Inn is exceptional. It is.

Located on a quiet street in Grass Valley, the 1866 Colonial Revival classic looks much as it did when gold baron Edward Coleman lived here. Wrapped by a wide veranda and draped in baskets of ivy, the two-story clapboard house presents a picture of homeyness, framed by a green wrought-iron fence.

Inside, a maze of hallways, entranceways, and stairways lead to a breakfast room, two parlors, and seven guest rooms. Each is graced with antiques, lace curtains, and floral wallpaper; some have sloped ceilings, skylights, and fireplaces.

Breakfast belongs in the gastronome's hall of fame. Served in the

Murphy's Inn (Courtesy Murphy's Inn)

breakfast room or delivered to a guest room, it includes entrées such as Belgian waffles, eggs Benedict, and coddled eggs, as well as hand-squeezed juices and fresh-ground coffee.

In the hospitality business, however, greatness depends not on frills but on the graciousness and skills of the innkeeper. Marc receives rave reviews. Having grown up in a family of innkeepers, Marc explains his success simply by declaring, "I guess innkeeping is in my blood."

In 1984, Marc invited Rose, his new bride, to join his innkeeping family. She immediately took to the business and is largely responsible for the decor of The Hanson Suite, which is the newest guest facility, located in the Donation Day House across the street.

Without any hestitation, I can recommend a visit to Murphy's Inn. It boasts all the ingredients of a fine bed and breakfast.

*   *   *

Murphy's Inn, 318 Neal Street, Grass Valley, CA 95945 (916-273-6873). Seven guest rooms in 1866 house, five with private baths. One guest room in Donation Day House with private bath. Rates range from $48 to $88 (subject to change). VISA/MasterCard. Children with prior approval; no pets; no smoking. Weddings, receptions, and special occasions welcome. From State Route 49, take Colfax 174 exit. Then turn left on South Auburn to a left on Neal Street.

RED CASTLE INN

Blushing bright red and dripping with icicles, the four-story Red Castle Inn peeks through dense ponderosa pines. Its Prospect Hill perch could easily be the setting for fairy tale dreams.

Nevada City, however, sprawls distant horizons from the nearest fairyland. This is gold country: rugged land that hides its wildness behind a mask painted in natural beauty. This is where John Williams came in 1849, braving the perils of prairie crossing for a chance to make his fortune.

By the 1850s, Williams was reaping the riches of success. The Red

Red Castle Inn (Courtesy Red Castle Inn)

Castle Inn became his monument to fame. Hauling lumber and bricks up Prospect Hill by wagon, Williams and his family were able to move into the mansion in the winter of 1860. The *Nevada Morning Journal* called the new brick structure, the "most prominent ornamental improvement" in the area.

Since 1963, this gingerbread Gothic Revival has served as an inn. Today's owners, Conley and Mary Louise Weaver, continue the tradition established here two decades ago of preserving the past while catering to the comforts of today's guests.

While the eight guest rooms boast antique furnishings such as crystal chandeliers, canopy beds, and mirrored armoires, the Conleys have wisely avoided the temptation to turn the inn into a stuffy museum. They have accomplished this in several ways.

First, six of the accommodations feature private baths. Although some are closet-size, the modern amenities add convenient touches. On a more social level, the living room welcomes conversation. The overstuffed furniture is comfortable and permits eye-to-eye contact without having to rearrange the room.

Comfort is also stressed at breakfast, which is a leisurely affair that lasts from 7:30 A.M. to 11:00 A.M. Served buffet-style in the foyer, trays of home-baked breads and muffins accompanied by seasonal fruit and an occasional special dish may be taken back to your room or eaten in the living room. Additional homey embellishments, such as fresh flowers and dishes of candy, make personal statements in each guest room. Finally, there are touches of whimsy scattered about, like the carved arms-and-hands towel rack in one of the bathrooms.

*   *   *

Red Castle Inn, 109 Prospect Street, Nevada City, CA 95959 (916-265-5135). Eight guest rooms, six with private baths. Rates range from $55 to $95 (subject to change). No credit cards. Children with prior approval; no pets; smoking in designated areas only. Although the castle can be seen from downtown, it is not easily located by car. From State Route 49, take the Sacramento Street exit. Then take a right at the gas station; wind your way up the hill to a left on Prospect Street.

The Interstate 5 Corridor

W ith Mount Shasta peeking over its shoulder, Interstate 5 cuts through the soul of Northern California. From the south, it slips past the capital city of Sacramento, through California's agricultural heartland, up and over the Shasta-Cascade wonderland, to the Oregon border.

The highway and its tributaries reach out to touch the length and breadth of this diverse land. Together they serve primarily as conduits for travelers, taking them to places beyond the roar of the corridor. Aside from the business of government in Sacramento and the recreational opportunities on and around Mount Shasta, tourists find little reason to pause and explore this land of the working man.

Still, there are places of interest and things to see and do. A trip to this part of California, far from the maddening crowd, could bring unexpected rewards.

GETTING TO KNOW
THE INTERSTATE 5 CORRIDOR

SACRAMENTO

The Sacramento and American rivers join hands here, before taking their act on the road ninety miles east to San Francisco. Their waters nourish the rich soils of the valley and welcome thousands of boaters and anglers. However, when made angry by heavy rains and distant melting snows, the rivers also can loose their vengeance on the capital city and nearby farming communities.

Sacramento rose from modest beginnings. But at the tender age of ten years, it sprouted nearly overnight from a lonely outpost to a boomtown. Its seed was planted on 12 August 1839, by John Sutter, who chose a knoll near the rivers' confluence to put down stakes. By winter, Sutter's Fort comprised several tents, grass huts, and a forty-foot-long adobe building.

With the help of Indian labor, Sutter's Fort grew. But it still resembled little more than a wilderness outpost. There were few signs that soon a thriving city would blossom nearby.

Gold proved to be both the demise of Sutter's Fort and the beginning of Sacramento City. By June of 1849, Sutter's agricultural enterprises were being trampled by miners heading into the Sierra Nevada mountains. But a new community, called Sacramento City, had grown from a vacant plot of land to a town of over two thousand citizens and two hundred homes. With gold bringing entrepreneurs and speculators, as well as flashing Sacramento in the limelight, it was no surprise that in 1854 fledgling California chose this flourishing community to be its capital city.

Today, Sacramento continues at a boomtown pace. It is the seventh fastest-growing metropolitan area in the United States. While it still hangs onto its past—the historical reconstruction of Old Sacramento and the Victorian homes that span out for twenty blocks in every direction—Sacramento is also a modern metropolis, featuring fine restaurants and a thriving night life.

CHICO

This is a rural community, located 175 miles northeast of San Francisco. Although not a tourist town, California State University, Chico, draws visitors from throughout California to its campus. And like all universities, its students and faculty create a demand for art, entertainment, and fine food. In addition, Chico's nearness to the Sierra Nevada foothills ensures an abundance of recreational opportunities.

RED BLUFF

Red Bluff is an agricultural town whose setting is less than memorable. However, it is friendly and quiet, so a good place to spend the night. There are also a number of historical homes here to view. And Lassen Volcanic National Park is only fifty miles east, while Shasta-Trinity National Recreation Area lies about that same distance to the north.

A PRACTICAL GUIDE TO THE CORRIDOR

THE CLIMATE

Sacramento's temperatures range from a low of 39 degrees in January to a high of 90 degrees in July, while Mount Shasta ranges from 24 degrees to 85 degrees in those same months respectively. During the winter, snowfalls can be expected in the mountains, while periods of heavy rain or fog may blanket the valley.

YOUR CLOTHES

This country is mostly rural and recreational; leisure clothes will suffice most of the time. For Sacramento, however, some formal attire is suggested.

VISITOR INFORMATION

For more information, contact the following: Sacramento Convention & Visitors Bureau, 1311 I Street, Sacramento, CA 95814 (916-442-5542); Lassen County Chamber of Commerce and Tourism Council, 75 North Weatherlow, P.O. Box 338, Susanville, CA 96130 (916-257-4323); Shasta-Cascade Wonderland Association, 1250 Parkview Avenue, Redding, CA 96001 (916-243-2643).

POINTS OF INTEREST

OLD SACRAMENTO. Between Capitol Mall and I Street (916-443-7815). This revitalized historic district sits on twenty-eight acres alongside the Sacramento River. There are restaurants, clubs, shops, and museums here.

CALIFORNIA STATE RAILROAD MUSEUM. Second and I streets, Old Sacramento (916-445-4209). Historical artifacts and restored locomotives and railroad cars.

STATE CAPITOL. Tenth Street and Capitol Mall, Sacramento (916-324-0333). Open daily at 9 A.M.

CROCKER ART MUSEUM. 216 O Street, Sacramento (916-449-5423). The first art museum in the West. Open Tuesday through Sunday.

CALIFORNIA ALMOND GROWERS VISITOR CENTER. 17th and C streets, Sacramento (916-446-8409). Two thousand almond products, cooking demonstrations, and tours. Closed on weekends and holidays.

SACRAMENTO HISTORY CENTER. Front and I streets, Sacramento (916-447-2958). Exhibits display Sacramento's past.

LAUGHS UNLIMITED. 1124 Firehouse Alley, Old Sacramento (916-446-5905). Good comedy club.

BIDWELL MANSION STATE HISTORIC PARK. 525 Esplanade, Chico (916-895-6144). A palatial Victorian mansion located next to a twenty-four hundred-acre park.

WILLIAM B. IDE ADOBE STATE HISTORIC PARK. 3040 Adobe Road, Red Bluff (916-527-5927). An 1848 adobe house.

LASSEN VOLCANIC NATIONAL PARK. State Route 36 from Red Bluff, State Route

44 from Redding, and State Route 89 from Dunsmuir lead to the 106,000-acre park. Lassen Peak last erupted ten thousand years ago. Excellent for driving tours, picnicking, hiking, swimming, trout fishing, plus winter downhill and cross-country skiing.

BRIDGE BAY BELLE. This sixty-four-foot sternwheeler departs daily from Bridge Bay Marina just north of Redding for two-hour tours of Lake Shasta (916-275-3021).

SHASTA DAM. From Interstate 5, take the Project City/Shasta Dam Boulevard exit (916-275-4463). The second largest dam in the United States. Guided tours are conducted daily. Take the walkway of the "Three Shastas" for spectacular views.

LAKE SHASTA CAVERNS. Tours begin at the O'Brien Recreation Area, fifteen miles north of Redding (916-238-2341).

LEWISTON AND TRINITY LAKES. Take State Route 299 west from Redding and State Route 3 north. Beautiful scenery, excellent fishing.

CASTLE CRAGS STATE PARK. These granite crags, which were formed 225 million years ago, stand some six thousand feet. Rock climbing, sight-seeing, and picnicking. Located six miles south of Dunsmuir.

MOUNT SHASTA. Located fifty miles north of Redding. For the best views, take the Mount Shasta City exit off Interstate 5 to the Everett Memorial Highway, which climbs to the eight thousand-foot level.

RESTAURANTS OF NOTE

The following restaurants are listed by location, beginning in Sacramento, then including Chico and Red Bluff.

WULFF'S. 2333 Fair Oaks Boulevard, Sacramento (916-922-8575). This may very well be Sacramento's finest restaurant. It is so popular that reservations should be made a week in advance. French cuisine is excellent, and the desserts are very special.

SCHOONER'S. 28th and N streets, Sacramento (916-452-7427). This is a casual, neighborhood restaurant, which is known for its tender back ribs and fresh fish.

JOAN LEINEKE. Alhambra and H streets, Sacramento (916-448-2761). The three-piece suit crowd congregates here for lunch. Nouvelle cuisine is pricey but excellent.

INDIA RESTAURANT. 729 J Street, Sacramento (916-448-9046). Modest decor, moderate prices, and good food.

MOVABLE FEAST. 601 Munroe Street, Sacramento (916-971-1677). An intimate restaurant that serves elegant French fare. Sauces are light.

BASQUE NORTE. 3355 Esplanade, Chico (916-891-5204). For the adventurous eater. Lots of grilled food served in a European family-style setting. Try the tomato garlic soup.

FREDUCINNI'S. 1020 Main Street, Chico (916-895-1981). Good Italian food. Tuesday is pasta-and-jazz night. Wine tastings are regularly scheduled.

THE OAKS BAR & GRILL. 243 West 2nd Street, Chico (916-895-3964). Good old-fashioned American food.

FRANCISCO'S. Located on Antelope, just east of Interstate 5, Red Bluff (916-527-5311). Standard Mexican fare adored by the locals.

GREEN BARN. Located just east of Francisco's on Antelope, Red Bluff (916-527-3161). Steaks and seafood.

WHERE TO STAY

AMBER HOUSE

Amber House is the kind of class operation you would expect of an inn located just seven blocks from the State Capitol, where government officials and business people come to discuss and conduct affairs of state. Since Sacramento is not known as a tourist town, Amber House caters to the needs of commercial travelers to a greater degree than the average inn. It does so with a flair.

Owned and operated by Bill McOmber, Amber House is a 1905 California craftsman-style house located on a quiet tree-lined street. The two-story structure was built as a private residence but transformed into an inn in 1981. Framed by two old elms, its clinker brick stairway, wide front porch, and colorful flower boxes create a homey yet stylish setting.

Upon entering the inn, classical music draws guests toward the living room. A brick fireplace, alderwood box beam ceiling, large sunny windows, and bright walls, which complement the dark woods, leather chairs, and stuffed sofas make up the setting.

In the adjacent room, shards of blue light stream through stained-glass windows across the oval dining room table. In the mornings, a gourmet breakfast is served here on hand-painted Limoges china placed amidst candlesticks and crystal.

The four guest rooms—Wicklow, Lindworth, Chelsea, and Meersbrook—are upstairs. Wicklow's delft blue wallpaper and dark wood furnishings are stylish but make it the darkest room in the house. Lindworth features a gorgeous and romantic bath, complete with skylight, stained-glass window, and a seventy-year-old porcelain bathtub with brass and ivory fixtures. Chelsea is a very warm and cozy front room. Meersbrook conjures up visions of the deep south: its French windows, tongue-and-groove wood paneling, wicker furniture, and white antique

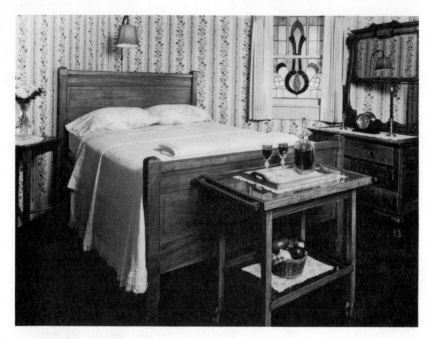

Amber House (Steve Simmons)

iron bed make this former sun porch very popular.

Despite the formal elegance of Amber House, this is a very friendly inn. Dishes of almonds, as well as green plants and fresh flowers, warm up the guest rooms, while decanters of California sherry or carafes of wine invite downstairs socializing. Bill's knack for understanding guests is very satisfying. He knows when to be gregarious but also senses when to give his visitors privacy.

*   *   *

Amber House, 1315 22nd Street, Sacramento, CA 95816 (916-444-8085). Four guest rooms, two with private baths. Robes are provided for guests who share a bath. Rates range from $70 to $85 (subject to change). VISA/MasterCard/American Express. No children; no pets; no smoking. Limited off-street parking available. From Interstate 80 traveling east, take the Sacramento Downtown/Jefferson exit. Go to the end of Capitol Mall, turn right on 9th, left on N and left again on 22nd.

THE BRIGGS HOUSE

Sometimes what goes on behind the scenes is as interesting as the performance on stage. If you have any interest in innkeepers and innkeeping, then the evolution and day-to-day operation of The Briggs House should grab your attention.

Although partnerships, often of the romantic variety, are common in the bed-and-breakfast industry, this is the only inn I know of ruled by two relatively large coalitions—one that owns the property and one that manages it.

In some instances, people belong to both groups. Still, the idea of a coalition running something as personal as an inn seemed unworkable to me. For instance, how do the partners ever agree on things such as decorating schemes, breakfast menus, and work schedules? Surprisingly, they do. And the inn runs smoothly.

In fact, this is a quality, well-managed bed and breakfast. The decor is both historical and charming, breakfast is leisurely and good, service is friendly and caring, and amenities equal and in some instances surpass those of other inns.

The Briggs House is located on a tree-lined residential street a few blocks from the State Capitol. It is a cube-type Colonial Revival built in 1901. Throughout most of the house's life, it has served as a private residence, although it did have a stint as a boardinghouse. The current owners purchased the home in June of 1981 for the purpose of opening an inn.

The main house features five guest rooms, a living room, and a library. Dark wood trim, wood floors, and deep blue walls and curtains create a somber ambience in the common rooms, but a wealth of literature,

The Briggs House (Courtesy The Briggs House)

an upright piano, and a large red brick fireplace do their best to offset this.

The guest rooms have a much lighter sense, particularly the Sunrise Room with its pale blue colors, lace coverlet, and private sun porch. The most elegant room is the Heritage Room, which features a French antique bed and matching dresser, as well as a collection of antique laces under glass. For maximum privacy, the backyard Carriage House offers two accommodations. All rooms boast robes, stationery, clocks, diaries, and flowers.

The backyard presents a comfortable setting for relaxing in the hot tub and sauna or taking a sunny breakfast. Orange and fig trees shade the brick patio, while camellias, pomegranate, and jasmine add lush colors and fragrances.

*   *   *

The Briggs House, 2209 Capitol Avenue, Sacramento, CA 95816 (916-441-3214). Five guest rooms in the main house, two with private baths. Two guest accommodations in the Carriage House, both with private baths. Rates range from $55 to $90 (subject to change). VISA/MasterCard/American Express. Children with prior approval; no pets; smoking in common rooms only. Small weddings, receptions, and meetings welcome. Off-street parking available. From Capitol Mall, take a right on 9th, left on N, then left again on 22nd to Capitol Avenue.

BULLARD HOUSE

Years of abuse—first by apartment dwellers then by college students—left this 1902 two-story redwood home gasping for breath. A jungle of ivy strangled its columned porch, while neglect scarred its insides. Built as a lovely private home, the house stood derelict.

Then in 1982, Pat and Patricia Macarthy breathed new life into this old house. With the help of the Butte-Glenn Medical Auxiliary, who chose the home as their "Decorator Dream House," the Macarthys transformed the building into a comfortable home.

They hacked away the ivy; planted grass, small trees, and flowers; laid stepping stones and filled brick planters with yellow marigolds; and put on lots of fresh paint. Inside, Pat and Patricia stripped walls to their bare frames, installed new plumbing and wiring, stripped paint, tore up linoleum, and revived wood floors.

Following three months of dedicated restoration and renovation, the interior decorators arrived. Eager to create a "Decorator Dream House," the designers worked diligently.

Finally, in November 1982, Pat and Patricia opened their new home, called Bullard House in honor of Pat's great-grandparents, to bed-and-

Bullard House (Cathleen McCampbell)

breakfast guests.

The four upstairs guest rooms are cheery under their ten-foot ceilings and windows that welcome lots of sunshine. An eclectic blend of antiques, wicker, lively wallpapers, light paints, green plants, and fresh flowers create a homey feeling.

Downstairs, the parlor, living room, and dining room combine comfort and elegance. The presence of Pat and Patricia add the necessary friendly touches.

Bullard House, although lavish in its luxurious furnishings, feels much more like a private home than an inn. It fits in well with the relaxed community of Chico.

*　　*　　*

Bullard House, 256 East 1st Avenue, Chico, CA 95926 (916-342-5912). Four guest rooms share one bath. Rates are $60 (subject to change). No credit cards. No children; no pets; no smoking. From State Route 99, take the East 1st Avenue exit to the corner of Oleander.

THE FAULKNER HOUSE

Downtown Red Bluff looks like a commercial for "Small Town, U.S.A." Its buildings shun showiness for simple practicality, while shops cater to the needs of townsfolk rather than those of tourists. It seems farfetched that a Victorian presence exists here. But it does.

The gingerbread Faulkner House rises just two blocks from Main Street. The two-story Victorian boasts a spired tower and is wrapped by a veranda.

The house was built in the 1890s by a jeweler who lived in it for nearly forty years. And like the story told straight-faced by fictionalized used-car salesmen, only three owners have sat in her since. Mary and Harvey Klingler, the most recent owners, purchased the house in 1983 and began operating a bed and breakfast here in October 1984.

Four guest rooms make up the home's second floor. The coziest and most charming is the Tower Room. Tucked into its intimate confines are an iron and brass double bed and a tiny antique dresser. Tall windows look out on the neighborhood.

The adjacent Wicker Room has tall sunny windows, pale blue wallpaper, white wicker chairs, and a white iron and brass bed. The remaining two rooms, Rose and Arbor, represent the home's most palatial accommodations. Both are furnished in antiques.

The parlor, living room, and dining room make up the first floor. With its very Victorian decor, the parlor is more for looking than sitting. But the bright and cheery living room, boasting a green tile fireplace and the fattest couch I have ever sat on, is just right for relaxing. In the mornings, breakfast is served in the formal dining room.

Mary and Harvey are relatively new to the bed-and-breakfast game, and in many ways that is refreshing. Both reflect an unbridled enthu-

The Faulkner House (Courtesy The Faulkner House)

siasm for their guests and are eager to cater to needs. Location may be their one drawback.

Most of us probably never give Red Bluff a second thought when making travel plans. I know the idea had never occurred to me. But The Faulkner House offered me a new perspective on the area. You might also find it a good place from which to explore the nearby sights.

*   *   *

The Faulkner House, 1029 Jefferson Street, Red Bluff, CA 96080 (916-529-0520). Four guest rooms share one bath. (There is an additional bathroom downstairs for busy times of the day.) Rates range from $45 to $50 (subject to change). No credit cards. No children; no pets; no smoking. From Interstate 5, take any Red Bluff exit to Main Street downtown. Then turn west on Union Street to Jefferson Street.

The North Coast

*T*he north coast stretches four hundred miles from San Francisco to the Oregon border. It bridges the hot-tub crowd of "Marvelous Marin" with the country style of Crescent City. In between, the surf washes over and around seastacks and crashes against steep cliffs, while steady breezes ripple grass-covered slopes and sweep away fog that blankets the valley vineyards and giant redwoods.

It is a diverse landscape that boasts great winding lengths of highway, where signs of human habitation are often only fleeting glimpses of grazing sheep or weathered barns. Here, the land is rugged and jobs are scarce.

With San Francisco fading in the rear view mirror, travelers should leave U.S. 101 for the roller-coaster trip along State Route 1. This is the string that gathers Marin's pearls before traipsing north. Hugging the coastline much of the time, it twists and turns slowly, joining quaint towns such as Bodega Bay and Mendocino.

Some two hundred tortuous miles north of San Francisco, it rejoins U.S. 101 in the tiny community of Leggett. From here to Eureka, the attraction changes from untouched shoreline to old-growth redwoods. Just north of Garberville, the Avenue of the Giants leaves the rush of the highway for a more leisurely drive through the towering forests. In Eureka, the highway kisses the Pacific again. Between Eureka and Crescent City, the traveler is welcomed into the best of both worlds, as the ocean and the redwoods take turns appearing on center stage.

GETTING TO KNOW THE NORTH COAST

MARVELOUS MARIN

When describing Marin County, it would be easy to reach into a bag full of hyperbole. Instead, just let it be said that "Marvelous Marin" has it all.

Along its 115 miles of coastline live many of the world's best educated and best paid people. A quick look around confirms that Marin is a haven for the smart set, where leisure plays an important role.

For many travelers, discovering Marin means a visit to the Mediterranean-like city above the bay—Sausalito. Reached either by automobile or San Francisco's Red & White Fleet, Sausalito's villas, hotels, galleries, restaurants, and boutiques beckon from the slopes of wooded hills.

Little Lombard Street, home to Village Fair—a multilevel complex of international shops—and Bridgeway—downtown's National Historic Landmark District—represent the main shopping areas. The north side of town, known as the Marinship, still harbors evidence of Sausalito's days as a haven for artists, writers, and craftsmen. However, many of the artisans have left for quieter and more affordable towns, so now the best time to view their work is during the Sausalito Art Festival over Labor Day Weekend.

West of Sausalito, along the county's Pacific borders, much of Marin has been set aside for parks. The two largest, Golden Gate National Recreation Area and Point Reyes National Seashore, dominate more than seventy-eight thousand acres. This is Marin's wild side. Here travelers will find sandy beaches, grassy dunes, deep bays, ocean-battered cliffs, and forested hills. Mount Tamalpais, which climbs above State Route 1, offers viewpoints that overlook all these splendors.

Continuing north, the highway winds along the coast and down to Stinson Beach. Ideal for picnics, beachcombing, surfing, and sunbathing, this forty-five hundred-foot stretch of sand hosts large crowds on sunny days.

Then it is on to the Point Reyes National Seashore. At Olema take Sir Francis Drake Highway to park headquarters and the Bear Valley Information Center. After loading up with maps, follow the highway through the Old World town of Inverness to Point Reyes Beach. The breakers here are man-killers, but the scenery is magnificent in its grandeur.

POINT REYES STATION

This colorful community, with its three-block-long main street, resembles a western movie set. There are galleries and gift shops here, as well as a few restaurants. Its central highway location makes Point Reyes Station a good place from which to explore the natural wonders of Marin.

NORTH TO OREGON

State Route 1 waves good-by to "Marvelous Marin" just south of the artist community of Bodega Bay and eventually rejoins U.S. 101 for its final meander to Oregon. With the exception of a few communities, travelers are left alone with California's scenery.

MENDOCINO

Mendocino is a place to feel. It is a place for walking, seeing, smelling, and relaxing. For many of us, it is the place where Americans, purported to be New Englanders, met the Soviets face to face in the comedy classic, "The Russians Are Coming."

Having grown up in New Hampshire, I understand why Hollywood comes here to photograph a typical East Coast town. Mendocino looks more New Englandish than my old hometown does.

Built in the nineteenth century by men of the sea, the town's clapboard buildings, water towers, and wooden sidewalks are planted on a rocky headland that juts into the Pacific. After the whalers built the town, lumberjacks came to harvest the tall redwoods that once stood here. Later came artisans escaping gentrification, flower children looking to revive a dying culture, and finally, urban professionals trying to go home again.

Today, these disparate groups live in harmony and welcome tourists to their tidy town. Galleries, performing arts, good food, leisurely strolls along the boardwalks, and quiet walks along the grass-covered cliffs make Mendocino a magical getaway.

FORT BRAGG

This is the largest coastal town between San Francisco and Eureka. It is also the place you stay when there is no room in Little River or Mendocino. Although some of the inns here are first-rate, their setting combines highway traffic with industrial architecture.

Still, there are things to see and do, and the coast awaits but a short drive away. In addition, Noyo Fishing Village does offer the ambience travelers seek on trips to the ocean.

FERNDALE

Ferndale is a living museum of Victoriana. Settled in the mid-1800s by European farmers, the village remains a tribute to their turn-of-the-century prosperity. In 1897, the farmers exported some 965,000 pounds of butter and 188,000 pounds of wool. These early settlers took their profits and built the ornate Victorian homes that line the streets today. Having been painstakingly restored, Ferndale's gingerbread palaces represent some of that era's finest architectural examples.

EUREKA

Eureka, the forest capital of Humboldt County, sits behind the "Redwood Curtain." This town of twenty-three thousand infuses itself as much with its architectural past as it does its artistic present.

To discover Eureka's history, travelers must leave the honky-tonk capitalism of U.S. 101 and weave up and down its tributaries. In both residential and commercial neighborhoods they will find houses of architectural significance—many reflecting the influences of New England. There are examples of Queen Anne, Italianate, Greek Revival, Gothic Revival, Craftsman, and French Second Empire, just to name a few.

Although Eureka's Old Town celebrates its architectural history, the neighborhood mirrors today's world. Shunning its rough frontier past, this spruced-up area boasts boutiques, antique shops, restaurants, and trendy bars. It is also home to Romano Gabriel's Wooden Sculpture Garden, one of two works of California folk art, which are internationally acclaimed.

Art is no stranger to Eureka. With the highest per capita population of artists in California, Humboldt County is a thriving center for the arts, and its focus—Eureka—boasts an array of museums, galleries, and theaters. Perhaps the zaniest tribute to art in all of California, the "Great Arcata to Ferndale Cross-Country Kinetic Sculpture Race" runs annually on Easter Weekend and draws enthusiastic crowds to Eureka.

A PRACTICAL GUIDE TO THE NORTH COAST

THE CLIMATE

Temperatures throughout this region remain mild, some might even say cool, year-round ranging from the 30s in the winter, to the 60s in the summer. Moisture, however, can be a problem. Winter brings onslaughts of heavy rain, while summer welcomes long visits by layers of fog.

YOUR CLOTHES

Leisure clothes are appropriate most of the time. In some of Marin's towns, you might wish to avoid clothes that border on casual extra-ordinaire. Throughout the coastal area, restaurant attire varies from leisure to dressy. Good, dry walking shoes are a necessity as is rainwear.

THE REDWOODS

Coast redwoods *(Sequoia sempervirens)* often grow to more than three hundred feet high and can live for up to two thousand years. U.S. 101 from

Crescent City to just south of Willits accesses these giant wonders as do State Routes 116 and 128, which bridge U.S. 101 and State Route 1.

Redwood National Park stretches from just north of Eureka to just south of Oregon. Other parks to explore are Richardson Grove State Park; Founders Grove, two miles north of Weott on the Avenue of the Giants; and nearby Rockefeller Forest.

WHALE WATCHING

California Gray Whales make their annual migration from Alaska to their breeding waters in Baja California during December and January and return to their arctic feeding grounds from March through May. California's northern coast offers several good locations for viewing these giants.

The best time to watch whales is in January. While they normally surface every three to five minutes, it is their spout that is usually seen first. From shore, the Point Reyes Lighthouse offers an excellent vantage point. Other good spots are Fort Ross State Historic Park, Gualala Head, Mendocino Headlands State Park, Noyo Harbor (Fort Bragg), Clam Beach (twelve miles north of Eureka), and Castle Rock near Crescent City.

For tour boat information, contact: Captain John's, P.O. Box 155, Half Moon Bay, CA 94019 (415-726-2913); Oceanic Society Expeditions, Fort Mason Center, Building E, San Francisco, CA 94123 (415-441-1106); or Blue & Gold Fleet, Box Z-2, Pier 39, San Francisco, CA 94133 (415-781-7890).

VISITOR INFORMATION

For more information, contact the following: Redwood Empire Association, One Market Plaza, Spear Street Tower #1001, San Francisco, CA 94105 (415-543-8334).

POINTS OF INTEREST

GOLDEN GATE NATIONAL RECREATION AREA. From the Golden Gate Bridge, take Alexander Avenue exit to Conzelman Road. Hiking, fishing, and nature tours.

MUIR WOODS NATIONAL MONUMENT. Located three and a half miles west of Mill Valley (415-388-2595). Old-growth redwoods.

THE MARIN MUSEUM OF THE AMERICAN INDIAN. 2200 Novato Boulevard, Novato (415-897-4064). Exhibits of California's Indians, including a collection of Indian art. Closed Mondays.

MOUNT TAMALPAIS. Magnificent views of the Bay Area. The summit road branches off to the right of State Route 1 just south of Stinson Beach.

POINT REYES NATIONAL SEASHORE. One hundred and fifty miles of trails. Beachcombing, fishing, whale watching, and picnicking. Visit the Coast Miwok Village (415-663-8013), Point Reyes Lighthouse (415-669-1534), and Bear Valley Visitor Center (415-663-1092).

MENDOCINO ART CENTER. Located on Little Lake between Williams and Kasten streets, Mendocino (707-937-5818). Exhibits, shows, concerts, and classes.

FORD HOUSE. 735 Main Street, Mendocino (707-937-5397). Pictorial history of logging and growth of Mendocino.

KELLEY HOUSE HISTORICAL MUSEUM & LIBRARY. 45007 Albion Street, Mendocino (707-937-5791). Historical exhibits.

CALIFORNIA WESTERN RAILROAD "SKUNK" TRAINS. Depart from the Fort Bragg depot on the corner of Pine and Main (707-964-6371). Trains run forty miles from Fort Bragg to Willits. Excellent way to see the redwood country.

GUEST HOUSE MUSEUM. 343 North Main Street, Fort Bragg. Logging equipment plus pictures and artifacts depicting the area's history.

MENDOCINO COAST BOTANICAL GARDENS. 18220 North Highway 1, two miles south of Fort Bragg (707-964-4352). Seventeen-acre botanical garden with ocean access.

MACKERRICHER STATE PARK. Three miles north of Fort Bragg on the Mendocino Coast (707-964-3438). Wildflowers, harbor seals, fishing, hiking, and picnicking.

CAPETOWN, CAPE MENDOCINO. From U.S. 101, take Mattole Road through Petrolia from the south or through Ferndale from the north. This is a long, lonely stretch of beach. Very primitive.

LOLETA CHEESE FACTORY. 252 Loleta Drive, Loleta (707-733-5470). Cheese tasting and viewing area.

CLARKE MUSEUM. Third and E streets, Eureka (707-443-1947). Collection of Indian basketry, pioneer relics, historical photographs, maritime exhibit, and Victoriana.

HUMBOLDT BAY HARBOR CRUISE. Departs from foot of C Street, Eureka (707-442-3738). Seventy-five minute tour of Humboldt Bay.

OLD TOWN. 1st, 2nd, and 3rd streets between C and G in Eureka. Victorian buildings, shopping, and eating.

TRINIDAD. Quaint fishing village north of Eureka. Excellent salmon fishing.

PRAIRIE CREEK REDWOODS STATE PARK. Located fifty miles north of Eureka. Grazing territory of Roosevelt elk.

REDWOOD NATIONAL PARK. Write 1111 Second Street, Crescent City, CA 95531 (707-464-6101).

RESTAURANTS OF NOTE

The following restaurants are listed by location, beginning with

Marin County.

ALTA MIRA. 125 Bulkley Avenue, Sausalito (415-332-1350). An 1890 hotel specializing in steaks and seafood.

CAFÉ MED. 2656 Bridgeway, Sausalito (415-332-8083). Moderately priced dinners (pasta, fish, and veal). Good desserts.

CASA MADRONA RESTAURANT. 801 Bridgeway, Sausalito (415-331-5888). California-French cuisine. Fresh foods. Scenic views.

SCOMA'S OF SAUSALITO. 588 Bridgeway, Sausalito (415-332-9551). The views of San Francisco alone are worth the price of admission.

THE OLEMA INN. Sir Francis Drake Boulevard and Highway 1, Olema (415-663-8441). Continental and California cuisine served in 1876 hotel.

STATION HOUSE CAFE. Third and Main streets, Point Reyes Station (415-663-1515). Good American food.

MANKA'S CZECH RESTAURANT. 30 Callendar Way, Inverness (415-669-1034). Excellent food. Try the roast duckling with caraway sauce.

SALMON POINT RESTAURANT. 3000 North Highway 1, Albion (707-937-0272). Ocean views. Steaks, chops, and seafood. Homemade ice cream.

LITTLE RIVER RESTAURANT. 7750 Highway 1, Little River (707-937-4945). Creative food. Friendly ambience. Fresh fish.

CAFÉ BEAUJOLAIS. 961 Ukiah Street, Mendocino (707-937-5614). Excellent natural and fresh foods. Odd hours.

MACCALLUM HOUSE RESTAURANT. 45020 Albion Street, Mendocino (707-937-5763). Pricey but good food. Seafood is excellent.

THE RESTAURANT. 418 North Main Street, Fort Bragg (707-964-9800). Consistently good food. Steaks and seafood.

WHARF RESTAURANT. 780 North Harbor Drive, Fort Bragg (707-964-4283). Touristy. Specializes in seafood. Good water views.

ROMAN'S. 315 Main, Ferndale (707-725-6358). Good Mexican fare.

LAZIO'S. Foot of C Street, Eureka (707-442-2337). Not fancy, just the best seafood in town. Located in an old cannery.

RAMONES. 409 Opera Alley, Eureka (707-444-3339). Continental cuisine in a romantic setting. Good scallops and prawns.

THE SAMURAI RESTAURANT. 621 Fifth Street, Eureka (707-442-6802). Superb Japanese food. Excellent service.

WHERE TO STAY

HOLLY TREE INN

The Holly Tree Inn is located on the edge of rugged Point Reyes National Seashore. It sits within a secluded nineteen-acre country estate planted with holly trees, mountain laurel, and lilacs.

The two-story home was designed by a Swedish immigrant in 1939 so that it would meld with its natural surroundings rather than overwhelm them. Today's owners, Diane and Tom Balogh, have taken advantage of this environment. Visitors to this area are seeking an unspoiled and tranquil getaway and that is exactly what the Baloghs offer.

But Holly Tree offers more than merely a setting. Since it first opened its doors to guests in July 1979, making it the first bed and breakfast on the peninsula, the inn has prided itself on hospitality and comfort.

"After all these years, we like running an inn just as much as the day we first opened," Diane says, and adds, "We just keep getting better."

The entire second floor is for the use of guests. Its focal point is the spacious living room, which opens through French doors onto a shaded porch. Overstuffed sofas and chairs dressed in Laura Ashley prints ring a large brick fireplace and vintage rugs garnish oak floors. The dining room, where country breakfasts are served in front of another brick fireplace,

Holly Tree Inn (Courtesy Holly Tree Inn)

sits just beyond the living room.

The four guest rooms occupy each corner of the house, offering views of the grounds. Like many of today's inns, antiques, quilts, and Laura Ashley prints adorn the accommodations; however, the rooms are somewhat unique in that each boasts a private bath.

What draws me most to this inn is its location and intimate size. I seek places that both blend with their environment and offer comfortable guest facilities, and the Holly Tree Inn fits that mold.

*   *   *

Holly Tree Inn, Box 642, Point Reyes Station, CA 94956 (415-663-1554). Four guest rooms, all with private baths. Rates range from $60 to $85 (subject to change). VISA/MasterCard. Children with prior approval; no pets; no smoking. The inn is located on #3 Silverhills Road, Inverness Park. From State Route 1, turn west onto Sir Francis Drake Boulevard toward Inverness. Then take the first left onto Bear Valley Road (unmarked) and the first right onto Silverhills Road (also unmarked).

GLENDEVEN

Glendeven is a stately New England farmhouse, which stands behind a redwood fence and one hundred-year-old cypress trees. It fathers over an estate that looks and feels crisp and fresh: the restored hay barn, an adjacent water tower, and the newest building, Stevenscroft, pose without a single hair out of place. Eucalyptus scents the air; acacias, camellias, and a variety of flowers burst with color.

Inside the farmhouse blossoms an elegance that only lyricists would associate with farm life. It is certain that the sweaty brows and callused hands of tillers of the soil have been absent from this place for many years.

The spacious sitting room is flooded in sunlight that cascades through a wall of windows and washes over rich furnishings and a grand piano. French doors lead to the brick terrace, where garden furniture looks out over a meadow.

Within this setting, six of Glendeven's ten accommodations welcome travelers. On the main floor, the Garden Room and the popular Eastlin Suite, featuring French-door views of the distant bay and a classic rosewood Louis XVI bed, make their appeal to the discriminating guest. Bayview, aptly named, Goldcrest, and King's Room make up the second floor, while one story above, ocean views mark The Garret, a unique attic room.

The two-story redwood Stevenscroft was created in 1984 to offer guests the kind of commodious accommodations that only Eastlin offers in the farmhouse. Besides each of its four rooms being large, they all have

Glendeven (Steve Simmons)

wood-burning fireplaces and private baths.

Like any inn, Glendeven will not please every visitor. In its case, travelers to the coast may find location a drawback. Unlike nearby Mendocino, which delights in its seascape setting, Glendeven nestles in a rural landscape. But the ocean is only five minutes away, and Glendeven is among the coast's most elegant inns.

* * *

Glendeven, Little River, CA 95456 (707-937-0083). Ten guest rooms, eight with private baths. Rates range from $60 to $110 (subject to change). Credit cards by special arrangement. The higher rate is for combining Goldcrest and King's Room into a roomy suite. Children with prior approval; no pets; no smoking in guest rooms. For farmhouse guests, breakfast can be taken in the sitting room or delivered to the guest rooms. Stevenscroft guests receive their breakfasts delivered to their rooms in a basket. Glendeven sits one and a half miles south of Mendocino on State Route 1.

THE VICTORIAN FARMHOUSE

The Victorian Farmhouse takes advantage of its rural location, two miles outside of Mendocino, to offer a private setting that seems more like a visit to a relative's home than one to an inn.

Innkeepers George and Carole Molnar purchased the inn in 1985, so, although George's Budapest family were innkeepers, the Molnars are rookies. But they are naturals and have the caring instincts necessary to help guests feel at home. They also have the desire and motivation to be successful.

In 1982 the Molnars decided innkeeping was for them. It took them three years of searching, however, before they found the right Northern California home. Then they came upon this 1877 two-story farmhouse. The building had been a bed and breakfast since the late 1970s, so after purchasing the home it was less a matter of restoration and more one of taking the plunge.

"It's a lot more work than we expected," Carole says, "but this is the life we wanted to live."

A downstairs bay-windowed parlor greets guests. But it feels more like a reception area than a place to relax, so it is the guest rooms where guests will spend their quiet times. The farmhouse offers four accommodations while the barn boasts two more. All rooms have quilts, fresh flowers, and breakfast nooks.

In the main house, the upstairs Emma Dora looks out over the treetops to the Pacific. It has a queen brass bed, a cozy sitting alcove, floral wallpaper, and a redwood ceiling. Dennen also looks toward the ocean. It features a brass king bed and a large, sunny bathroom that overlooks a tiny apple orchard alongside Schoolhouse Creek. The Victorian, with its

The Victorian Farmhouse (Len Cook)

French wood-burning stove and private sitting room, and Garden, whose breakfast nook has a garden view, sit downstairs. The barn's rooms feature open beams and a country ambience.

The Victorian Farmhouse is an ideal getaway for those seeking a pastoral setting. If you have ever lived in an old country home, you will relive the feelings here.

*   *   *

The Victorian Farmhouse, 7001 North Highway 1, P.O. Box 357, Little River, CA 95456 (707-937-0697). Six guest rooms, all with private baths. Rates range from $67 to $75 (subject to change). No credit cards. No children under ten; no pets; no smoking. Breakfast is delivered to the rooms on trays. Private parking available. The inn is located two miles south of Mendocino on State Route 1.

THE HEADLANDS INN

Mendocino takes me back to my youth in New England: the quiet strolls; the great breaths of air that clear the mind of worry; the know-thy-neighbor attitude that is so often misunderstood by outsiders. It is more a state of mind than a place of things.

That is also true of The Headlands Inn. The feelings begin even before you step inside this tall, lean three-story house. There is serenity blossoming in the sun-drenched flower garden, an order imposed by the weathered picket fence, and a welcoming that beckons from the wide front porch.

Inside, the house seems to open its arms in greeting. There is no front desk, just a friendly Irish setter slapping his tail on the carpet and the smells of bread baking in the old-fashioned kitchen. Stairs invite, almost plead, with you to explore, to discover the warmth within these walls.

It is hard to imagine that this home was once a small one-story barbershop, which sat on Main Street more than a century past. To provide living quarters for his family, the barber added a second story in 1873. Following stints as a restaurant, then a small hotel, the building was moved to its present location in 1893. In August 1979, the home began its career as a bed-and-breakfast inn.

The Headlands is large enough so that guests can savor their privacy, yet it still harbors a sense of intimacy. The innkeepers are warm and caring without being intrusive. And the decor is elegant but not stuffy.

Accommodations include five rooms in the house and a large cottage in the rear of the building. All of the rooms have fireplaces, individual electric heat, and private baths. The innkeepers provide down comforters and pillows, extra blankets, fresh flowers, green plants, and clocks.

The Headlands Inn (Lewis Green)

Each of the rooms is unique and often a surprise. Room six offers spectacular views of the ocean; room three opens through a Dutch door onto a private deck; room two features a terrific bay window sitting area that looks out to the Pacific; and the cottage is distinguished by its deep steeping tub.

The Headlands Inn is a charming old home in a quaint seaside village. There is freedom to live and to think here, and the calm that encourages both.

*   *   *

The Headlands Inn, P.O. Box 132, Mendocino, CA 95460 (707-937-4431). Five rooms and a cottage, all with private baths. Rates range from $68 to $90 (subject to change). No credit cards. No children; no pets; no smoking. The inn is at the corner of Howard and Albion streets.

JOSHUA GRINDLE INN

The Joshua Grindle Inn features a relaxed environment within spectacular scenery. Everything about it says "first-class."

Still, all too often credit for quality inns falls on the shoulders of tangible things—the setting, the architecture, the antiques, the fireplaces, the art. I cringe at that perspective. Anyone can purchase a historic home and fill it with antiques and works of local artists. None of that guarantees success. Innkeepers are the key; their attitudes and philosophies make the difference. Joshua Grindle's innkeepers, Bill and Gwen Jacobson, understand this.

"We try to get a feeling for individual guests," Bill says, "and make ourselves available. But we don't want to be intrusive. The guests don't come here to see us."

So true. Fortunately, this philosophy melds with elegant accommodations, offering travelers the best of two worlds.

This 1879 two-story New England-style farmhouse sits on a knoll overlooking Mendocino. A white picket fence embraces the sprawling front lawn. Inside the house are five guest rooms. All are decorated in seventeenth- and eighteenth-century country antiques made of pine and cherry. The Master and Library rooms boast fireplaces. Throughout the house, you feel the quiet elegance of New England.

Around back, in the shade of one hundred-year-old cypress trees, sit the Cypress and the Water Tower. Each offers two accommodations. Franklin stoves warm Cypress, while wood stoves keep the chill out of the Water Tower.

There is not a bad accommodation here, so choice depends upon personal preference. The farmhouse features a more attached, New England climate, perhaps a slightly more elegant look. The outbuildings

Joshua Grindle Inn (Steve Simmons)

provide additional privacy.

*   *   *

Joshua Grindle Inn, 44800 Little Lake, P.O. Box 647, Mendocino, CA 95460 (707-937-4143). Nine guest rooms, all with private baths. Rates range from $67 to $94 (subject to change). VISA/MasterCard. No children; no pets; smoking in guest rooms only. Breakfast is served around a nine-foot pine harvest table in the farmhouse and includes home-baked breads and muffins. Private parking available. The inn is located just off State Route 1 on the north side of town.

WHITEGATE INN

This 1880 two-story white frame house is typical of large New England homes. However, its homey looks, lush flower gardens, and hand-carved picket fence belie a tattered past in which even the earliest days were filled with insecurities.

After the house was built, its owner realized he could not afford to live here. To save himself from having to sell the building, he leased it to a doctor who ran a clinic and hospital out of the home. Finally, in 1894 the house began serving its original purpose as a private residence. The turbulent 1960s, however, saw the building returned to questionable status, first as a boardinghouse, then as a holistic health center. Since 1979, the house has been a bed-and-breakfast inn.

It continues, however, to be a turnstile for innkeepers. The most recent change occurred in the spring of 1986, when Patricia Patton became the inn's newest owner. Like previous managers, Patricia is maintaining the high standards set at the Whitegate since its early days as an inn. She brings a world of travel to Mendocino from her experiences in the Diplomatic Corps, where she served in Paris, Vienna, Taipei, and Jeddah.

In at least one way, Patricia should feel right at home. The inn is a people place. The atmosphere makes for easy conversation; the parlor invites guests to gather. Its wood stove and mammoth redwood doors lend an air of warmth, while the nineteenth-century English antiques and Oriental wallpaper add touches of class.

Each of the six guest rooms is charming. Downstairs, The Cypress Room features redwood floors and a Franklin stove, while The Rose Room is bright and sunny. Upstairs, The French Room boasts tall windows with ocean views, a hand-painted Italian chandelier, and a magnificent antique French bedroom set. The Tulip and Blue rooms are a little dark but cozy, while The Garden Room is light and airy and boasts a fireplace.

The Whitegate has an old-fashioned romantic feeling about it. You can envision women sashaying down the stairway to the glances of

Whitegate Inn (Courtesy Whitegate Inn)

mustachioed men. Today, the house shines as it would have in its early days if history had been kinder to it.

*   *   *

Whitegate Inn, 499 Howard Street, P.O. Box 150, Mendocino, CA 95460 (707-937-4892). Six guest rooms, four with private baths. Rates range from $65 to $95 (subject to change). No credit cards. No children under thirteen;

no pets; no smoking. Sunday breakfasts include an old-fashioned Christmas tradition featuring homemade waffles. The inn is located on the corner of Howard and Ukiah streets.

THE GREY WHALE INN

Bed and breakfast is a fairly recent phenomenon on the West Coast, and when they first began appearing here, tradition often dictated the setting: Mom and Pops, cozy bed-and-breakfast homes, were far more common than were inns. Nevertheless, The Grey Whale Inn felt no insecurities about opening its doors in 1978. Like its namesake, the large inn overshadowed most of the other fish in the sea. Even today, with the growth of bed-and-breakfast inns on the rise, The Grey Whale has reason to celebrate its differences.

This weathered redwood structure was built in 1915 to serve as the north coast's major health-care facility. Known as the Redwood Coast Hospital, it cared for the sick and welcomed new babies into the world until 1971. Then the building lapsed into decline until 1978, when John and Colette Bailey responded to an ad in *The Wall Street Journal* proclaiming the old building was for sale.

"We had been looking to get into business for ourselves," Colette says. "When we got here and saw the building, we knew this was the perfect place for an inn."

But first there was work to be done. For several months, John and Colette worked eighteen-hour days, seven-day weeks. John fixed everything that did not move, while Colette sewed from morning to night. While all this was going on, they also worked as innkeepers on a small scale, for they opened a few rooms as soon as they moved in.

Today, The Grey Whale Inn boasts a total of fourteen rooms and suites in an environment that stresses privacy. This inn specializes in "letting the guests make the first move." It is not that the innkeepers and staff are not friendly and willing to meet guests' needs, they are. But visitors will not be running into the hosts at every corner.

Thirteen rooms sit off of wide hallways on three floors, while an apartment-size suite shares the lower level with the inn's recreation room. Decor is eclectic and furnishings are comfortable. There are a few antiques scattered about but even they serve practical functions and are not present just for looks. The original art that adorns walls and tables provides ample sustenance for the eyes.

While the inn's name implies a seaside perch, such is not the case. The Pacific rushes to shore several blocks away. However, some of the rooms, particularly Sunset, do look out across rooftops to the ocean.

The Grey Whale Inn (Brett Behrens)

The size and unique atmosphere created by this former hospital, which by the way still retains some of its hospital features—such as a surgery lamp in The Whale Watch Suite—offers travelers a bed-and-breakfast experience in a small hotel atmosphere.

*   *   *

The Grey Whale Inn, 615 North Main Street, Fort Bragg, CA 95437 (707-964-0640). Fourteen guest rooms, all with private baths. Several suites available. Rates range from $60 to $90 (subject to change). VISA/MasterCard/American Express. Children with prior approval; no pets; smoking permitted. Private parking available. Main Street is also State Route 1. The inn is located on the north side of town.

THE GINGERBREAD MANSION

If The Gingerbread Mansion had been a painting, it would hang beside the world's greatest works. As it is, the mansion's face has adorned the covers and pages of North America's finest magazines and newspapers.

Renowned as Northern California's most photographed Victorian, The Gingerbread Mansion is, in my eyes, the most beautiful bed-and-breakfast inn on the West Coast. Its peach and yellow three-story frame is elaborately trimmed and garnished with carved spools, ornate brackets, scalloped shingles, a lacy widow's walk, and a spired turret.

The mansion's magic is magnified by its setting. Sculpted shrubs and

The Gingerbread Mansion (Courtesy The Gingerbread Mansion)

hedges commingle with colorful blossoms in the front yard, while an English-style garden, complete with fountain, flourishes to the side.

Inside, four parlors, a formal dining room, and the Gingerbread Suite make up the main floor, while seven guest rooms and a two hundred-square-foot gardenlike bath make up the second level. Obviously, this is a large kingdom to reign over. Still, owners Wendy Hatfield and Ken Torbert manage to rule with a soft and gentle touch.

Beginning with the dictum that the way to a guest's heart is through their stomach, the smells of fresh food fill the mansion much of the time. The day begins with trays of coffee, tea, and juice, which await on hallway buffets. Between 8:30 A.M. and 9:30 A.M. breakfast of homemade breads, muffins and cakes, local cheeses, and seasonally fresh fruit is served. Then later in the day, afternoon tea, starring home-baked gingerbread and special cakes, takes center stage.

In the evening, beds are turned down and hand-dipped chocolates are left at bedsides. Other touches, including reading lamps, luggage racks, electric blankets, robes, umbrellas, and even rubber boots are enlisted to serve in the mansion's army of amenities.

Rarely do such works of art surface in the hospitality industry. The Gingerbread Mansion by any standards is a masterpiece.

*   *   *

The Gingerbread Mansion, 400 Berding Street, Ferndale, CA 95536 (707-786-4000). Eight guest rooms, five with private baths. Rates range from $65 to $95 (subject to change). VISA/MasterCard. No children under ten; no pets; no smoking. From U.S. 101, take either Mattole Road at Fernbridge or Grizzly Bluff Road at Rio Dell. Once in Ferndale, turn on Brown to Berding.

CARTER HOUSE

San Francisco's "Painted Ladies" represent the standard bearers of America's Victorians. Their gingerbread frills and lively colors are constantly being mimicked. However, it is important to note that these bright facades are not dipped in historical fact but instead reflect a recent trend.

According to innkeeper Mark Carter, the first Victorians often featured drab exteriors. And infected with a desire to build an authentic Victorian mansion, Mark raised the Carter House between 1980 and 1982.

The result is quite a shock to eyes accustomed to today's gay

Carter House (Courtesy Carter House)

Victorian style. Based upon the plans of an 1884 San Francisco home, the Carter House's unpainted redwood boards and scalloped shingles create a lackluster finish on what otherwise is a magnificent structure.

Once inside the mansion's great front doors, a cheery elegance replaces the flat exterior. Three open parlors, awash in sunlight streaming through large bay windows, boast marble fireplaces and Victorian antiques. But frills and clutter, usually associated with that period and often lending a stuffy museumlike air, have been eliminated by understating the decor. The patina of oak floors, the richness of oak and redwood trim, and the beauty of Oriental rugs are all allowed their day in the sun. Bringing life to the entire setting are fresh flowers, green plants, and an array of contemporary paintings and ceramics by local artists.

Each of the seven guest rooms carries on this level of elegance. European antiques, hardwood floors, Oriental carpets, and original art distinguish the accommodations. In addition, all rooms have robes, comforters, digital clocks, and good magazines.

While every room makes its own impression, The Suite is in a class by itself. Its spacious setting welcomes a marble fireplace, wing chairs, and a beveled-glass, hand-carved armoire. And the bathroom's Jacuzzi adds just the right touch of decadence.

Building the Carter House and turning it into an inn seems a stroke of genius. But the inn's evolution is really a fable of whimsy.

Mark, a developer of some note, built the mansion as a private residence. "But I got a little carried away," he says, sporting a sheepish smile. "Suddenly I was broke and couldn't even furnish the place."

So, like any desperate homeowner, he turned his castle into a business. First, it was an art and antique gallery, then he added three guest rooms and by 1984 Mark and his wife, Christi, moved next door so their pride and joy could become a full-fledged, seven-room bed-and-breakfast inn.

*   *   *

Carter House, 1033 Third Street, Eureka, CA 95501 (707-445-1390). Seven guest rooms, four with private baths. Rates range from $65 to $150 (subject to change). VISA/MasterCard/American Express. No children under ten; no pets; no smoking. Breakfast is a four-course gourmet meal. In Eureka, turn west off U.S. 101 onto L Street to Third.

Oregon

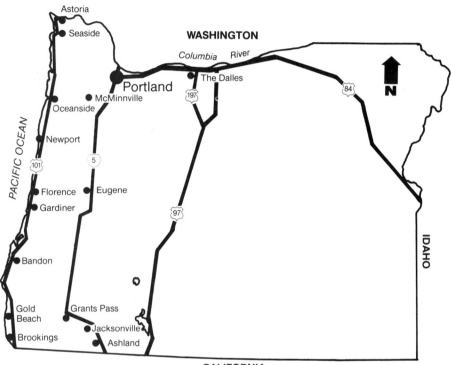

ASHLAND
    Chanticleer Inn
    The Miners Addition
    The Morical House
    Romeo Inn
ASTORIA
    Rosebriar Inn
BANDON
    Cliff Harbor Guest House
    Spindrift
BROOKINGS
    Sea Dreamer Inn
EUGENE
    Campus Cottage
    Griswold Bed & Breakfast
GARDINER
    Guest House at Gardiner by the Sea

GOLD BEACH
    Endicott Gardens
GRANTS PASS
    The Handmaidens' Inn
JACKSONVILLE
    McCully House Inn
MCMINNVILLE
    Mattey House
NEWPORT
    Ocean House
OCEANSIDE
    Three Capes
SEASIDE
    The Boarding House
THE DALLES
    Williams House

Portland

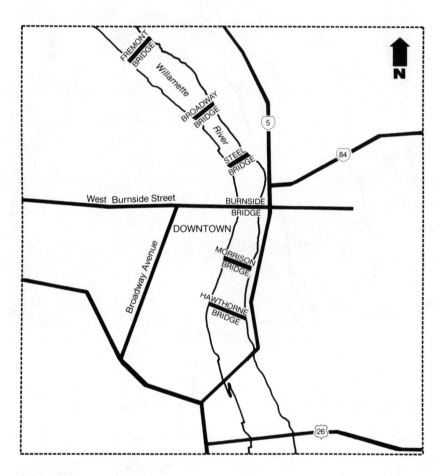

Allenhouse
Corbett House

Portland

---

*P*ortland feels like a favorite pair of slippers—comfortable. It lacks the push and shove of most modern metropolises, preferring to ease rather than jump forward.

Still, there is growth, albeit cautious. It can be seen in the changing skyline; it can be heard on downtown streets where jackhammers pound out modern tunes.

Within the last decade, Portland has welcomed the construction of a number of image-changing structures. There is the magnificent Performance Arts Center; the colorful Michael Graves' masterpiece—the Portland Building—with its seven-ton copper statue Portlandia crouching above the entrance; the downtown bricked mall along Fifth and Sixth avenues; the light-rail commuter line linking downtown to bedroom communities on the east side; and the RiverPlace development, a community of the 1980s whose elegant hotel, pricey restaurants and shops, and classy condominiums toss their shadows on the Willamette River.

Nevertheless, compared to most other West Coast cities, Portland's urban renewal is more like a nose job than a face lift. Portlanders prefer it that way. In fact, they look to Seattle, a place where change is occurring at breakneck speed, as the fast lane. A curious admonition to those of us who think of Seattle as just a bit sleepy, despite its transforming skyline.

As a result of Portland's prudence, the city's reputation for livability is alive and well. The downtown is compact and built to a scale that invites both sunlight and fresh air. It welcomes walking and a leisurely pace. Some seventy-five hundred acres of parks scatter greenbelts across the city's landscape, creating a country backdrop for an urban scene. Cars seldom clog city streets and freeways mostly slash over and around Portland rather than through it.

To put it succinctly, Portland is a quiet community. In most ways, it is more like a town cradling its people than a city throbbing with bright lights.

GETTING TO KNOW PORTLAND

Portland's downtown is easily explored on foot at a leisurely pace in one day. This is due to the vision of early pioneers from New England, who admired walkable cities.

Begin your tour at Pioneer Courthouse Square. Once the site of the old Portland Hotel, it is now a gathering place ringed with columns and dotted with benches. Broadway—home of Nordstrom, a fashionable department store, and the Performing Arts Center—makes up its western border. One block farther west, Park Avenue hosts the Oregon Historical Center and the Portland Art Museum. All are within six blocks of the Square.

Running along the Square's eastern horizon is the city's bricked transit mall, Fifth and Sixth avenues. Reserved for public transportation and pedestrians, these broad boulevards cut through the soul of Portland's shopping and business districts.

For people who enjoy shopping and a touch of history, there are two other locations worth exploration. At 110 Southwest Yamhill, between First and Second in the Yamhill Historical District, the Yamhill Market sprawls. The smells of fresh seafood and the sounds of shoppers browsing arts, crafts, and gifts waft through its open spaces. Eight blocks north on Second, life in Portland's Old Town echoes about its cast-iron-front buildings. Here visitors find historic structures, unique shops, and interesting restaurants. Between May and December, a must stop on the edge of Old Town is the corner of Waterfront Park, just under the Burnside Bridge. On weekends, the Saturday Market wraps young and old alike in arts, crafts, entertainment, and food.

In June, the City of Roses celebrates its sobriquet with the Portland Rose Festival. It is a time of parades, auto races, mini-festivals, and carnivals.

Just about any time is a good time to explore one of Portland's parks. Its most spectacular commons, Washington Park, makes up 145 acres in the city's West Hills. Its views of Mount Hood rising above downtown and the blooms of both the rose and the Japanese gardens make this a special place. The best views of the city and mountains, however, are from 1,073-foot Council Crest Park in southwest Portland. For a wilderness experience, no other urban greenbelt can top Forest Park, which boasts miles of hiking and riding trails.

As a travelers' destination point, Portland's critics might contend, "A great place to live, but I wouldn't want to visit there." That attitude is shortsighted at best. The city may not flash with pizazz, but stars do twinkle here—perhaps not as bright as in some other metropolises, but they are still here.

In addition, Portland makes a grand place to wine, dine, and repose while exploring the pleasures of nearby Mount Hood, the Columbia Gorge, or the wine country. All are within a two-hour drive of downtown.

A PRACTICAL GUIDE TO THE CITY

THE CLIMATE

Temperatures tend to be mild year-round, 30s and 40s in deep winter, 70s and 80s in summer. From as early as October to as late as May, do not be caught without an umbrella.

YOUR CLOTHES

As I have said, this is a relaxed city. Casual clothes are appropriate most of the time. However, theater patrons sometimes put on the ritz, as do some nightclub and restaurant goers.

DRIVING AND PARKING

This is an easy city to drive around. There are enough parking garages and lots for everyone. Before exploring the city, stop at the Convention and Visitors Center for a map.

PUBLIC TRANSPORTATION

Tri-Met's (503-233-3511) bus service downtown is free and offers frequent stops.

VISITOR INFORMATION

For more information, write or call: Greater Portland Convention and Visitors Association, 26 Southwest Salmon Street, Portland, OR 97204 (503-222-2223).

POINTS OF INTEREST

YAMHILL MARKET. 110 Southwest Yamhill. An urban marketplace featuring fresh foods and unique shops.

OREGON HISTORICAL CENTER. 1230 Southwest Park Avenue (503-222-1741). Changing historical exhibits.

PORTLAND ART MUSEUM. 1219 Southwest Park Avenue (503-226-2811). Excellent exhibit of Northwest Coast Indian art.

PORTLAND CENTER FOR THE VISUAL ARTS. 117 Northwest Fifth Avenue (503-

222-7107). Two galleries of contemporary works, performance events, and lectures.

MORGAN'S ALLEY. 515 Southwest Broadway. Small boutiques and restaurants.

OLD TOWN. Along Second Avenue from Southwest Ankeny to Northwest Everett. Historic buildings, unique shops, and restaurants.

PERFORMING ARTS CENTER. Broadway and Main (503-241-0788). Construction scheduled for completion in April 1987. A world-class center for the performing arts.

WASHINGTON PARK. Located in Portland's West Hills, off U.S. 26 West. Home of Japanese Gardens and the International Rose Test Garden.

WASHINGTON PARK ZOO. Take U.S. 26 West to Washington Park (503-226-1561). Natural habitats. Known for its elephant herd.

OREGON MUSEUM OF SCIENCE AND INDUSTRY (OMSI). Adjacent to Washington Park Zoo (503-222-2828). Hands-on displays, reptile exhibit, and Kendall Planetarium.

WESTERN FORESTRY CENTER. Adjacent to OMSI (503-228-1367). An examination of forest resources and the timber industry.

PITTOCK MANSION. 3229 Northwest Pittock Drive (503-248-4469). A restored French Renaissance mansion. Antique furnishings and objets d'art from the seventeenth, eighteenth, and nineteenth centuries. Good city views.

RESTAURANTS OF NOTE

Portland boasts a fine array of restaurants. The following represent some of the city's best.

ALEXIS. 215 West Burnside (503-224-8577). Noisy and authentic Greek taverna. Kalamarakia is excellent. Large servings of all dishes.

BRASSERIE MONTMARTRE. 626 Southwest Park (503-224-5552). The fare is moderately good but do come here for nightly live jazz.

BREAD AND INK CAFE. 3610 Southeast Hawthorne (503-239-4756). A neighborhood restaurant, whose name derives from the daily baking of breads and the drawing talents of one of the owners. Daily specials are excellent.

CHEN'S DYNASTY. 622 Southwest Washington (503-248-9491). Extensive menu. Excellent food.

COUCH STREET FISH HOUSE. 105 Northwest Third (503-223-6173). Fresh seafood that can be very good. Ignore the other entrées.

GENOA. 2832 Southeast Belmont (503-238-1464). Set menu. Set seatings. Simple decor. Great northern Italian food.

THE HEATHMAN RESTAURANT. Southwest Salmon at Broadway (503-241-4100). An excellent hotel restaurant. Regional seasonal cuisine.

HUNAN. 515 Southwest Broadway (503-224-8063). Excellent Szechuan cuisine.

INDIGINE. 3723 Southeast Division (503-238-1470). Small dining room. Excellent food. Three-course dinners Tuesday through Friday. Set feast on Saturday.

L'AUBERGE. 2601 Northwest Vaughn (503-223-3302). One of Portland's best. Excellent French specialties featuring local veal, lamb, and quail.

LE CUISINIER. 1308 West Burnside (503-224-4260). Only eight tables provide an intimate setting for inventive dishes. Entrées are superb. Regarded by some critics as Portland's best restaurant. Reservations a must.

THE RINGSIDE. 2165 West Burnside (503-223-1513). Best steaks in town. A good spot for celebrity watching. Long lines likely.

A THYME GARDEN. 1705 Northeast Couch (503-238-3934). Menu represents specific regions of Europe and changes frequently. Dinners served Thursday through Saturday only.

WHERE TO STAY

ALLENHOUSE

The seeds for bed-and-breakfast inns are planted in many different ways. Some germinate in an atmosphere of entrepreneurship, others sprout in the shadows of corporate burnout, while still others flourish in a climate of fun. Allenhouse took root over a bottle of wine and friendship.

"I had been managing a small restaurant," Barbara Allen says, "and was really looking for something else. One evening I was sipping wine with a friend and said, 'Wouldn't it be wonderful to run a bed and breakfast?'"

For Barbara, those words were all she needed to open the doors to innkeeping. In August 1985, she purchased this 1914 three-story house. Its residential location just five minutes from downtown and its grand proportions seemed an ideal environment for a bed-and-breakfast inn.

Before opening, however, the house required some refurbishing. Barbara revived every square inch of the place. For starters, she painted, papered, polished, and furnished with antiques. Not surprisingly, there are still more changes and decisions to be made—things such as guest room decor and whether to add more private baths are, at this writing, still in a state of flux.

The downstairs boasts three common areas. Hardwood maple floors, mauve walls, and the textured plaster ceiling give the living room its

Allenhouse (Dana Olsen)

character. And despite a forest of shrubs and bushes embracing the house's facade, lots of natural light brightens the stuffed furnishings. The sun-room looks out on a lush backyard. Through French doors, guests pass into the adjacent dining room. Here, oak trim surrounds a large table that stands on a Persian rug.

The four guest rooms sit off an open upstairs hallway. Polished maple floors and fresh flowers weave a common thread through the rooms. However, each accommodation reflects an individual decor.

The North Room features a double canopy bed with a satiny down comforter. Rattan chairs and an exotic bird wallpaper establish a tropical setting. The Master Room has an antique double mahogany bed and matching dresser. The Suite features iron and brass beds while the South Room is furnished very much like a child's room.

*   *   *

Allenhouse, 2606 Northwest Lovejoy Street, Portland, OR 97210. (503-227-6841). Four guest rooms, one with a private bath. Rates range from $58 to $63 (subject to change). VISA/MasterCard/American Express. Children with prior approval; no pets; smoking in sun-room only. Take Burnside west to 23rd Avenue, turn right, then left on Lovejoy.

CORBETT HOUSE

Corbett House is a traditional bed and breakfast with a nontraditional hostess. While most innkeepers are caring and friendly, few are as captivating as Sylvia Malagamba. She combines an honest interest in her guests with a self-portrait that induces others to pay attention.

Once you discover Sylvia's innate curiosity and her guest house's raison d'etre, the idea of late night, early morning klatches seems natural. In fact, they are probably the primary reason for her exceptionally high return rate.

"I run this house like an inn," Sylvia says. "I have respect for my guests and their needs, including privacy. But I happen to live here too, so sharing conversation seems natural.

"Actually, I've started calling this place Doormat University," Sylvia continues, "because I've just learned so much from my guests."

Many of Sylvia's guests are business people, so it is important to note that privacy is available here. The home's location and ambience do promote a very quiet atmosphere.

The two-story 1920s Art Deco house sits on a knoll in a residential neighborhood on Portland's southwest side. It rises above John's Landing and the Willamette River, three miles from downtown, with Mount Hood towering to the east.

The home's interior reflects a lived-in, comfortable style. The living room features a blend of stuffed furniture, metal sculptures, paintings, and floral arrangements. There is also a brick fireplace.

Corbett House (Lewis Green)

All three guest rooms occupy the second floor. Two front bedrooms boast views of Mount Hood and the Cascades and have access to a tiny balcony.

The only way to describe decor is to call it eclectic, although there is a Mediterranean thread and an Asian influence that run through the house. In addition to the comfortable beds and unique settings, there are guest robes in a hallway closet and an honor refrigerator stocked with soft drinks and mineral water in the hall.

Breakfast is a leisurely affair served in the modest dining room or on the balcony. It features natural and healthful foods, including seasonal fruit, home-baked breads, and whole wheat croissants.

This is a cozy environment: the house is small so visitors should expect a European bed-and-breakfast experience.

*   *   *

Corbett House, 7533 Southwest Corbett Avenue, Portland, OR 97219 (503-245-2580). Three guest rooms share two baths. (There are plans for a room with a private bath.) Rates range from $40 to $55 (subject to change). VISA/MasterCard/American Express. Children with prior approval; no pets; no smoking. From Interstate 5 south of downtown, take the Corbett Street exit south to the top of the hill.

The Oregon Coast

*O*regon's pristine wilderness wears a Jekyll and Hyde mask. While rugged beauty lures outdoor activists to its mountains, lakes, and rivers, Oregon's provincial and protective nature often ignores even basic commercial trappings, which sometimes discourages the average tourist.

Yet the Oregon Coast has struck a balance between preservation and people. It conserves its shoreline, while at the same time provides needs for travelers.

For some 350 miles, stretching between Northern California and the Columbia River, U.S. 101 carries auto-tourists through Oregon's royal jewels. It sweeps past beaches and hugs the edges of rugged cliffs. It makes hairpin turns around the sides of forested mountains and looks down on craggy ocean pinnacles. And it greets sandy dunes, rocky headlands, sheltered coves, deep inlets, romantic lighthouses, and migrating wildlife.

The south coast—between Brookings and Bandon—boasts Oregon's least explored beaches and miles of open seascapes. And from Coos Bay (the largest natural harbor between San Francisco and Washington's Puget Sound) to Astoria, seaside communities and diverse landscapes share the spotlight with the Pacific.

GETTING TO KNOW THE OREGON COAST

BETWEEN BROOKINGS AND PORT ORFORD

Along this seventy-mile stretch of Oregon's coastline, the scenery is absolutely breathtaking and there are enough viewpoints to satiate the hunger of even starved sightseers.

Brookings' mild temperatures keep this town in full bloom nearly year-round. Azaleas reach their peak in time for the Azalea Festival over Memorial Day Weekend, and lilies, the area's top money crop, color the fields in June and July. Still, fishing and beachcombing share the town's top billings as far as travelers are concerned.

Ocean fishing, rock fishing, and surf casting abound, with charter boats available for bottom fish as well as silver and Chinook salmon. Except for salmon, any type of ocean fish can be caught off the jetty at the mouth of the Chetco River without a license. In the river itself, trout are abundant in spring, while steelhead and salmon run in the fall.

Beachcombers delight in the variety of shells and marine life that dot the beach. In addition, myriad parks in and around Brookings offer a treasure trove of discoveries.

The 141-acre Harris Beach State Park melds sandy beaches, sea stacks, thick shrubs, and tall firs. The view from Harris Butte sweeps the Pacific in three directions. Two miles north, 11-mile-long Samuel H. Boardman State Park provides a number of convenient viewpoints for the auto-tourist. Indian Beach is a good place to stretch car-stiff legs. A short trail snakes through salal and spruce to an ocean overlook. History tells us this was once a gathering place for Indians, who came here to catch shellfish and make arrowheads. Eight miles east of Brookings sprawls Loeb State Park. Located alongside the Chetco River, the park features groves of old-growth Oregon myrtle trees and coast redwoods.

Gold Beach, though half the size of Brookings, outpoints its southern cousin in the tourism arena. The number of motels winking alongside U.S. 101 testifies to that.

This is a popular port for sport fishing. But it is Gold Beach's location at the mouth of the Rogue River that keeps motel parking lots full. Besides its famed runs of steelhead and salmon, which attract herds of plump seals and sea lions, the wild and scenic Rogue throbs with jet boats bouncing with tourists being whisked into the back country.

Leaving Gold Beach and traveling north again, the scenery once more captures the attention of visitors. Six miles south of Port Orford rises the second highest peak on the Oregon Coast, 1,756-foot Humbug Mountain. Strong hikers should take the three-mile trail from the park to the mountaintop. Others must be satisfied with less lofty sea views from the shadows of myrtles, alders, and maples.

Port Orford seems like little more than a bend in the highway. Here, seafood stands hawk fresh fish brought in by fleets of fishing boats, which use this natural deep-water harbor as a base.

Five miles north of Port Orford, the turnoff to Cape Blanco leads to the most westerly point on the coast and a lighthouse that has been in operation since 1870. Named by a Spanish sailor in 1603, who was paying tribute to the chalk white cliffs, the cape offers travelers good views of migrating gray whales, particularly in December.

BANDON

As is true of many Northwest communities grappling with a

changing economy, Bandon suffers from an identity crisis. Like Eve, it has several faces. There is its community face—quiet, conservative, protective. Then there is its chamber-of-commerce smile—the one that alternately calls itself Bandon-By-The-Sea, the Cranberry Capital of Oregon, and the Storm Watching Capital of the World. Each boast is a little bolder; each one puts another nail in the coffin of a reclusive lifestyle.

All of the self-promotion has reaped results: the tourists are coming. And when they arrive, the chamber and the hospitality industry do their best to ensure visitors like what they see. As a result, Old Town, the victim of earlier fires, has been restored to cater to guests, and of course the town's ego.

To people traveling U.S. 101, the title Bandon-By-The-Sea may be puzzling. For whether you are coming from Port Orford or from Coos Bay, the ocean remains mostly out of view.

Nevertheless, Bandon does have a spectacular seaside setting. To enjoy it, abandon U.S. 101 for Beach Loop Drive, either at Beach Junction Market, one mile south of downtown, or at the entrance to Old Town.

This narrow country lane accesses smooth beaches alive with sea birds. At Face Rock, sea stacks rise out of the waters like whales frozen in midbreach. Legend explains these granite monoliths—called Face Rock, and Cat and Kittens—by telling the tale of the defiant Indian maiden Ewauna and her precious pets. Because Ewauna resisted the amorous advances of Seatka, the evil spirit of the ocean, she and her friends were frozen in time.

Back in Bandon, on the waterfront, Old Town relives its own history, as well as celebrating its present. Fresh-fish stores and bait shops commingle with gift shops and arts and crafts shops.

THE CENTRAL COAST

Just north of Bandon, after crossing the Coquille River, the smart traveler leaves U.S. 101 for the scenic drive along Seven Devils Road and Cape Arago Highway to Charleston.

At Cape Arago there are opportunities to watch ships from distant lands calling on the harbor of Coos Bay. Also, binoculars provide views of sea lions padding about Seal Rocks. A half-mile north, the restored gardens of Shore Acres State Park bloom with a variety of flowers, including roses, dahlias, azaleas, and rhododendrons. In addition, the glass-walled observation shelter looks down on the ocean as it washes over the cliffs. The next stop should be Sunset Bay, which offers excellent photo opportunities, picnicking, and swimming.

Other than the Oregon Coast Music Festival in July—highlighting world-class musicians performing folk to classical—there are few reasons for tourists to spend time in the industrial cities of Coos Bay and North

Bend. Next along U.S. 101, however, awaits the Oregon Dunes National Recreation Area.

Interrupted only by the Umpqua River and several smaller streams, rolling mounds of sand, some reaching heights of five hundred feet, stretch from North Bend to Florence. The National Dunes Recreation Area Visitor Center in Reedsport is the best place to obtain maps and guides to this area. They will show you which of the beaches are open to vehicles and how to access them from the highway. If a glimpse of the dunes is all your curiosity requires, visit Honeyman State Park three miles south of Florence.

The community of Florence displays the Bandon Syndrome: there is the real, nondescript town along the highway, and there is also the more poetic Old Town. Old Town is the place to visit. Its historic buildings, variety of restaurants, and touristy shops sit alongside the north bank of the river in the shadow of the Siuslaw River Bridge. A walking tour map is available from the Chamber of Commerce.

Although tourist spots usually leave this writer less than impressed, Sea Lion Caves, twelve miles north of Florence on U.S. 101, is an experience worth exploring. An elevator takes people down 208 feet into one of the largest sea caves in the world. Here visitors can observe both playful pups and burly bulls.

Between Florence and Newport there are a number of uncrowded beaches, waysides, and viewpoints. The most spectacular panorama along this stretch stands eight hundred feet above the rolling sea just south of Yachats (Ya-hots), which is Indian for "at the foot of the mountain." First called Cape Perpetua in 1778 by Captain James Cook, this perch spans the beaches and rocky headlands below.

Newport sits at the crossroads of U.S. 101 and U.S. 20 and, like Bandon and Florence, the old surpasses the new. Restaurants, pubs, gift shops, bait and tackle stores, and fishing boats sit along the historic Bayfront area. In addition to these sites, Yaquina Bay's tideflats offer excellent clamming and its piers good crabbing. The beaches north of the bay represent some of the finest agate-hunting grounds in the world.

Depoe Bay, which claims to have the world's smallest harbor, rests some twelve miles north. Whether true or not, watching fishing boats navigate the narrow channel, even on the calmest days, makes for one of the best shows on Oregon's coast. Farther north, Lincoln City, a commerical embarrassment to Oregon's flight from pretension, makes up the final leg of the central coast.

THE PORTLAND CONNECTION

Several broad highways bridge Portland to the north coast, which partially explains its popularity. However, the hidden treasures, diverse landscape, and historical nature of this final one hundred-mile-trek also deserve credit.

Just north of Oretown, leave the highway and follow the bike route called Three Capes Loop. Each of the three capes has its own charm: Cape Kiwanda is a haven for artists, hang gliders, and dory fishermen; Cape Lookout juts two miles out into the ocean, and the foliage is similar to that of a coastal rain forest; and Cape Meares is the site of the famous Octopus Tree, a twisted Sitka spruce that has been featured in "Ripley's Believe It or Not." Before reaching Cape Meares, visit the seaside hamlet of Oceanside and Three Arch Rocks National Wildlife Refuge. Murres, gulls, cormorants, puffins, petrels, and guillemots bring these rocks to life.

Then it is back to the highway, past the Tillamook Cheese Factory, and up 1,661-foot Neahkanie Mountain. During whale migration, this lofty perch offers excellent whale-watching opportunities for those with binoculars.

SEASIDE

Seaside's nearby southern neighbor, Cannon Beach, draws accolades and notice for its June Sand Castle Contest, its December Dickens Weekends, its arts community, and its photogenic Haystack Rock. Still, Seaside deserves a closer look, especially by those who have rejected its commercial lean.

The amusement centers, gift shops, and annual "Miss Oregon" pageant continue to play to large crowds. But the beach and the two-mile-long concrete promenade that fronts it are really the community's luminaries.

Seaside's beach is mostly flat, just a lot of sand welcoming the Pacific. But it is the kind of beach where a kite can be flown, a Frisbee tossed, a sand castle built, or a love affair kindled. It is quiet, it is peaceful, and it is gentle.

Separating the beach from a long gray line of bungalows, the promenade welcomes leisurely walks and conversation. It is a place for strolling among strangers who are ready to become friends. While most of Oregon's coast offers excuses to enjoy anonymity, Seaside's promenade encourages congregations.

ASTORIA

Astoria boasts no sun-splashed beaches or spectacular rocky head-lands. In fact, it borders on not even being a close relative of the coastal family. Still, its location at the mouth of the Columbia River gives it a seagoing, salty flavor. And it is a city with a colorful past, which is what makes this town attractive to tourists.

In 1792, Captain Robert Gray discovered the mouth of the Columbia River. Thirteen years later, members of the Lewis and Clark expedition wintered just south of present-day Astoria at Fort Clatsop. Then in 1811, John Jacob Astor established a fur-trading post where Astoria now stands. These were Astoria's beginnings.

Today, this working-class town of eleven thousand is a blend of classic architecture and museums dedicated to history.

Begin all tours from atop the 125-foot Astoria Column sprouting on Coxcomb Hill. The reward for climbing the 166 steps is the panoramas of Astoria, the Columbia River, the rolling coastal mountains, and the Pacific. Then take in the area's museums. Finally, walk Franklin and Grand avenues for looks at historic homes.

A PRACTICAL GUIDE TO THE OREGON COAST

THE CLIMATE

Temperatures tend to be mild, 50 degrees to 70 degrees year-round. Summer can mean dense morning fog; winter heavy storms. September and October usually feature the most reliable weather.

YOUR CLOTHES

Nothing but casual clothes are required along the coast. Comfortable, dry walking shoes, sweaters, and jackets are musts.

WHALE WATCHING

December is usually the best time for this activity along the Oregon Coast. Choose coastal headlands that jut out into the ocean. Early morning hours and a calm ocean favor your chances of spotting gray whales. Look for their blow—water blown into the air when the whale exhales.

CHARTER FISHING

Ocean salmon seasons usually begin in mid-May and run to mid-September. Tuna are normally caught in late summer; bottom fish year-round. Charter boats moor in all the major ports. Telephone ahead at least one week for reservations. Contact the Oregon State Tourism Division for a list of Oregon Coast charter boat operators.

Visitor Information

For more information, contact the following: Oregon Tourism Division, 595 Cottage Street NE, Salem, OR 97310 (800-547-7842 outside Oregon, 800-233-3306 inside Oregon).

Points of Interest

HARRIS BEACH STATE PARK. Located just north of Brookings. Sandy beaches, rocky outcroppings, and good views.

SAMUEL H. BOARDMAN STATE PARK. Located about two miles north of Harris Beach State Park. Excellent viewpoints and picnicking.

JERRY'S ROGUE RIVER JET BOAT TRIPS. Located in Gold Beach (503-247-7601). Trips up the Rogue River.

WEST COAST GAME PARK. Located on U.S. 101, seven miles south of Bandon (503-347-3106). More than 350 exotic animals, including many that enjoy human contact.

THE CONTINUUM CENTER. 175 Second Street, Old Town, Bandon (503-347-4111). An exhibit called The Immortality Principle. A working hologram. A marvelous bookstore.

COQUILLE RIVER HISTORICAL MUSEUM. 390 First Street Southwest. Located in the old Coast Guard building on Old Town Bandon's waterfront. Excellent displays. Indian artifacts.

SHORE ACRES STATE PARK GARDENS. Located just north of Cape Arago. Magnificent botanical gardens.

SOUTH SLOUGH NATIONAL ESTUARINE SANCTUARY. Located just south of Charleston (503-888-5558). Features a variety of habitats and wildlife.

OREGON DUNES NATIONAL RECREATION AREA. Stretches from North Bend to Florence (503-271-3611).

SEA LION CAVES. Located on U.S. 101, twelve miles north of Florence (503-547-3415). Elevator takes visitors down to a large cave.

CAPE PERPETUA. Located near Yachats alongside U.S. 101. Ocean views, visitor center, beaches, and saltwater fishing.

MARK O. HATFIELD MARINE SCIENCE CENTER. Marine Science Drive, Newport (503-867-3011). Museum displays. Aquaria exhibits.

YAQUINA BAY LIGHTHOUSE. Yaquina Bay State Park, Newport. Excellent ocean views and bird watching opportunities.

OREGON UNDERSEA GARDENS. 267 Southwest Bay Boulevard, Newport (503-265-7541). Underwater exhibits of sea life.

THREE CAPES SCENIC LOOP. Skirts U.S. 101 between Cloverdale and Tillamook. Excellent for auto-touring and bicycling.

PIONEER MUSEUM. Junction of U.S. 101 and State Route 6 in Tillamook (503-842-4553). More than twelve thousand displays. Lifelike exhibits.

CAPE MEARES LIGHTHOUSE. Cape Meares State Park west of Tillamook. Free tours during the summer.

TILLAMOOK CHEESE FACTORY. Located on U.S. 101 just north of town. Tours.

ECOLA STATE PARK. Located just north of Cannon Beach. Hiking, picnicking, and excellent ocean views.

CLATSOP COUNTY HISTORICAL MUSEUM. 8th and Exchange, Astoria (503-325-2563). An excellent example of Victorian architecture, which includes a collection of period exhibits.

COLUMBIA RIVER MARITIME MUSEUM. 1792 Marine Drive, foot of 17th Street, Astoria (503-325-2323). Nautical artifacts, ship models, and fishing tools.

RESTAURANTS OF NOTE

The following restaurants are listed by location, beginning on the south coast.

MAMA'S AUTHENTIC ITALIAN. 703 Chetco Avenue, Brookings (503-469-7611). Excellent pasta, savory sauces, great pizza, and Mama, a gentle Philadelphian who will win your heart.

NOR'WESTER SEAFOOD. Port of Gold Beach (503-247-2333). Good selection of seafood. Views of the port.

THE TRUCULENT OYSTER. 236 Sixth Street, U.S. 101, Port Orford (503-332-9461). Locals brag that this is the best seafood in the area.

ANDREA'S OLD TOWN CAFE. 160 Baltimore, Old Town, Bandon (503-347-3022). Menu changes daily. Intimate setting. Food is homemade and fresh and tastes like it.

BANDON BOATWORKS. South Jetty Road, Bandon (503-347-2111). Great ocean views. Service superb. Fresh fish. Excellent rack of lamb.

HURRY BACK. U.S. 101 and Commercial, Coos Bay (503-267-3933). Fresh seafood. Café ambience.

SEAFOOD GROTTO. 8th and Broadway, Winchester Bay (503-271-4250). Seafood. Popular with the locals.

FOREST HILLS RESTAURANT & LOUNGE. 1 Country Club Drive, Reedsport (503-271-3414). Steaks and seafood. Overlooks golf course.

CANYON WAY RESTAURANT & BOOKSTORE. 1216 Southwest Canyon Way, Newport (503-265-8319). Excellent quiches, fresh seafood, homemade pasta.

SALISHAN GOURMET DINING ROOM. Salishan Lodge, Gleneden Beach (503-764-2371). Elegant dining. Magnificent wine list. Food receives rave reviews. Coat and tie recommended. Pricey.

BAY HOUSE. 5911 Southwest Highway 101, Lincoln City (503-996-3222). Fresh seafood. Excellent desserts.

DAGGATT'S AT TOLOVANA. 3400 South Hemlock, Tolovana Park, Cannon Beach (503-436-1111). Good views of ocean and Haystack Rock. Fresh seafood, steaks, and chicken.

THE CRAB BROILER. U.S. 101 and U.S. 26, Seaside (503-738-5313). The name says it all—crab is the specialty of the house.

DOOGER'S SEAFOOD & GRILL. 505 Broadway, Seaside (503-738-3773). Fresh seafood. Good clam chowder.

THE SHIP INN. 1 Second Street, Astoria (503-325-0033). Fresh seafood. Some English foods. Views of the Columbia River.

WHERE TO STAY

SEA DREAMER INN

Like so many of us, Judy and Robert Blair have an ongoing love affair with the Oregon Coast. The romance began with vacations to Brookings and culminated in 1985 when they left their Nevada home to purchase a 1912 redwood Colonial home here. Almost immediately, they began preparing it for bed-and-breakfast travelers.

"We had no idea what we were getting into," Judy says. "Neither of us had ever stayed in a bed and breakfast. But so far it's been fun, and we've met lots of interesting people."

Sea Dreamer, named after the Blair's thirty-foot Bahama Islander, sits on a tree-lined knoll above U.S. 101. Its blue two-story frame looks across lily fields to the rocks of McVay Park and the ocean beyond.

Guests entering the house discover a comfortable and attractive living room. Sunlight streams through an ocean-view bay window, across overstuffed chairs and antiques, to a stone fireplace wearing a wood-burning stove insert. During holidays, the room boasts decorations celebrating the season.

A formal dining room, where hearty homemade breakfasts are served, is nearby. Breakfast features such items as seasonal fruit, breakfast meats, special egg dishes, home-baked breads or muffins, and local preserves.

Developing first-class accommodations takes time and money. And while Sea Dreamer's guest rooms are comfortable and showing signs of polish, on my visit they were not yet the equal of the common rooms. But the house is loaded with potential, and improvement plans are brewing. Bob and Judy specifically mentioned that high on their list are the replacement of some worn shag carpets and a few tired chairs.

In the meantime, the four guest rooms have hidden characters, which

Sea Dreamer Inn (Lewis Green)

are slowly being revealed. In addition, all the beds boast lamb's wool mattress covers, and each room has individually controlled heat.

Located just south of Brookings, Sea Dreamer Inn makes a comfortable getaway for those exploring the south coast. I expect it will soon qualify as an elegant one as well.

*   *   *

Sea Dreamer Inn, 15167 McVay Lane, P.O. Box 1840, Brookings, OR 97415 (503-469-6629). Four guest rooms, two with private baths. Rates range from $50 to $60 (subject to change). VISA/MasterCard. No children; no pets; no smoking. McVay Lane loops the highway just north of the Winchuck River, three miles from the California border.

ENDICOTT GARDENS

As I drove up the gravel driveway onto a wooded lot, Endicott Gardens came into view. At first, I thought I had made a wrong turn: surely this nondescript ranch-style house was not the bed-and-breakfast inn I had heard so much about. Then I realized it had to be, and that really caused me a problem. You see, I was allowing a "snob factor" to influence my judgment. How could this plain contemporary home, which actually appeared somewhat cluttered, be a first-class bed and breakfast? The answer was quickly forthcoming.

Responding to my knock on the door, Mary Endicott—the most gregarious, warm person imaginable—welcomed me into her living room. Knitting sat about fat chairs, and the newspaper sprawled across the floor. But the fireplace glowed, and Mary's smile soon had me melting.

"I used to try to keep this place looking special," Mary says. "But we live here, you know."

And that is the key to this home's success: Mary and Stewart Endicott live here. You are visiting their home; they are welcoming you as their guests. Endicott Gardens represents bed-and-breakfast tradition.

The four guest rooms are in the wing of the house, off a short hallway. Each is painted plain white, furnished simply and boasts nothing more than comfort. When Mary and Stewart started in this business, that's all bed and breakfast ever promised.

When the Endicotts built the house in 1974, the plans included turning the building into a lodge. That never happened. Then in 1979, a struggling reservation service in need of guest homes encouraged Mary to try bed and breakfast. She did. Soon the agent was out of business, but Endicott Gardens was flourishing. It has been a success ever since.

One of the real joys here, besides the Endicotts and a large home-cooked breakfast, is the backyard. Flower gardens dot the manicured

Endicott Gardens (Lewis Green)

lawns, fruit trees create delicious fragrances, and nearby rolling hills form a verdant horizon.

Discovering the joys of Endicott Gardens took some courage on my part. Yet for travelers who do not need gilding, this may just be the best bed-and-breakfast experience they will ever have.

*   *   *

Endicott Gardens, 95768 Jerry's Flat Road, Gold Beach, OR 97444 (503-247-6513). Four guest rooms, all with private baths. Rates range from $45 to $55 (subject to change). No credit cards. Children with prior approval; arrangements can be made for pets; smoking permitted. From U.S. 101, just north of downtown Gold Beach, take Jerry's Flat Road 3.8 miles to a hidden, gravel driveway on the right.

CLIFF HARBOR GUEST HOUSE

Bill and Doris Duncan's two-story cedar-framed home perches on a wind-swept grassy bluff, which overlooks the ocean. Seabirds float around granite monoliths, while sea lions scamper around the base of rocks.

This scenic spot is perfect for a vacation retreat, which is exactly what the Duncans had in mind when they built the house in 1977. At the time, they were still living in Eugene and the house was being used sparingly. But in the early 1980s, a nearby motel, which was experiencing overflow, asked the Duncans if they would be interested in renting one of their rooms. They agreed to let the motel book what is now The Cliffside Studio. It was so successful that by 1984 they had added The Harbor Suite, published a brochure, and become a full-fledged bed and breakfast.

When I asked the Duncans what motivates them to share this lovely spot, Bill quickly answered, "We've just had marvelous guests. We're really having a wonderful time doing this."

Although there are only two accommodations, Cliff Harbor is not typical of a "Mom-and-Pop" operation.

The downstairs Harbor Suite makes up much of the rear of the house. A private entrance off a sweeping deck, which is sheltered by dunes, enters a spacious suite. It is enclosed on three sides by walls of windows and includes a queen bed, color television, window seats, high canted ceiling, and a private bathroom.

For views, The Cliffside Studio earns higher marks. Located in an upstairs alcove adjacent to the main living area, this suite is wrapped by windows that look out to sea and north across the Coquille River to the Bandon lighthouse. There are two double beds, a color television, a metal fireplace, a private entrance and bathroom, and a completely stocked kitchen that has everything except home-cooked food.

Cliff Harbor Guest House (Courtesy Cliff Harbor Guest House)

Both accommodations receive breakfast. However, if guests of Cliffside wish a full morning meal, like the one prepared for The Harbor Suite, there is a $10 surcharge. Otherwise, a continental breakfast is delivered to Cliffside.

Cliff Harbor Guest House sits on the sea and offers travelers a rare opportunity to enjoy a vacation home without dealing with a mortgage. Beyond that, it offers the size of a small private home with the privacy of a larger inn.

*   *   *

Cliff Harbor Guest House, Beach Loop Road, P.O. Box 769, Bandon, OR 97411 (503-347-3956 or 344-4132). Two guest rooms, both with private baths. Rates range from $59 to $65 (subject to change). No credit cards. Children with prior approval; no pets; smoking in Cliffside only. Located on Beach Loop Road, just southwest of Old Town.

SPINDRIFT

It is as peaceful as a newborn baby cuddling in thick virgin wool. A fire crackles on the brick hearth; the smell of just-brewed coffee wafts from the kitchen. Don Smith, who would look right at home on a Maine fishing dock, rocks casually in an overstuffed swivel chair.

His horizon is the world. It sweeps in from distant lands, swirling

Spindrift (Charlie Kloppenburg)

about Face Rock and the Oregon Stacks. Then, as if surrendering its untamed energy in a gesture of friendship, the Pacific deposits its rolling froth upon the sand.

This is Spindrift. Don and Robbie Smith's home since 1976 and a bed and breakfast since 1980. It is cozy and homey—more traditional than innlike. It was meant to be. The Smiths were looking for a seaside retreat, not a lodge.

"I wanted to recapture my past in Maine," Don says. "I wanted to live on the coast but didn't want to deal with cold weather."

At Spindrift vacationers can sit on the deck of this cedar-frame beach house, which perches atop a fifty-foot bluff, and let summer sea breezes wash over them, or they can visit in the winter and be awed by the Pacific as it hurls itself against Spindrift's wall of windows.

Guests of the Smiths can expect to be pampered. Besides being personally indulged by the hosts, overnighters will find their room garnished with a down quilt, digital clock radio, fresh flowers, a jar of candy, bathrobes, extra blankets, tide tables, visitors guide, post cards, and stationery.

While both rooms are comfortable, Seaview must be the accommodation of first choice. Tall picture windows offer ocean views, while a brick fireplace keeps the room warm.

*　　　*　　　*

Spindrift, 2990 Beach Loop Road, Bandon, OR 97411 (503-347-2275). Two guest rooms—Seaview has a private bath, Surfsound shares a bath with the Smiths. Rates range from $45 to $59 (subject to change). VISA/MasterCard. Children with prior approval; no pets; no smoking. A full and large breakfast is served. About one mile south of 11th Street, turn west on Seabird Drive to a right on Beach Loop Road.

GUEST HOUSE AT GARDINER BY THE SEA

Gardiner is and always has been a mill town. It is one of those nondescript, working-class highway communities that travelers enter, then blink and forget.

But Gardiner is different. First, it sits at the southern end of Dune Country. Second, it boasts a secret treasure, an undiscovered bed and breakfast that is both charming and warm.

Sitting on the hillside that rises above the mill and the highway, the century-old Guest House features no views, lakes, or beaches on its front step. But owner and world traveler Kathleen Dunaway has created a bed and breakfast that does not need any of those things to favor guests.

In fact, there are extras here rarely found in guest houses, which will help guests forget they cannot see the ocean. To begin with, children are welcome, which is in itself unusual. But beyond just accepting young ones, Kathleen provides a small nursery, complete with crib and a twin bed. In addition, she offers a main-floor exercise room, which includes a Jacuzzi.

Although the house is a little dark inside, attributable to all the cedar paneling and dark furnishings, it feels warm. The living room's bay window and large brick fireplace, and the dining room setting of china, crystal, and linen help establish hospitality.

Both upstairs guest rooms also reflect cordiality. A rose floral

Guest House at Gardiner by the Sea (Lewis Green)

comforter and matching drapes add fresh touches to the Rose Room, while a great bay window and pale blue walls make the Blue Room a cozy abode. Both rooms are furnished with antiques and boast baskets of fruit and fresh flowers.

*   *   *

Guest House at Gardiner by the Sea, 401 Front Street, Gardiner, OR 97441 (503-271-4005). Two guest rooms, Blue Room has a private bath. Rates range from $35 to $55 (subject to change). No credit cards. Children with prior approval; no pets; no smoking. Breakfast is rich and hearty. Front Street runs two blocks east of U.S. 101, parallel to the highway.

OCEAN HOUSE

Surrounded by firs and pines and embraced by lawns and gardens, this large country home sits on a bluff that overlooks Agate Beach. A private path winds through the gardens and down the hillside to the sands and tide pools below. The setting offers an environment ideal for people who love the ocean, while also indulging those who like a taste of the beach but do not want sand and sun with every course of their meal.

Innkeepers Bette and Bob Garrard moved to their Newport home in 1965 to enjoy Oregon's coast and to raise a family.

"We love the coast," Bette says, "and it's such a good place to bring up children."

But children grow up, leaving parents lonesome and houses mostly empty. When the Garrard's children left, Bette and Bob decided to fill their rooms with bed-and-breakfast guests. Since 1984, they have been doing just that.

The overnight accommodations include three upstairs bedrooms, named for the Garrard's daughters, plus one downstairs. Although all of the rooms are comfortable, Michele's Room is definitely the star. It features a queen-size bed dressed with a down comforter and garnished with lots of frills. Wicker furniture, off-white walls, and windows that open to the sea create a bright and cheery scene. There is also a private deck.

Downstairs, a large living room looks out to the Pacific. Leather sofas and chairs, a beam ceiling, and a brick fireplace make the room comfortable.

Unlike most of Oregon's bed and breakfasts in setting but similar to them in atmosphere, Ocean House is more traditional than professional. That and location make up much of the home's charm.

*   *   *

Ocean House, 4920 NW Woody Way, Newport, OR 97365 (503-265-6158 or

Ocean House (Lewis Green)

265-7779). Four guest rooms, two with private baths. Rates range from $40 to $70 (subject to change). VISA/MasterCard. No children under twelve; no pets; no smoking. Breakfast is full and hearty. As you enter the Agate Beach area on U.S. 101, look for the country lane on the ocean side that hides just north of the Jack Pot store.

THREE CAPES

Oceanside stretches between the waves and the hills. It is well beyond the sights and sounds of passing motorists traveling north and south on U.S. 101. Few travelers ever discover the town's charms; few experience the untouched beauty of its beach.

The hamlet's narrow, winding lanes; its one- and two-story frame beach houses; the tiny grocery store and friendly tavern; the wide, empty beach and the birds of Three Arch Rocks; and the cliffs that rise nearly straight out of the ocean make up Oceanside's environment.

Three Capes is a contemporary home that sits on a steep hillside overlooking the town, the beach, and the rocks. Both accommodations are downstairs, with their own private entrances. Except for breakfast, guests will have little contact with their hosts, Ross and Kathy Holloway.

These young people moved to Oceanside in the early 1980s. They purchased the home in 1984 and immediately began the task of re-

Three Capes (Lewis Green)

modeling. (As of this writing, work is still going on.) The first bed-and-breakfast guests arrived in May 1985.

The Holloways are friendly and full of life. But they foster a deep respect for their guests' privacy and understand that people do not visit Oceanside to party. Most come here for the solitude.

While the house seems modest from the outside, the accommodations are warm and homey. They feature plush carpets and delicate wallpapers, good beds, lots of reading materials, green plants, and ocean views. In addition, there are clocks, comforters on the beds, and baskets of toiletries in the bathrooms.

Oceanside's environment demands a bed and breakfast with soft and subtle qualities. Anything more would intrude upon the sounds of nature. Three Capes does little to interrupt the mood; instead it complements the setting.

*   *   *

Three Capes, 1685 Maxwell Mountain Road, Oceanside, OR 97134 (503-842-6126). Two guest rooms, both with private baths. Rates are $50 (subject to change). No credit cards. Children and pets with prior approval; no smoking. During the week a continental breakfast is offered, while a full family style meal is served on weekends. From Tillamook take Third Street west. Follow the signs to Netarts and Oceanside. In Oceanside, turn right at the stop sign, then left up Maxwell Mountain Road.

THE BOARDING HOUSE

The Boarding House is the best bed-and-breakfast inn on the Oregon Coast. In fact, if it were almost anyplace else other than its present location—perhaps somewhere along the beach or at least away from its neighboring lumber company—it would be a perfect ten.

Originally built in 1898 as a private residence, this two-story stick-style Victorian has withstood the test of time. It survived the great fire of 1912, stood up under the burden of being a World War II boardinghouse, and smiled through several renovations that actually doubled its size.

Today, owners Dick and Carol Rees have the house looking better than ever.

"When we first bought the house in 1983," Dick says, "we thought we would slowly refurbish it. Then we decided to do it right from the start."

Doing it right meant stripping back the interior to its roots. The Rees refurbished and redecorated. They put in new plumbing, wiring, and heating. The result is a masterpiece.

Guests step from the wrap-around porch into a living room bathed in natural light, which even overcomes the fir tongue-and-groove wainscoting, dark trim, and wood floor. There is usually a fire crackling in the brick fireplace, which stands before Victorian and Eastlake furnishings. The country atmosphere extends to the adjacent dining room.

Each of the six guest rooms boasts an individual style, but brass and white iron beds, antique appointments, and down quilts dominate. Modern comforts include private, though sometimes small, bathrooms, as well as color televisions, thick towels, and clocks.

Breakfast features seven different menus. Entrées range from French toast sandwiches made with Philadelphia cream cheese and walnuts to

The Boarding House (Lewis Green)

special egg casseroles.

Still, innkeepers make a bed and breakfast glitter, and the Rees'
friendliness is infectious. This combination of personal caring and
character of style embraces this old house and creates a bed and breakfast
that is easy to recommend.

*   *   *

The Boarding House, 208 North Holladay Drive, Seaside, OR 97138 (503-
738-9055). Six guest rooms, all with private baths. Rates range from $35 to
$55 (subject to change). VISA/MasterCard. Children with prior approval;
no pets; no smoking. Small meetings and weddings welcome. Holladay
parallels the highway and runs through Seaside's downtown. The inn sits
on the north side of town.

ROSEBRIAR INN

Rosebriar Inn boasts a colorful past—so dramatic, in fact, that now
that stability has reentered this old house's life, you can almost hear sighs
of relief whispering down its winding stairway.

Built in 1902 by Frank Patton, a prominent local banker, the home
wore a residential face for nearly half a century. But then it began taking

Rosebriar Inn (Kay Green)

on the airs of Lon Chaney. For the next thirty years, it went through change after change.

First, after the Archdiocese of Portland purchased it, this white clapboard structure grew to nearly double its original size. For nearly two decades, fourteen nuns roamed these spaces, which they called Holy Name Convent. Then it became a home for girls before being completely abandoned in the late 1970s. By the time Ann Leenstra and Judith Papendick came to the rescue, the structure was suffering from institutional drabness and neglect and seemed ready for a quiet and somber burial.

Instead, armed with will and a vision, Ann and Judy marched past the columns of this neoclassical Greek building and through the entranceway to do battle with decay. They stripped floors and scraped walls, then refinished the oak hardwoods and hung rolls of wallpaper. Next they furnished with antiques and reproductions, adorned with Oriental rugs, and garnished with green plants. Their hard work and good taste produced a quality bed-and-breakfast inn.

Rosebriar's nine guest rooms make it one of Oregon's largest bed and breakfasts. The rooms must be described as charming rather than elegant. They are simply and sparingly furnished. However, large windows, floral-print wallpapers, and rich wood trim add character and style.

On the other hand, the living and dining rooms are luxurious. Brass chandeliers, antique lace curtains, vintage rugs, and antique appointments conjure up a time of wealth.

Overall, the home is a perfect getaway for historic Astoria. It offers visitors an opportunity to share directly in this town's past.

*   *   *

Rosebriar Inn, 636 Fourteenth Street, Astoria, OR 97103 (503-325-7427). Nine guest rooms, two with private baths. All rooms without private baths have sinks. Rates range from $36 to $48 (subject to change). VISA/ MasterCard. Children and pets with prior approval; no smoking. There is a conference room available for small gatherings. Private off-street parking available. From downtown, drive up 12th Street, then turn left on Franklin to Fourteenth Street.

Oregon's Heartland

*I*nterstate 5 draws a long black line through the heart of Oregon, bridging the world of Shakespeare with the City of Roses. As it runs its course between two mountain ranges, the highway carries travelers from Ashland's "Land of Will," through the rugged Rogue River Valley, across the fertile Willamette Valley, to the state's largest city. To the east, the Cascade Mountains rise, offering up their gifts of outdoor adventures. To the west, Oregon's wine country flourishes. In between, the towns and cities of Oregon reflect a quiet existence.

GETTING TO KNOW
OREGON'S HEARTLAND

ASHLAND

In 1935, a school teacher with a vision and a reluctant group of city fathers willing to risk four hundred dollars delivered Ashland from obscurity into the bright lights of fame. With that money and some half-hearted support, Angus Bowmer produced the very first festival of Shakespeare. A half-century later, the Oregon Shakespearean Festival lures some two hundred and fifty thousand people annually to the streets of Ashland and, in addition, attracts international attention.

The festival, which runs from February to October and features not only the plays of Shakespeare but also the works of playwrights such as Williams and Albee, represents Ashland's main attraction. Infusing the town with creative blood, an entire arts community and hospitality industry has grown up around the theater.

Within this town of fifteen thousand, there are several excellent galleries and museums, including the Hanson Howard Galleries and the Shakespeare Art Museum. As for amenities, while shopping is limited to a few small but unique shops, lodging and dining opportunities are exceptional.

There can be little argument that the flags fluttering atop the Elizabethan Stagehouse mark Ashland's headliner. But there is no actor whose looks can equal, nor are there any words written by mortals that can describe, the quiet beauty of Lithia Park. Its one hundred acres invite moments of reflection and hours of pleasure. There are white swans floating in tiny ponds, sloping lawns, and a band shell that hosts a variety of entertainment. In addition, there are trails that walk among stately trees and wooded commons made for picnicking.

JACKSONVILLE

In 1852, following the discovery of placer gold in nearby creeks, Jacksonville became the Oregon Territory's first boomtown. But it soon fell on hard times: gold was quickly mined out, small pox struck, flood and fire swept over the town, and as a final insult, the railroad passed this struggling community by.

But Jacksonville survived. Today, its past can be recaptured with a visit to the County Museum, located in the old Jackson County Courthouse. Next door, a children's museum, which is housed in an old jail, features hands-on exhibits.

In all, there are more than seventy-five historic buildings, most built before 1900, that dot Jacksonville's streets. The most interesting is the 1880 U.S. Hotel, whose first guests were President Rutherford B. Hayes and friends.

In addition to its historical significance, Jacksonville boasts a contemporary event well worth attending—the Britt Festivals. From June through August, five festivals—classical, musical theater, dance, bluegrass, and jazz—perform to enthusiastic crowds. The shows are held under the stars on an outdoor stage.

GRANTS PASS

Grants Pass grew up around the railroad and today continues to reflect a working-class demeanor. It is a town slashed by U.S. 199 and trimmed by Interstate 5. The town's merchants have responded to the invasion of motorized vehicles by creating a highway jungle of gas stations, fast-food outlets, and honky-tonk.

Nevertheless, Grants Pass's location at the midpoint of the wild Rogue River, fifty miles from the Oregon Caves and less than ninety miles from Crater Lake, makes it a convenient base for tourists. If you are planning to explore the Rogue River, this is the place to put your trip together. Grants Pass headquarters more than twenty-five outfitters eager to take you rafting or fishing. (Call 800-547-5927, outside Oregon, or 503-476-7717, inside Oregon, for a brochure.)

While in this area, there are several scenic drives that are musts. The Redwood Highway, U.S. 199, winds up and around the Kalmiopsis Wilderness Area, past the exit to Oregon Caves, to the Jedediah Smith Redwoods State Park seventy-five miles from Grants Pass. Heading northwest from Grants Pass, the Merlin-Galice Road offers spectacular views of Hellgate Canyon and the Rogue River.

EUGENE

Eugene is a university town replete with cultural attractions, sports events, greenbelts, and shopping. Its major cultural facility is the Hult Center for the Performing Arts, which hosts the Oregon Bach Festival during June and July. Running, especially along the Prefontaine Trail, tops the sports' line. For views and picnicking, two parks—Skinner Butte to the north and Spencer Butte to the south—represent the best choices. Shoppers should visit the Fifth Street Public Market, where Eugene's craftspeople share the three-story stage with fresh fish and produce vendors.

The countryside east of Eugene demands exploration. State Routes 126 and 58 lead to the rivers, lakes, forests, and mountains of the Cascades. Besides hiking, fishing, canoeing, and natural sights, there are nine covered bridges that can be reached from these roads. (The Eugene Springfield Convention & Visitors Bureau can provide maps. 800-452-3670, inside Oregon, or 800-547-5445, outside Oregon.)

WINE COUNTRY

In recent years, Oregon's wines, particularly its Pinot Noir, have been cheered for their fine quality. Although more than fifty wineries dot the state, their greatest concentration flourishes along the gently rolling slopes that border 99W between Amity and Newberg and extending north to U.S. 26. For a brochure with maps and information about tours, write or call: Oregon Winegrowers Association, P.O. Box 6590, Portland, OR 97228-6590 (503-224-8167).

THE COLUMBIA GORGE AND THE DALLES

The eighty-five-mile-long Columbia River Gorge slices a magnificent gap through the Cascade Mountains. Before the construction of dams and navigational locks, the river plunged and boiled toward the Pacific, often sending barges and steamers to toothpick heaven.

Today, however, the Gorge invites quiet reflection and recreation. Steep bluffs and overlooks, such as 720-foot Crown Point, offer views of the deep canyon. Outdoors activists can choose from miles of hiking trails that crisscross the mountainsides, or they can trade in their boots for bicycles for rides along the old Columbia River Scenic Highway. In the Gorge's grasp, the tamed river teems with anglers after walleyed pike and sailboarders seeking the wind.

There are two ways for auto-tourists to explore the Gorge. One is quick—Interstate 84—the other spectacular—the Columbia River Scenic Highway. The first leg of the old highway (the Scenic Highway) can be picked up fifteen miles east of Portland at Troutdale via Exit 16; it rejoins Interstate 84 two miles east of Horsetail Falls. The second leg begins about six miles east of Hood River in Mosier at Exit 69; it ends at The Dalles. This road is narrow, winding, and dotted with sightseers scanning the cliffs for waterfalls, so be alert.

The Dalles is a historic city. In the 1840s it marked the end of the Oregon Trail. After gold was discovered in 1860, the town prospered as an outfitting center for prospectors. Today, it is an agricultural center ringed by hillside cherry orchards and wheat fields.

Just as there are two routes to discover the Gorge, there are two ways to explore The Dalles. With a walking tour map supplied by the chamber (503-296-2231), you can discover a number of historic buildings. The chamber can also provide self-guided driving tour maps. These drives explore The Dalles and beyond, putting travelers in touch with much of this countryside. For especially good scenic views, particularly of Mount Hood, be sure to take Skyline Road out of The Dalles to a lofty viewpoint.

A Practical Guide to Oregon's Heartland

The Climate

Mostly you can expect year-round mild temperatures, with cloudy days and wet weather in the winter. Summer days in and around Ashland and Grants Pass can be quite warm, while winter days are often milder and drier than farther north. Summertime temperatures in the Gorge and The Dalles will average in the 80s and 90s. Some snow can be expected in winter.

Your Clothes

Casual clothes are appropriate most of the time. Attire for the Shakespearean Festival depends upon whether you are attending the outdoor stage or one of the indoor theaters. In all cases, however, comfort rules. For the Britt Festivals, be sure to carry a blanket and a light jacket.

No matter where you go in western Oregon, always have good walking shoes, wet weather gear, and a sweater or light jacket. Frankly, in Oregon I seldom find need for anything more than a respectable pair of jeans or cotton trousers, cotton shirts, wool sweaters, my favorite tweed jacket, occasionally a tie, and a sturdy but honorable pair of all-purpose shoes. My wife, sans the tie and the jacket, dresses similarly, although a skirt or a dress always travels in her wardrobe.

VISITOR INFORMATION

For more information, write or call: Oregon Tourism Division, 595 Cottage Street Northeast, Salem, OR 97310 (800-547-7842, outside Oregon, 800-233-3306, inside Oregon).

POINTS OF INTEREST

OREGON SHAKESPEAREAN FESTIVAL. P.O. Box 158, Ashland (503-482-2111). Three theaters celebrate Shakespeare and an array of other great playwrights from February to October. Special events also scheduled.

SHAKESPEARE EXHIBIT CENTER. Main and South Pioneer streets, Ashland (503-482-2111). An exhibit of props, costumes, and photographs.

SHAKESPEARE ART MUSEUM. 460 B Street, Ashland (503-488-0332). Paintings and drawings based on Shakespearean themes.

HANSON HOWARD GALLERIES. 505 Siskiyou Boulevard, Ashland (503-488-2562). An excellent range of works in a comfortable setting.

LITHIA PARK. Begins behind the Elizabethan Stage, Ashland. Duck ponds, trails, lawns, tennis courts, and band shell events.

BRITT FESTIVALS. P.O. Box 1124, Medford (503-773-6077). A series of festivals performed on an outdoor stage in Jacksonville. Features classical, musical theater, dance, bluegrass, and jazz.

CRATER LAKE. Oregon's only national park, located seventy-four miles from Medford via State Route 62. For information call 503-594-2211. It is the single, most spectacular vision in the Northwest. The deep blue waters cradled by steep cliffs seem to reflect life itself. The lake is six miles long, four and a half miles wide and 1,932 feet deep. The cliffs making up the crater rise 500 to 2,000 feet above the water. You can tour the caldera from above by car along Rim Drive. If you wish guided tours, rangers and bus tours leave regularly from Crater Lake Lodge. Or you can get a closeup look aboard one of the boat trips that launch from Cleetwood Cove.

OREGON CAVES. Located at the end of State Route 46, twenty miles southeast of Cave Junction. Guided tours.

OREGON BACH FESTIVAL. University of Oregon School of Music, Eugene (503-686-5667). A celebration of Bach performed in June and July.

MCKENZIE RIVER VALLEY. Take State Route 126 east from Springfield. Hiking, fishing, rafting, swimming, and skiing. For a gorgeous scenic drive, take State Route 242 to Sisters (road open only in summer).

MOUNT HOOD. Located about an hour's drive east of Portland via U.S. 26. Scenic views, hiking, climbing, year-round downhill skiing.

STERNWHEELER *COLUMBIA GORGE*. From June through September, the sternwheeler moors at Cascade Locks, 45 minutes east of Portland on Interstate 84 (503-374-8427 or 503-223-3928). Daily trips up the Columbia River.

CROWN POINT. Located east of Corbett off the old Scenic Highway. Commanding views of the Gorge.

LARCH MOUNTAIN. Take Larch Mountain Road from the old Scenic Highway just east of Corbett. There are breathtaking views of the Cascades at the top.

MULTNOMAH FALLS. Located between Bridal Veil and Ainsworth Park. The second highest waterfall in the United States at 620 feet.

BONNEVILLE DAM. Off Interstate 84. Displays.

HOOD RIVER BOAT BASIN. Excellent sailboarding.

FORT DALLES MUSEUM. Garrison and 15th, The Dalles. Historic memorabilia and an excellent collection of horse-drawn vehicles.

RESTAURANTS OF NOTE

The following restaurants are listed by location, beginning in Ashland.

CHANGE OF HEART. 139 East Main, Ashland (503-488-0235). Only fresh ingredients go into the French and American dishes served here. Menu changes weekly. Elegant and cozy setting.

CHATA. 1212 South Pacific Highway, just north of Ashland in Talent (503-535-2575). Delicious Eastern European cuisine, mostly Polish. Home-baked breads and desserts. Folksy atmosphere.

CHATEAULIN. 50 East Main, Ashland (503-482-2264). Caters to the theater crowd, so can be busy before the curtain rises. Small and intimate French dining. Seasonal foods prepared superbly. Professional service.

GEPPETTO'S. 345 East Main, Ashland (503-482-1138). This is one of my personal favorites. The pasta is good, sauces savory, conversations lively, and prices reasonable. Locals start lining up for dinner at this cozy café by 6 P.M.

WINCHESTER INN. 35 South Second, Ashland (503-488-1115). A restored Victorian home. Soups and salads delicious. Entrées usually good. A "fine dining" environment.

JACKSONVILLE INN. 175 East California Street, Jacksonville (503-899-1900).

Located in the lower level of this historic building in a setting of sandstone walls and old photographs. Seven-course meals or à la carte. Good continental food. Good wine list. Magnificent desserts.

MATSUKASE. 1675 Northeast Seventh Street, Grants Pass (503-479-2961). In a town not famous for gourmet food, this simple Japanese restaurant, which creates excellent food, is a real find.

PARADISE RANCH INN. 7000 Monument Drive, Merlin (503-479-4333). Seasonal regional cuisine served in elegant surroundings.

CAFE ZENON. 898 Pearl Street, Eugene (503-343-3005). Fresh fish. Good soups. Great desserts. The chef relates well to herbs and spices.

THE EXCELSIOR CAFE. 754 East 13th Street, Eugene (503-342-6963). Located in a Victorian house. Good American food using local ingredients. Menu changes frequently.

POPPI'S. 675 East 13th Street, Eugene (503-343-0846). Simple, somewhat funky decor. Excellent Greek peasant food, especially the kalamarakia and the moussaka.

LA MAISON SURRETTE. 729 East Third, McMinnville (503-472-6666). Open weekends only. Located in a century-old Victorian home. Elegant dining. Fresh local ingredients. Continental cuisine.

NICK'S ITALIAN CAFE. 521 East Third, McMinnville (503-434-4471). An authentic and noisy northern Italian trattoria. Reservations needed well in advance. Excellent food.

COLUMBIA GORGE HOTEL. 4000 West Cliff Drive, Hood River (503-386-5566). The restaurant, located in a restored luxury hotel, has a commitment to excellence. Good views. Fresh local ingredients. Elegant dining.

WHERE TO STAY

CHANTICLEER INN

The Chanticleer Inn is the quintessential prototype for bed-and-breakfast inns. Everything here is as it should be: the guest rooms have charm but do not overwhelm, furnishings are both attractive and comfortable, breakfast is superb without being decadent, the library offers good reading and practical local information, and the innkeepers attend to guests' needs without smothering them with pampering.

Innkeepers Jim and Nancy Beaver came to Ashland in 1980. They had been living in San Francisco, where Jim worked for NBC News and Nancy labored as a personnel manager for United Vintners. Like so many of their peers, the Beavers sought to escape the corporate world, and bed and breakfast seemed the way to do it. They purchased this modest 1920

Chanticleer Inn (Kay Green)

California-style bungalow and, following extensive renovation, opened with six accommodations in July 1981. They added a guest suite in 1985.

Chanticleer may very well be the most popular bed and breakfast in the Northwest. I know of people who tried for two years to obtain a summer reservation here before finally meeting with success. Nothing could offer better testimony to Chanticleer's allure.

The gray clapboard house sits on a residential street, a few steep blocks from downtown. The dun-colored Cascade foothills form a distant backdrop to the manicured lawns and laurel hedge.

Chanticleer's essence, its elegant simplicity, greets guests as soon as they enter the living room. Sunlight filters through lace-curtained windows, while breezes enter through a narrow screen door. Next to a stone fireplace are bookshelves crammed with reading material. Stuffed furniture circles an oak coffee table.

The guest rooms occupy all three levels of the house. Their names are Aerie, Fleur, Maitre, Rosette, Pertelote, Jardin, and Chanticleer. Each is different but all are furnished with antique beds and boast touches such as scented soaps, fresh flowers, and green plants. The home's air conditioning can be a godsend on sunny summer days, but before retiring turn it off and open windows to the calm outside.

Chanticleer receives rave reviews. Mine can be added to a long list of others. Even other innkeepers praise the Beavers' efforts. There is no mystery to their success. Chanticleer is an inn, not a museum.

*   *   *

Chanticleer Inn, 120 Gresham Street, Ashland, OR 97520 (503-482-1919).

Seven guest rooms, all with private baths, Chanticleer is a two-bedroom suite with a private yard. Rates range from $69 to $99 (subject to change). No credit cards. Children with prior approval; no pets; no smoking in guest rooms. Although reservations are difficult to obtain in summer, they are available. In the off-season and during midweek, rooms are usually easily booked. Breakfast is full and served in a bright, sunny dining room. Off-street parking available. Turn west off Main Street (State Route 99) onto Gresham.

THE MINERS ADDITION

Miners lived hard lives. They traveled great distances, over difficult terrain, with little to look forward to but grueling work. Still, slivers of hope that one day the glitter of gold would fill their pans kept dreams alive. The Miners Addition is dedicated to those illusions and the men who held them.

An old metal ore car sits outside the two-story frame house, a pick and shovel are etched in the glass of the front door. Inside, both upstairs guest rooms bear the names of local mines—Sterling and Maltern—while

The Miners Addition (Julia Gross)

mining artifacts and old black-and-white photographs adorn the hallway.

While history garnishes The Miners Addition, the happy truth remains that this is a place to reflect on the past, not to experience it. There is nothing grueling about this bed and breakfast. Comfort and relaxation dominate the environment; owner Carolyn Morris makes sure of that.

In some ways, Carolyn relates to southern Oregon's miners. She, too, was looking for a dream when she left San Francisco office life in 1982. But her vision revolved around independence, not gold. She wanted to create a life-style for herself rather than have one created for her.

As a result, she has created a bed and breakfast that reflects her friendly and caring style. The Miners Addition encourages guests to be themselves but also asks visitors to allow themselves to be pampered just a bit. Carolyn likes to provide little extras.

In the evenings, she serves hors d'ouevres and a beverage before guests go out for dinner. Upon their return, cookies and tea are waiting. Carolyn also caters picnics. While her guests stroll through Lithia Park or the streets of Ashland, she packs them a picnic basket filled with cheese, fruit, homemade soup, and wine, which she then delivers to the park. Carolyn does ask that guests reserve this service twenty-four hours in advance.

While the extras are attractive, the accommodations are modest and comfortable. A country atmosphere pervades the setting with iron and brass beds, patchwork quilts, rocking chairs, floral-print wallpapers, and wood trim painted blue.

*   *   *

The Miners Addition, 737 Siskiyou Boulevard, Ashland, OR 97520 (503-482-0562). Two guest rooms, both with private baths. (Sterling's shower is in the hall.) Rates are $60 (subject to change). No credit cards. Children with prior approval; no pets; no smoking. Breakfast is full. Off-street parking available. The inn is located just south of downtown.

THE MORICAL HOUSE

The Morical House reflects a dignified elegance that demands close examination. The craftsmanship that went into this renovated country farmhouse produced an inn of quality. Owners Joe and Phyllis Morical purchased the three-story gabled house in 1982. Despite its sound structure, the building was suffering from years of gentle decline. The Moricals restored its health by stripping the structure down to its studs. Then they spent nine months creating a modern home within an old frame.

The Morical House opened its doors to guests in December 1982. With

The Morical House (Helga Motley)

the house wearing a fresh luster, the Moricals turned their attention on the grounds. By spring the lawns wore a manicured look, and the more than one hundred varieties of trees, shrubs, and flowers bloomed with life.

Today, Phyllis, an energetic lady filled with enthusiasm, runs the inn like an aunt who wants to make sure everything is just right. She prevents the home's refined air from overwhelming its country side.

The downstairs reflects both sides of the house's personality. Two common rooms open off of a large entranceway. The parlor, while containing an excellent library, seems more suited to looking than sitting. It has tall windows dressed with lace curtains and red valances. Adding to the Victorian feel, an antique Eastlake pump organ sits beneath a stained-glass window. On the other hand, the dining room, which opens through French doors to a sun porch, exudes a friendly down-home charm. The mountain views add to the feeling.

All five guest rooms occupy the upper levels. Number five tucks itself into the slopes and angles of the third floor. It boasts a strong feeling of privacy and offers good views of the hills and Mount Ashland. The 1870 cottage-painted furniture, a queen brass bed, and the raspberry color scheme distinguish the setting. On the second floor, numbers one and two also have views of the hills.

The house's location can be seen as both an advantage and a drawback. The grounds and country environment are tranquil. But its setting north of downtown takes it out of Ashland's mainstream. A five-minute drive, however, or a brisk fifteen-minute walk brings the theater and restaurants to the inn.

*   *   *

The Morical House, 668 North Main Street, Ashland, OR 97520 (503-482-2254). Five guest rooms, all with private baths. Rates are $65 (subject to change). VISA/MasterCard. Children with prior approval; no pets; smoking permitted. Breakfast is full. Off-street parking available. The inn is located north of downtown on Main Street (State Route 99).

ROMEO INN

If Norman Rockwell were to recreate suburbia on canvas, the portrait would look like the Romeo Inn. This home mirrors the American Dream as portrayed by the Merchants of Advertising. There is the corner lot, pruned and preened, and planted with tall pines. A rambling Cape Cod clapboard house with a view of the valley sits atop a knoll—truly a slice of Americana.

As we step inside the house, we find a decor best described as eclectic and comfortable. The living room sports peach walls, plush sofas, and a white brick fireplace. In the early evening hours, it becomes the setting for homemade cookies, hors d'oeuvres, and liquid refreshment.

Then we pass through French doors to the private patio. The

Romeo Inn (Harold K. Berninghausen)

swimming pool is deep blue, a swirl spa whirrs, guests relax on garden chairs, and barbecued hamburgers sizzle on the grill.

Back indoors, fresh flowers, perched atop two wooden tables, bathe in the sun washing through the dining room's bay window. In the morning, a large home-cooked breakfast fills the room with smells of bread and fresh-ground coffee.

Four guest rooms make up the accommodations. Downstairs, number one looks and feels like a suite. It boasts a large brick fireplace, both a king and a twin bed, a desk, two comfortable chairs, a canted ceiling, and views of the foothills. Number two is also comfortable but too dark. Upstairs numbers three and four feature hand-stitched quilts, antique furnishings, and floral-print wallpaper.

Although Romeo Inn seems the perfect appellation for a bed and breakfast in Shakespeare country, its name actually refers to the Romeos, previous owners who first opened the home to guests. Wisely, the current owners—Bruce and Margaret Halverson—retained the title.

*   *   *

Romeo Inn, 295 Idaho Street, Ashland, OR 97520 (503-488-0884). Four guest rooms, all with private baths. Rates range from $80 to $90 (subject to change). No credit cards. No children; no pets; no smoking. The location is in a quiet neighborhood, somewhat removed but still close to downtown. From Main Street, go west on Sherman, right on Iowa, left on Idaho, to the corner of Idaho and Holly.

McCully House Inn

This two-story, white clapboard Classical Revival home has been a Jacksonville landmark since 1861. Built as a mansion for one of the town's prominent citizens, it was one of Jacksonville's most expensive and palatial homes during its boomtown days. The house was so costly, in fact, that its owner, Dr. J. W. McCully, allegedly fled town to avoid creditors, leaving his wife Jane to take in boarders and open the town's first school.

Today, the restored mansion reflects the quality of its earlier life. Antiques, polished wood floors, vintage rugs, and lace curtains create a setting of luxury.

In the downstairs parlor, a square grand piano recalls the days when this room was reserved for special guests, such as the preacher. In the adjacent dining room, there are a Chippendale fireplace, Victorian frieze, and Battenburg lace curtains. Across the hall, the family sitting room is comfortable with overstuffed furniture and a wood stove insert.

Except for the downstairs suite, which was a back porch added in the 1960s, guest rooms recall the turn of the century. The Doll Suite tucks into an attic space, which once hosted the Jacksonville Doll Museum. Today, its narrow rooms, vaulted ceilings, and willow chairs seem quaint. The Girls' Room was once the McCully daughter's bedroom. An exposed

McCully House Inn (Mark T. Dennett)

brick chimney separates two double spool beds. The McCully Room, formerly the master bedroom, is the inn's most elegant accommodation. It has a free-standing claw-footed tub, a brick fireplace, and a Renaissance Revival bed.

Historical homes ooze charm, but there are always tradeoffs. Here, it is the bathrooms. While all four rooms feature private facilities, only Kathy's Suite and The McCully Room's tub offer freedom of space.

Still, that is a small sacrifice in return for a journey through time. And the perfect bed and breakfast is rare indeed.

*   *   *

McCully House Inn, P.O. Box 387, Jacksonville, OR 97530 (503-899-1942). Four guest rooms, all with private baths. Rates are $65 (subject to change). VISA/MasterCard. Children with prior approval. No pets; no smoking. Breakfast is full. McCully House Inn is located at California and Fifth streets, on the edge of downtown.

THE HANDMAIDENS' INN

Do not let the Grants Pass address fool you. This three-story cedar house is out in the country.

The Handmaidens' Inn (Jody Hammer)

Located some five miles from downtown in a subdivision at the base of the Siskiyou foothills, Handmaidens' Inn sits with its back to the woods. Its face looks across a yard dotted with scrub oak and past a narrow country lane. A small farm and the rolling hills sprawl beyond the road.

The home is so young, it still smells new. Built in 1983, it was purchased by current owners Bette and Jody Hammer one year later. Shortly thereafter, they opened their doors to bed and breakfast.

Most of their guests are highway travelers on their way to someplace else, and this home is ideal for that kind of visitor. The modern conveniences and amenities provide a boost to tired minds and bodies that need recharging.

Guests can lay back in the family room, which opens onto a large deck, and enjoy the brick fireplace, listen to the stereo, or watch the color television. If an evening of reading is preferred, the nearby sitting room offers a quiet, private corner of the house.

Although the contemporary look is never very far away, the Hammers have added touches of country to the three guest rooms. The coziest of the accommodations is The Peach Parlor, which is decorated in rosy apricot tones, with peach comforters on the twin beds. Abigail's Sitting Room is perfect for the traveling business person. It features a desk, digital clock radio, telephone, and color television, as well as a view of the hills. The most spacious room is Elizabeth's Suite. It has a private balcony and a large private bath with a skylight.

Recommending a bed and breakfast such as Handmaidens' entails some risks: it is not ideally located; it can be difficult to find; and the building is contemporary with no historical or architectural significance. Nevertheless, the accommodations are comfortable, the amenities good, and the hospitality is excellent.

*   *   *

The Handmaidens' Inn, 230 Red Spur Drive, Grants Pass, OR 97527 (503-476-2932). Three guest rooms, one with a private bath. Rates range from $45 to $65 (subject to change). No credit cards. No children; no pets; no smoking. From Interstate 5 south, take Exit 58; from Interstate 5 north, Exit 48. Drive to State Route 99 (Rogue River Highway), where southbounders should continue south and northbounders north. At Cloverlawn, go west and zigzag to the second Summit Loop sign. Turn left, then proceed to Red Spur Drive.

CAMPUS COTTAGE

Hyperbole awaits around every corner, eager to gobble up travel writers and spit them out into the hands of their critics. We learn to be

Campus Cottage (Courtesy Campus Cottage)

cautious; to avoid overplay. But sometimes a place or an innkeeper or a combination of the two impress so much that it is impossible to control the excitement. That is the way I feel about Campus Cottage.

Frankly, there is really nothing all that special about the house. It is cute and charming, all right, but not a candidate for the pages of "Architectural Digest."

On the other hand, the innkeepers are terrific. Owner Ursula Bates and her associate, Susie, are the kind of people who make guests feel good. They are intelligent, interesting, and fun. And as long as they are running Campus Cottage, it will remain one of Oregon's finest bed and breakfasts.

Ursula opened Campus Cottage in July of 1982, making it the first guest house in Eugene. At first her neighbors, none of whom knew what a bed and breakfast was, thought she was crazy. Then, as guests began arriving, Ursula's image returned to the sane end of the scale. Today, with all the attention she has received, Ursula is seen as a minor celebrity.

In recent years, however, Ursula has begun delivering her bed-and-breakfast philosophy to other parts of the country. These workshops have taken her away from Eugene. That is how Susie came into the picture. In some ways, she now runs the inn.

Susie is a college student, but not an 18-year-old bubble-gummer who drowns guests in sweet syrup. Like many of us, she discovered education several years after the shock of high school finally wore off. Susie has an engaging personality, is knowledgeable about the area, has a good sense of humor, and knows how to make a tasty breakfast.

Now, about the house. It is a 1922 blue, one-story bungalow with three guest rooms. It sits on a grassy lot across the street from fraternity row; despite that, the neighborhood is quiet.

Inside, the common areas boast hardwood floors and overstuffed furniture. All of the accommodations are comfortable. The Suite is sunny, with lots of windows, plants, and flowers; The Guestroom is a cozy blue abode; and The Cottage is spacious, with a private deck. The atmosphere throughout is country.

Above all else, Campus Cottage reflects friendliness. It is a people place. Ursula and Susie rise to the top and make this a special inn.

*   *   *

Campus Cottage, 1136 East 19th Avenue, Eugene, OR 97403 (503-342-5346). No credit cards. Three guest rooms, all with private baths. Rates range from $63 to $83 (subject to change). Children with prior approval; no pets; smoking permitted. From Franklin Boulevard in Eugene, take either Agate or Alder to 19th Avenue.

GRISWOLD BED & BREAKFAST

This 1910 two-story shingled house does not look like much from the outside, although the neighborhood is tree lined and pleasant enough. Even the inside is modest by today's standards. But the hospitality and relaxed style of the innkeepers are quite special indeed.

Phyllis began her bed-and-breakfast career in the early 1980s, when she opened a reservation service. However, booking guests into other people's homes did not give her the kind of satisfaction she was looking for.

"I was missing so much," Phyllis says. "I never got to meet and enjoy the guests. Now I have it all."

As you might expect, guests here are treated like family, and that sometimes means doting attention. It also means caring and friendliness.

The accommodations, two upstairs guest rooms, have been nicely done. In fact, they overshadow the rest of the house. The Blue Room is light and airy. Its windows look out on the trees and houses of West Broadway. Pale blue walls, a queen brass bed, and a stuffed armchair create a restful setting. The Peach Room receives morning sun and is furnished with an antique Eastlake bed and matching dresser. There are baskets of towels and toiletries in each room for use in the large hall bathroom.

Phyllis speaks with pride of her homemade breakfasts. Served on a formal setting of china, they include seasonal fruits, sweet breads, jellies and jams, and a special entrée.

For the money, Griswold's represents a true bargain. It is a throw-

Griswold Bed & Breakfast (Courtesy Griswold Bed & Breakfast)

back to tradition and early guest house philosophy.

*   *   *

Griswold Bed & Breakfast, 522 West Broadway, Eugene, OR 97401 (503-683-6294). Two guest rooms share a hall bath. Rates range from $35 to $39 (subject to change). No credit cards. No children; no pets; smoking in common rooms only. From Franklin Boulevard, take Sixth Street to Jefferson, then left on West Broadway.

MATTEY HOUSE

This mansion stands on ten acres of lawns, farmland, and a fledgling vineyard. It strikes a lonely yet regal figure, and one has to wonder how such a grand lady ended up in this otherwise modest countryside, which just happens to produce some of the world's finest wines.

Mattey House goes back to a time when grapes were something farmers ate in the midst of a hot summer day—to 1892, when cattle roamed this land and orchards produced fruit, bringing ranchers and farmers wealth. Then, the land, sixty acres in all, belonged to Joseph Mattey. He built this two-story Queen Anne house so that his family could live in style.

In 1984, Gene and Susan Irvin purchased the home so bed-and-

Mattey House (Charles Blakeslee)

breakfast travelers could delight in its turn-of-the-century elegance. The Irvins had been scouring the wine countries of California and Oregon for two years before happening upon Mattey House. As soon as they saw it, the light turned green and the mansion became theirs.

The exterior reflects gingerbread craftsmanship. Garnishing the dusty rose, cream, and deep brown house are a wrap-around porch, scalloped shingles, ornamental brackets, and stained-glass windows. Inside, oak floors glisten throughout the house, while red cedar makes up the baseboards, trim, and columns. Victorian furnishings appoint the living room, which is distinguished by a blue tile fireplace, a Bradbury and Bradbury frieze, and a decorative ceiling. Tones of luxury continue to reverberate in the dining room, with its oak table and Belgian carpet.

At this writing, two guest rooms occupy the upstairs, although future plans include expansion, should the law permit. Pinot Noir features two large bedrooms, ideal for couples traveling together. Riesling, with its Laura Ashley prints, creates a cozy, romantic setting. Both rooms boast robes, flowers, comforters, antiques, and reading lamps.

The setting here is one of peace and seclusion. Mattey House is an excellent base for exploring Oregon's wine country.

*　　*　　*

Mattey House, 10221 Northeast Mattey Lane, McMinnville, OR 97128 (503-434-5058). Two guest rooms, both with private baths. Rates range from $50 to $80 (subject to change). VISA. No children under thirteen; no pets; no smoking. Mattey Lane is east of McMinnville, off of State Route 99W. Since it is unmarked, you must look for landmarks, which the Irvins will tell you about.

WILLIAMS HOUSE

Don Williams brings new meaning to senior citizen. Except for some well-earned wrinkles and loss of hair, Don displays more wit and energy than most people half his age. He alone is worth a trip to this bed and breakfast.

But that is not meant to slight his wife Barbara, who is a gem in her own right, or to downplay the beauty of this large turn-of-the-century Victorian.

Built in 1899 by Judge Bennett, the mansion sits on a grassy knoll. Gables and turrets crown the frame building, while spools and sculpted shingles garnish it. A gazebo graces the backyard's rolling lawns, which are shaded by evergreens.

The decor is typical of Victorians—deep red carpets, period antiques, dark woods, and Oriental art. The walls are light, and the large windows welcome lots of sun. In addition, an absence of the clutter so often found in Victorians keeps the house livable.

The front parlor and the living room represent the mansion's most luxurious chambers. Tower windows and an ebony piano mark the parlor, while a veined marble fireplace highlights the living room.

Although the common areas mirror Victorian elegance, the three guest rooms fall short of this image. They reflect a more casual, comfortable style. Only the second-floor Georgian Room approaches the grandeur suggested by the house's facade and its sitting rooms. Here, a four-poster canopy bed and a fainting couch adorn the room.

With its ornate exterior and Victorian flavor, Williams House features the look sought by many bed-and-breakfast travelers. But a look is merely specious. The real focal point of any inn centers on its innkeepers and Williams House boasts two of the best.

*　　*　　*

Williams House, 608 West 6th Street, The Dalles, OR 97058 (503-296-2889). Three guest rooms, one with private bath. Rates range from $45 to $55 (subject to change). VISA/MasterCard. Children with prior approval;

Williams House (Courtesy Williams House)

no pets; smoking in common rooms only. Off-street parking available. Williams House is located on the western edge of downtown.

Washington

ANACORTES
   Channel House
BAINBRIDGE ISLAND
   The Bombay House
CHELAN
   Whaley Mansion
CONCRETE-BIRDSVIEW
   Cascade Mountain Inn
COSMOPOLIS
   The Cooney Mansion
LEAVENWORTH
   Brown's Farm
   Haus Rohrbach Pension
ORCAS ISLAND
   Blue Heron (West Sound)
   Kangaroo House (Eastsound)
   Turtleback Farm Inn
   Woodsong
PATEROS
   French House
PORT ANGELES
   The Tudor Inn

PORT TOWNSEND
   Arcadia Country Inn
   Hastings House Inn
   The James House
   Lizzie's
SAN JUAN ISLAND
   San Juan Inn (Friday Harbor)
   Wharfside Bed & Breakfast (Friday Harbor)
SPOKANE
   Blakely Estates
   Fotheringham House
WHIDBEY ISLAND
   Caroline's (Langley)
   Guest House (Greenbank)
   Home By The Sea (Clinton)
   Lone Lake (Langley)
   Pillars By The Sea (Freeland)
   The Saratoga Inn (Langley)
WHITE SALMON
   Inn of the White Salmon

Seattle

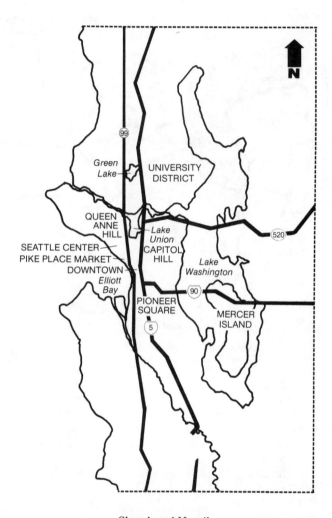

Chambered Nautilus
Chelsea Station
Galer Place
Gaslight Inn
Roberta's
The Williams House

Seattle

$\mathcal{S}$ eattle is a city of nature. Most cities' roots are planted in heritage, but Seattle's foundation is the earth itself. You can see and sense this from atop the Center's Space Needle—Seattle's symbol to the world but, more important, an emblem marking the city's cosmopolitan birthright.

Large bodies of water surround Seattle: Elliott Bay to the south, Puget Sound to the west, Lake Union to the north, and Lake Washington to the east. Mountains mantled by glaciers and snow form a towering backdrop. Hurricane Ridge and the Olympics rise above the Sound. And looking like an apparition of Tolkien, Mount Rainier dwarfs Seattle's man-made pinnacles, while the rugged Cascades cut a jagged swath through the state's heart to Mount Baker and the Canadian border far to the north. All this splendor embraces Seattle, making it one of the world's most beautiful cities.

But when Seattle looks in the mirror, it also sees conflict. This is a city teetering on the edge of greatness, which requires Seattle to ask itself an important question: can nature and commerce coexist in harmony?

The business and fashion districts are growing, great restaurants and theater are thriving, and professional sports have arrived in a big way. Still, the city's heart holds onto traditional Northwest values. A leisurely pace, one respectful of mind and body, dominates the city. Traffic jams, which strike at least twice daily Monday through Friday, do not create a cacophony of angry horns; department store sales, which occur nearly as frequently as traffic jams, do not inspire mob scenes played out by middle-class shoppers; and festivals, which erupt nearly as often as either jams or sales, do not transform celebrants into sadomasochists.

Seattle is easy to explore and, like almost any city worth visiting, should be discovered on foot. When combined with Metro buses, the monorail, and ferry boats, Seattle can be admired from head to toe with very little effort.

The city is divided conveniently into neighborhoods. First-time visitors should begin at the Seattle Center, where in 1962 Seattle declared its readiness to become a great American city.

GETTING TO KNOW SEATTLE

THE SEATTLE CENTER

The views from atop the Space Needle offer reasons enough for travelers to begin their city tours here. But there are also several other good arguments for making the Center a starting point. First, there is usually parking available (on nonevent days). Second, the monorail will speed you from the Center to downtown in ninety seconds and with absolutely no hassles. (There is only one place to get on and one place to get off.)

The Center was built in 1962 to host the Seattle World's Fair. Today, its seventy-four acres represent Seattle's cultural and festival heart.

Visitors could easily spend an entire day here. Under the high arches, you will find the Pacific Science Center. It hosts traveling exhibits, as well as hands-on computers, the StarLab Planetarium, environmental displays, laser shows, and an IMAX® Theater. Nearby, the Seattle Art Museum Pavilion usually features at least one interesting exhibit, often displaying works of regional artists. (It is free on Thursdays.) The adjacent Coliseum is home to the Seattle SuperSonics and welcomes concerts and exhibits throughout the year. On the northern edge of the Center stand the Bagley Wright Theatre, home of the Seattle Repertory Theater, and the Opera House, which hosts the prestigious Seattle Opera and the Pacific Northwest Ballet.

Before leaving, you might also wish to visit the amusements in Fun Forest and the shops and restaurants of the Center House. However, you would spend your time better by hopping aboard the monorail and heading for downtown.

PIKE PLACE MARKET

The Market took root in 1907 as a backlash to high food prices. By the 1930s, some fifty-five thousand shoppers tramped the Market's arcades daily, eyeing and buying the products of more than six hundred farmers.

However, urbanization, industrialization, and suburbanization combined with the internment of Japanese farmers to decrease the number of nearby farms and increase the popularity of malls and chains. By the 1960s, the Market was showing signs of shabbiness, and downtown developers saw this as an opportunity to tear down an eyesore and replace it with prime water view property. Seattle's citizens balked at the idea, and by 1971 the Market was designated a seven-acre historical district.

Today, this grab bag of mix-and-match architecture lures a cross section of Seattle's people and an army of tourists to participate in America's favorite participant sports—eating and shopping. Sprawling between Pike and Virginia, and Western and First, are the Northwest's freshest foods and some of its best shops. There are fish, fruit, vegetable, and meat vendors standing alongside craftspeople and artists hawking their wares. There are also funky stores, specialty shops, street musicians, bakeries, and restaurants.

The focal point for this hodgepodge of Northwest living is the Main Arcade, which stretches north, south, up, and down. The air is thick with smells of fish and herbs and the sound of commerce. The arcade is shoulder-to-shoulder people.

It is impossible and quite insane to attempt to complete exploration of the Market in one day. But, no matter what your approach is, be sure to get off the Main Arcade and beyond the vendors of Pike Place to the Market's hidden treasures. Walk down into the bowels of the Arcade and check out all the crannies and passageways.

In the vicinity of the big clock, you will find an information booth. Here, pick up the Market News, which contains a map. Now begin walking, with these tips in mind: (1) Never touch the produce. Instead, tell the farmers exactly what you need and when and how you plan to use it. They will select carefully and honestly for you. (2) Be aware that the high stalls are permanent vendors, who buy their produce wholesale, while the low stalls are local farmers, who grow their own foods. (3) Prices do vary, so shop around.

One final piece of advice—driving through the Market on Pike Place is foolish: traffic is usually slowed to a stop. If you must drive, try the parking lots along Western Avenue and walk up to the Market.

FASHIONABLE FIFTH AVENUE

Once the eyes and stomach have been pampered at the Market, it is time to take to the trendy trail. A brisk five-block walk east on Pike—past bellicose but harmless panhandlers and street kids—brings shoppers to fashionable Fifth Avenue and the department store district. Here, it is wise to keep a firm grip on pocketbooks, lest they begin throwing plastic money into the palms of eager sales people.

For the next several years, construction, dust, and noise may take some of the glitter off this Mecca for finery. Still, if you wish to dine off Seattle's fashion plate, this is the place.

Amidst maples and old-fashioned lampposts walk well-dressed shoppers and smart-looking executives. They appraise the windows and floors of retailers such as Nordstrom and Frederick and Nelson at Fifth and Pine, or The Bon at Fourth and Pine, or I. Magnin at Sixth and Pine. And for those suburbanites who break into cold sweats without the familiar feel of a mall, trendy Rainier Square, a multi-level arcade with more than fifty shops and restaurants, sits on the lower level of the forty-story Rainier Bank Tower at Fifth and Union. Here, such boutiques as Jaeger's, Polo of Seattle, and Totally Michael's cater to designer needs.

PIONEER SQUARE

In 1852 Seattle's first settlers abandoned wind-swept Alki Point for the protection of Elliott Bay. Over the years, this area grew up as Seattle's heart. But expansion and decay during the early and mid-1900s left the neighborhood, known until recently as Skid Road for the logging skids which once paved Yesler Street, gasping.

However, the area was rescued from the wrecking ball by declaring it a historic district in 1970 and renaming it Pioneer Square. Today, its brick buildings and cobblestone streets claim the city's largest concentration of art galleries, as well as shops, restaurants, and nightclubs.

Bounded by Cherry, Jackson, Alaskan, and Third, Pioneer Square is a compact neighborhood that is easy to tour. The Square itself (which is actually a triangle at First and Yesler) is a good place to start. For a guided tour, Bill Speidel's Underground Tours depart from Doc Maynard's Public House for entertaining and sometimes irreverent looks at the neighborhood.

From the Square, a walk down First delivers you to one of Seattle's most famous landmarks—The Elliott Bay Book Company. Besides a magnificent selection of books and magazines, the downstairs café is a gathering place for Seattle's quiche eaters and espresso sippers. Several other spots along First are also worth a look, including Grand Central Mercantile, the Northwest Gallery of Fine Woodworking, and the Pioneer Square Gallery. Before leaving the area, do not miss Waterfall Gardens at Second and Main or the views from atop the Smith Tower, once the tallest building west of the Mississippi, at Second and Yesler.

THE INTERNATIONAL DISTRICT

Located in the shadows of the Kingdome, the International District is small compared to similar neighborhoods in San Francisco and Vancouver. Perhaps this is why the few tourists who come here are obvious. Too bad, for the neighborhood is a living museum of Seattle's multicultural mix.

Narrow low-rises, many adorned with Asian script, line Jackson and King, between Fifth and Eighth. Chinese street lamps and pagodalike telephone booths dot the sidewalks. Breaths of ginseng, ginger, and barbecue sauce join the sing-song voices of Chinese, Vietnamese, and Korean shoppers as they walk from building to building. Barbecue ducks and sides of pork garnish the windows of the China Poultry Company on King; the smell of fresh shrimp fills Cho Dongnama; quail eggs, sharks fin soup, and pickled delicacies line the shelves of the Viet Hoa Market; and crates of produce adorn at least a half dozen storefronts.

If guided tours help your orientation, call Vi Mar Travel (206-447-

9230). Otherwise, begin your walk at the Wing Luke Memorial Museum at 417 Seventh Avenue South. Exhibits focus on the culture and history of Asians and Asian-Americans. Then work your way to the Bush Asia Center at Maynard and Jackson. Inside, you will find an array of shops. For spicy Korean food, try Han Il, then proceed downstairs for dessert at the Golden Bakery. Outside is Hing Hay Park, a tiny urban oasis with a grand pavilion, designed and created in Taipei. Do not leave the District without first shopping at Uwajimaya, a huge Japanese supermarket at Sixth and King, or before sampling the sushi at the Mikado Japanese Restaurant, located at 514 South Jackson.

SEATTLE'S WATERFRONT

Seattle's commercial fortunes float on its waterfront. Large ships from faraway lands import jobs and export American goods. This has been true since before the Alaskan gold rush.

You should begin your tour of the waterfront by sailing across the bay. The best and least expensive way is to walk aboard a Washington State Ferry bound for Winslow on Bainbridge Island. Ferries leave Pier 52 regularly, and the trip lasts thirty minutes each way. The other alternative is Seattle Harbor Tours (206-623-1445), which leave from Pier 56.

Back on land, you should explore the funky and zany Ye Olde Curiosity Shop at the foot of Yesler. It has the largest collection of bizarre items in Seattle. Then grab a bench and watch harbor life from Waterfront Park along Piers 57 and 59. While at Pier 59, stop in at the Seattle Aquarium. It features a touch tank, underwater dome, salmon ladder, and octopi, sharks, crabs, eels, and seals. Those bound for Victoria can board the Princess Marguerite at Pier 69, while those heading for shoppers' world can discover an array of opportunities at Pier 70.

CAPITOL HILL

This is my neighborhood, so forgive my prejudices. Quite simply, however, it is the most cosmopolitan area of Seattle. It is also the home of tree-lined residential streets, scenic overlooks, and a gorgeous park.

Broadway is where the action is. It is the only Seattle street that does not sleep. Boutiques, specialty stores, restaurants, and hair salons cram a six-block section that stretches from Denny to Roy. Fashion along these blocks ranges from punk to sophisticated. Capitol Hill's apartments, frame houses, and mansions shelter the elderly, yuppies, gays, lesbians, singles, preppies, punks, and all-American families.

Given a sunny day, some residents can be found at Volunteer Park. (Take Aloha north to a left on 14th Avenue.) Some will be walking the halls of the Seattle Art Museum, others will be smelling the flowers at the conservatory, but most will be enjoying the park's thick lawns, blooming gardens, lily ponds, stately trees, and panoramas of Elliott Bay.

UNIVERSITY DISTRICT

The thirty-five thousand-student, 680-acre University of Washington anchors this neighborhood. The campus alone—with its stately architecture and grassy commons—is in itself worth a visit. But for sheer daytime energy, nothing in Seattle, not even Broadway, can top University Way Northeast. Ethnic restaurants, fast-food outlets, trendy boutiques, unusual shops, and the city's best bookstore (the University Book Store) create a beehive of activity.

QUEEN ANNE HILL

Queen Anne Hill is actually two neighborhoods in one—Lower and Upper. Lower Queen Anne borders the Seattle Center and is home to several excellent restaurants. Upper Queen Anne is quiet and residential. Around its edges await the city's best views.

From First Avenue North, climb steep Queen Anne Avenue. Turn left on Highland Drive to Kerry Park. The city, sound, and mountain views from this vantage point are spectacular. More views await if you continue west past several mansions to the Betty Bowen Viewpoint, which is kitty-corner from the Parsons Memorial Garden. Continue north on Eighth, which accesses Seventh Avenue, and make your way around the crest of Queen Anne Hill for more views.

A PRACTICAL GUIDE TO THE CITY

THE CLIMATE

Temperatures remain relatively mild year-round, 70s in the summer, 40s in the winter. Rain and fog are a threat from November to May, but gray skies with light rain or drizzle are more likely. From Memorial Day until about mid-November, Seattle experiences many warm and sunny days.

YOUR CLOTHES

This city believes people should do their own thing. That means almost anything goes. However, fashionable and expensive attire can be a common scene at nightclubs, theaters, restaurants, and along Fifth Avenue. Comfortable shoes are a must. Remember, Seattle is built on hills.

DRIVING AND PARKING

Interstate 5 runs just east of downtown's high rises; it is nearly always crowded, and between 4 P.M. and 6 P.M. looks more like a parking lot. You should also avoid Interstate 90 and State Route 520, which cross Lake Washington, during these times. Hills and one-way streets can make driving challenging for people unfamiliar with Seattle. Street parking is difficult to find during the week; however, there are a number of lots and garages. Outdoor lots may be self-service—pay attention to signs threatening impoundment: they are serious. All in all, this is not a town in need of more cars.

PUBLIC TRANSPORTATION

This is the way to go. Metro buses are clean, inexpensive, and run on schedule. In downtown, rides are free. Maps displaying bus routes and numbers frequent downtown shops. In addition, bus drivers and passengers are friendly and helpful. Metro's twenty-four hour information number is 206-447-4800.

VISITOR INFORMATION

For more information, write or call: Seattle-King County Convention & Visitors Bureau, 1815 Seventh Avenue, Seattle, WA 98101 (206-447-4240).

POINTS OF INTEREST

SEATTLE CENTER. Bounded by Denny and Mercer, and First and Fifth. Call 206-625-4234 for information on activities. A seventy-four-acre park, which is the legacy of the 1962 World's Fair. It serves as Seattle's cultural and convention center. (At this writing, a new convention and trade center is under construction elsewhere.)

SPACE NEEDLE. Seattle Center (206-443-2100). Seattle's 605-foot symbol. Open to the public year-round. Two revolving restaurants at 500-foot level; observation deck at 520 feet. Views sans dining costs $3.50 per adult for the elevator ride.

CENTER HOUSE. Seattle Center. Home to a children's museum and more than fifty touristy shops and restaurants.

SEATTLE ART MUSEUM PAVILION. Seattle Center (206-443-4796). The traveling exhibits here deserve attention.

PACIFIC SCIENCE CENTER. Seattle Center (206-443-2880). Hands-on computers, planetarium, exhibits, laser shows, and IMAX® Theater.

PIKE PLACE MARKET. Bounded by Pike and Virginia, and Western and First (206-682-7453). The oldest continuously operating farmers' market in the United States. Fresh foods, ethnic restaurants, and unique shops.

MARKET PARK. At the foot of Virginia. A sunny and grassy oasis overlooking the bay to the mountains beyond.

PIONEER SQUARE. Bounded by Cherry, Jackson, Alaskan, and Third. The original center of Seattle, settled in 1852. The fire of 1889 destroyed the entire frame town, which was then rebuilt with brick. Shops, restaurants, and galleries.

KLONDIKE GOLD RUSH NATIONAL HISTORICAL PARK. 117 South Main, Pioneer Square (206-442-7220). A tiny museum depicting Seattle's role in the gold rush of 1897–1898.

WING LUKE MEMORIAL MUSEUM. 417 Seventh Avenue South, International District (206-623-5124). Exhibits focusing on the people of Asia and on Asian-Americans.

WATERFRONT STREETCAR. 1927 cars run on rails alongside Alaskan Way from Pioneer Square to Myrtle Edwards Park. They make several stops along the way. Good way to see the waterfront.

SEATTLE HARBOR TOURS. Pier 56 at the foot of Seneca (206-623-1445). Offers excellent tours of the waterfront, plus tours to Tillicum Village on Blake Island, which provide a look into the heritage of North Coast Indians.

THE SEATTLE AQUARIUM. Pier 59 (206-625-4358). Excellent displays of Puget Sound's sea life.

MYRTLE EDWARDS PARK. North of Pier 70. Biking and jogging paths, as well as a new fishing pier at the north end.

WASHINGTON PARK ARBORETUM. Located along Lake Washington Boulevard East. From downtown, take Madison over First Hill to the Boulevard. Sprawling park of trees, shrubs, and flowers. The Japanese Garden is located at the south end of the park. A great place for bicyclists.

WOODLAND PARK ZOO. Bounded by Phinney and Aurora, and North 50th and 59th (206-789-7919). From Interstate 5, take the 50th Street exit west. This is a zoo that is constantly being upgraded. Many animals are displayed in their natural environments.

GREEN LAKE. Located east of the zoo. A mecca for sun worshippers and fitness fans. Roller-skating, biking, jogging, sailboarding, fishing, tennis, picnicking, and swimming.

HIRAM M. CHITTENDON LOCKS. Take Northwest Market Street through Ballard to Northwest 54th Street. Joins Lakes Union and Washington to the Sound. Good picnicking. Fish-viewing area.

DISCOVERY PARK. Located on the northwest tip of Magnolia. Seattle's largest park at 520 acres. This is Seattle's best spot for nature lovers. Environments range from woods to beaches. Views from atop steep cliffs of the Sound and the Olympics.

RESTAURANTS OF NOTE

Seattle's restaurants are among North America's finest. Fresh regional foods are particularly good.

ALEXIS RESTAURANT. First and Madison (206-624-3646). Located in the posh Alexis Hotel. Elegant dining. Fresh Northwest foods superbly prepared.

DOMINIQUE'S PLACE. 1927 43rd Street East (206-329-6620). A cozy café setting overlooking Lake Washington. Classic French cooking using fresh Northwest ingredients. Extraordinary sauces.

IL BISTRO. 93-A Pike Street (206-682-3049). A café setting in the lower level of Pike Place Market. Northern Italian fare. Good pasta and rack of lamb.

INDIA HOUSE. 4737 Roosevelt Way Northeast (206-632-5072). Authentic Indian dishes. Tandoori specialties (barbecued dishes) are particularly good.

LABUZNIK. 1924 First Avenue (206-682-1624). Arguably the best restaurant in town. Only fresh ingredients. Roast duckling, veal Orloff, and roast lamb are magnificent. Elegant dining.

LE GOURMAND. 425 Northwest Market Street (206-784-3463). Chef Bruce Naftaly has become a Northwest legend. His restaurant is cozy; his food superb. Everything is grown, raised, or caught locally. Cuisine is country-French, and the menu changes every two weeks. Soups and salads are not to be missed.

LE TASTEVIN. 19 West Harrison Street (206-283-0991). Classic cuisine. Fresh seafood. The rack of lamb and the chicken breast are also good. Desserts are excellent. Located near the Center, so theatergoers crowd in here before curtain time.

MAMOUNIA. 1556 East Olive Way (206-329-3886). Sit on pillows or banquettes surrounding round tables of tin and prepare yourself for an authentic Moroccan experience. No utensils here, just superb lamb, chicken, and rabbit served with heaping helpings of couscous.

MIKADO. 514 South Jackson (206-622-5206). Excellent sushi bar. Light meals also commendable.

NIKKO. 1306 South King Street (206-322-4641). Some say the sushi bar has surpassed Mikado as Seattle's best. Superb sushi and excellent dinners.

THE PINK DOOR. 1919 Post Alley, Pike Place Market (206-682-3241). This funky, unpretentious little restaurant is one of my personal favorites. Best suited for lunch, however, as the dinner menu is skimpy. The cioppino and the pasta are very good. For dessert, the diplomatico, a rich cake, is wonderful.

RAY'S BOATHOUSE. 6049 Seaview Avenue Northwest (206-789-3770). May be the best seafood restaurant in town. Always fresh and delicious. Oysters and scallops are particularly tender and tasty. Very casual.

ROSELLINI'S OTHER PLACE. 319 Union Street (206-623-7340). This has long been considered one of Seattle's finest restaurants. Fresh Northwest ingredients only. Both the fish and the game are unequaled in excellence. The best wine list in Seattle. Clientele is dignified rather than trendy.

SALEH AL LAGO. 6804 East Green Lake Way North (206-524-4044). Central Italian cuisine in a simple setting. Good pasta and veal. Like The Pink Door, this is a restaurant to choose if you are in the area.

SETTEBELLO RISTORANTE. 1525 East Olive Way (206-323-7772). Northern Italian cuisine. The pasta and the wine list are very good.

WHERE TO STAY

GASLIGHT INN

Few bed-and-breakfast inns anywhere can equal the elegance and the amenities of Gaslight Inn. In these ways, it mirrors the light-hearted sophistication of its neighborhood—Capitol Hill.

Built in 1906, this glorious mansion served as a model home to prospective residents of this up-and-coming Seattle enclave. The home basked in the shine of its oak floors, the grandeur of its oak columns, the magnificence of its great stairway, and the radiance of its leaded and stained-glass windows.

However, as time went by, both the neighborhood and the home fell from grace. But the house had secret admirers. For fifteen years, Trevor Logan and Steve Bennett held deep passions for the mansion. Then in 1983, the building went on the market. Within twenty-four hours of its availability, Trevor and Steve had purchased it.

For two years, they tore away the residue of neglect and subdivision. They restored and remodeled. They scraped away layers of paint and removed false walls until its original luster shined through.

The downstairs rooms are elegant. A Persian carpet covers the oak floor of the parlor, which is furnished in leather and surrounded by jade green walls. There are VCR, color television, and stereo system. Another Persian carpet adorns the music room, which has a baby grand piano and oak window seat. The living room features more oak, with a marble fireplace and a brass gaslight chandelier.

In the fall of 1986, the inn offered eight guest rooms with at least one more planned. They occupy the second and third floors and range in decor

Gaslight Inn (Kay Green)

from turn-of-the-century antique, to rustic country, to classic contemporary. All boast refrigerators, sinks, televisions, digital clocks, quilts or comforters, fresh flowers, and original art.

Gaslight also features a second-floor solarium and a private thirty-three-foot in-ground heated pool. A terraced deck, complete with lounges, chairs, tables, and tanning pads, surrounds the pool.

The most complimentary thing I can say about Gaslight is that it equals some of San Francisco's best inns in scope and luxury. But the rates are so much lower (I suspect that may change) that San Franciscans can only look north with wonderment.

* * *

Gaslight Inn, 1727 15th Avenue, Seattle, WA 98122 (206-325-3654). Eight guest rooms (still in a state of flux), four with private baths (this, too, could change). Rates range from $35 to $55 (subject to change). VISA/MasterCard. Children with prior approval; no pets; smoking permitted. Some rooms feature city views. On-street parking. From Interstate 5, take Exit 166 to Denny Way. At the crest of Capitol Hill, turn right onto 15th Avenue.

ROBERTA'S

Roberta Mar runs a bed and breakfast because she loves people. From the moment visitors arrive to the time they wave goodbye, there are

Roberta's (Kay Green)

enough smiles, laughs, and "Oh, honeys" to pump up even the most stressed guests.

She is a former school teacher, with a degree in English from Seattle University. The idea of running a bed and breakfast came to her during trips to Ireland, where she stayed in guest houses.

"I thought this would be great fun," Roberta says, "and the idea of getting another real job was distressing. So far, this has been as brilliant as I had wished."

Her two-story frame house sits on a tree-lined residential street at the top of Capitol Hill. The house was built in 1903, features a wide veranda, which is draped by the blossoms of azaleas and rhododendrons.

There are four upstairs guest rooms. Magnolia and Plum overlook the neighborhood, with partial views of the Cascades. Although Magnolia's antique elegance has much to offer, the Peach Room is Roberta's pride. A black antique Franklin stove catches the eye first, then you notice how light and airy the room feels. The Blue Room represents the home's coziest, meaning smallest, accommodation.

Breakfast combines conversation and home-cooked food. It is served around an old oak table in the large kitchen. It is very possible that during your second popover or third cup of coffee, a neighbor or two may show up for a brief visit, testimony to the innkeeper's popularity.

The importance of sociability here cannot be overstated. If anonymity rates high on your list of needs, then another Seattle inn will better suit you. On the other hand, if you like making new friends, Roberta's can accommodate you.

*   *   *

Roberta's, 1147 16th Avenue East, Seattle, WA 98112 (206-329-3326). Four guest rooms share two baths. Rates range from $45 to $50 (subject to change). No credit cards. Children with prior approval; no pets; no smoking. On-street parking. From Interstate 5 south, take the Roanoke exit to 10th Avenue East. Take a left at Boston to 15th. Then turn left on Prospect to 16th. From Interstate 5 north, take the Denny exit. Take either Olive or Denny to a left on 15th Avenue. Then go right on Prospect to 16th Avenue.

CHAMBERED NAUTILUS

For Kate McDill and Deborah Sweet, owning and operating a bed-and-breakfast inn is a fantasy that evolved into reality. Like so many ideas, its roots grew out of necessity.

Kate was a student. One of her projects involved developing a budget for a private business. Believing two heads are better than one and usually a lot more fun, she enlisted Deborah's assistance. Together, the idea for developing a bed and breakfast blossomed. As they found themselves getting deeper and deeper into the project, they began thinking, why not? Running a bed and breakfast just might be their calling.

For the next year, they searched for the right house. Their efforts proved fruitless until they were just about to give up. Then Kate and Deborah found the perfect home. They bought it and spent the next ten weeks painting and remodeling. In the summer of 1983, Chambered Nautilus welcomed its first guests.

Their dream is a large, blue Georgian Colonial-style home in the heart of the University District. It was built in 1915 by Herbert and Annie Kay Gowen. Back then, before the ship canal was built and streets paved the neighborhood, the house overlooked a country setting, with the Cascades rising in the distance.

Today, the country has given way to apartments, houses, and a shopping center. But the neighborhood remains quiet, and the mountains continue their vigilance.

Upon arriving at the 22nd Avenue address, guests climb the stairs to this hillside perch. They enter a tiny foyer flanked by the living and dining rooms. After showing guests to their room, Kate and Deborah immediately make themselves available to help with itineraries—a valuable service in a town with so much to see and do.

All of the six guest rooms are on the second and third floors—four of them have porches. Softened with pastels, the rooms are furnished with a blend of American and English antiques. Rather than presenting a grand

Chambered Nautilus (Courtesy Chambered Nautilus)

or elegant ambience, however, the accommodations feel homey. They mirror the simple life, which recalls the country heritage of the home. Still, there are the extras that sophisticated travelers have come to expect—the robes, alarm clocks, reading lamps, fresh flowers, thick towels, extra pillows, and extra blankets.

Breakfast also dresses in a cultivated yet country fashion. The handsome dining room sets the scene; a fire crackling in the brick fireplace, bread baskets garnishing one wall, flowers adorning the oak table, and classical music calming the air. The fresh homemade foods include scones, just-ground coffee, and cheese-baked eggs.

*   *   *

Chambered Nautilus, 5005 22nd Avenue Northeast, Seattle, WA 98105 (206-522-2536). Six guest rooms share three hall baths. Rates range from $38 to $62 (subject to change). VISA/MasterCard/American Express. Children with prior approval; no pets; smoking on sun porch only. The inn welcomes receptions, luncheons, and meetings. Full catering services are available. On-street parking—which can be a hassle during school hours. From Interstate 5, take Exit 169 to 50th Street east. Turn left on 20th, to a right on 54th, to another right on 22nd.

CHELSEA STATION

It is a big step to go from running a sixty-room hospital to operating a five-guest room bed and breakfast. But then Dick Jones was not seeking

Chelsea Station (Courtesy Chelsea Station)

small changes. He and his wife Marylou were looking for different directions and inspirations. Still, Dick was at first surprised by his new life-style.

"The first time I knelt down to clean a toilet here was quite a humbling experience," Dick says.

That was in September 1984. Quite a few toilets have been cleaned since then, and Dick and Marylou have comfortably settled into the routine of innkeeping.

Chelsea Station is a two-story brick Federal Colonial that sits across from Woodland Park Zoo and near Green Lake. Although it was built in 1920 as a private residence, the house's lines create a sense of apartment living, not surprising since the building was converted into apartments shortly after being built. It remained that way until the Joneses purchased it in 1984.

Four of the accommodations, including two suite-size spaces, occupy the second floor. All the rooms feature homey touches, such as freshly cut flowers and scatter rugs. Privacy, which is natural to the building's layout, is stressed.

Lilac and Rose represent two of the most spacious rooms in town. Lilac overlooks the zoo's rose garden and boasts oak floors, a sitting area with overstuffed furniture, two twins made into a king-size bed, lots of windows, and a fake fireplace that somehow avoids being tacky. Rose is equally large and, in addition, features a completely stocked kitchen.

While privacy is stressed, and the house still has some leftover apartment in it, there is a feeling of warmth. It is reflected in Dick and Marylou's personalities and in their concern for guest comfort. This caring has spilled over in the form of amenities, such as the help-yourself-to-coffee-and-tea table and the hot tub.

If you are looking for a grand mansion adorned with museum pieces, Chelsea Station will not do. But if your needs revolve around tranquility, privacy, price, comfort, and convenience, this is the place.

*   *   *

Chelsea Station, 4915 Linden Avenue North, Seattle, WA 98103 (206-547-6077). Five guest rooms; Daffodil has a private hall bath, others share two hall baths. Rates range from $39 to $59 (subject to change). VISA/MasterCard/American Express. No charge for children under six; no pets; no smoking. House available for small weddings, parties, and meetings. On-street parking. From Interstate 5, take 45th Street west. Then take a right on Fremont, to another right on 50th. Go one block to Linden.

GALER PLACE

It was one of Seattle's first bed and breakfasts and remains one of the city's best. The major difference today from when Galer Place first opened its doors in the early 1980s, is that now the home sports a bit of jolly old England.

The English influence arrived in May of 1984, with new owner Chris Chamberlain. Along with her English accent, Chris brought the traditional afternoon tea. Served every day between 4 P.M. and 5 P.M., Chris

Galer Place (Courtesy Galer Place)

treats guests to strong tea, freshly baked Scottish shortbread, and friendly conversation.

This two-story frame house has been a familiar landmark on Queen Anne Hill since 1906. The home radiates a cozy, lived-in feeling. The closeness of the rooms and all the plants, flowers, books, magazines, and works of art deserve much of the credit.

The downstairs features the dining room and the parlor. Both rooms are small and welcoming. In the parlor, sunshine flows through the bay window, across a garden of plants, to stuffed furniture. A large, lace-covered table and a cut glass chandelier dominate the dining area.

Four guest rooms occupy the second floor. While all are furnished with antiques, each offers a special ambience. Mahogany is cozy and homey, Brass boasts a Victorian feeling, Oak is quiet and private, and Rattan features a South Seas atmosphere.

Everything about the house seems intimate, including the backyard garden. It is enclosed by a fence and has a terraced deck with a hot tub, lawn chairs, and a tiny table.

If there are any drawbacks to Galer Place, they revolve around location. Because it sits near Queen Anne's business district, the setting seems more commercial than residential. But all of this is lost inside the house or on the back deck.

To its credit, Galer Place creates an environment that many inns either fall short of or are simply not interested in: it is intimate while still professionally run.

*   *   *

Galer Place, 318 West Galer Street, Seattle, WA 98119 (206-282-5339). Four guest rooms—The Brass Room has a private bath, Oak a half-bath, and the others share a bath. Rates range from $43 to $55 (subject to change). VISA/MasterCard/American Express. No children under twelve; small pets with prior approval; smoking downstairs only. On-street parking. From Interstate 5, take the Mercer Street exit to Fifth Avenue. Turn right, then take a left on Roy, to a right on Queen Anne Avenue North. At the crest of the hill, turn left onto West Galer.

THE WILLIAMS HOUSE

To the south, the Space Needle rises in the foreground, with Seattle's glass-and-steel mountains creating a formidable backdrop. In the east, the Cascades duck behind the apartments and condominiums of Capitol Hill. This is how The Williams House sees the world.

Built in 1905 with traditional Victorian lines, the house sits atop Queen Anne Hill in a quiet neighborhood. A wide veranda and sun porch

The Williams House (Kay Green)

wrap two sides, while broad dormers dot the roof.

The Williams House has been the home and inn of Doug and Susan Williams since 1983. They are friendly and always happy to meet guests' needs, to provide insider's tips, or make arrangements for dinner reservations or theater tickets. However, Susan and Doug believe in and practice privacy. They are not doters. At The Williams House, guests should expect to make themselves at home.

The entire downstairs is available to guests. The large, bay-windowed living room boasts the elegance of Victoriana without the clutter. It is ideal for small weddings. The dining room feels formal but friendly, while the sitting room features overstuffed casualness. Readers and daydreamers will find much to admire on the sun porch.

All five guest rooms are upstairs. They have polished wood floors, large windows, vintage radiators, antique furnishings, and floral-print wallpapers. The Bay Room promises the best views, but there are also good scenes available from The English, Skyline, and Brass and Satin rooms.

There are several reasons to recommend The Williams House: its tranquil setting five minutes from downtown, its turn-of-the-century charm, and its professional service. Doting is not part of the package—a plus for some, a drawback for others. For that reason, The Williams House is best suited for those who cherish and respect privacy.

*   *   *

The Williams House, 1505 Fourth Avenue North, Seattle, WA 98109 (206-285-0810). Five guest rooms share two baths. Rates range from $45 to $60 (subject to change). VISA/MasterCard/American Express. Children with prior approval; no pets; smoking on sun porch only. Small weddings, receptions, and meetings welcome. Breakfast is expanded continental; eggs served on request. On-street parking. From Interstate 5, take Mercer Street exit to a right on Fifth Avenue. Turn left at Highland, then right on Third. At Galer Street, turn right to Fourth Avenue North.

Washington's Islands

*T*he first time I drove into the belly of a Washington State Ferry, a battle of emotions raged within me. To my left stood the largest trailer truck ever molded of heavy metal, while to my right stretched a parade of tour buses loaded with all of Iowa. And all around me, in bumper-to-bumper lines, sat several parking lots full of cars. It seemed all of Washington had decided to join me for a tour of the San Juan Islands. Was this really how I wanted to spend my vacation?

Realizing fate was out of my hands, I climbed the stairs to the passenger level. There, I bumped into schools of children running and saw hordes of unconcerned adults sitting on cushioned vinyl. I winced and walked out onto the deck. Out of harm's way, my fears were washed away by cool sea breezes, golden splashes of sun, and views of rolling isles.

This is the magic of Washington's islands: they pose peaceful and pristine, waiting to soothe nerves stretched to the point of snapping. They are places where pace is slow and time is measured by the raspy voices of ferries as they come and go.

No sojourner to Washington should leave without visiting at least one of its isles. And, as I learned on that first trip years ago, getting there is half the fun.

GETTING TO KNOW WASHINGTON'S ISLANDS

BAINBRIDGE ISLAND

In some ways, Bainbridge Island represents the best and the worst of Washington's islands. On the plus side, the island floats only a thirty-minute ferry ride from Seattle, making it a convenient quick country fix for city lovers. Unfortunately, that is also its negative side. Summer traffic on State Route 305, the main highway through Bainbridge, and in Winslow, the island's only town, is often heavy with cars, trucks, and bicycles. Not only do people come here to explore the island, but they are also using the highway and Agate Pass Bridge to reach the Olympic Peninsula.

Still, Bainbridge offers good bicycle and auto tours. (Cyclists be warned: the terrain is hilly.) With picnic packed and a map from the chamber of commerce in hand, head to either Fort Ward State Park, which sprawls alongside Rich Passage, or Fay Bainbridge State Park, which features views of Seattle. Before leaving the island, you might also wish to walk Winslow's main street. There are several interesting shops, and it does not take very long to check out the entire town.

WHIDBEY ISLAND

Fifty-mile-long Whidbey Island is so large that once you are within its hills and farmlands, it barely feels as if you are on an island at all. And that may be the reason why it does not attract more tourists. On the other hand, if local boosters succeed in luring travelers by the ferry loads, some of Whidbey's charm may get caught up in traffic-heavy byways and lost in quaint towns succumbing to tourist dollars.

Today, Whidbey Island remains tranquil and a haven for travelers who want to get away from it all, including other travelers. On its west side stretch miles and miles of open sandy beaches, ideal for beach-combing, sunning, or watching foreign ships ply the strait. On the east side, hidden harbors and mud flats offer a quiet, more private setting.

Like other Washington isles, Whidbey Island is perfectly suited for auto-touring, bicycling, beachcombing, boating, fishing, and picnicking. It also offers the appeal of small-town life. Six communities dot Whidbey; each welcomes visitors.

The largest of the towns is Oak Harbor, which is just a short drive south of twenty-five hundred-acre Deception Pass State Park. While the park is often crowded during the summer, its forests and beaches should be explored. Nearby Oak Harbor was once quiet and unassuming; however, the Navy landed in 1941. Now it is a good place for its twelve thousand residents to live but not worth a tourist detour.

Instead, visit nearby Coupeville, which was founded in 1852 by Captain Thomas Coupe. Today, the town revels in its past, showing off several historic buildings, including some Victorians. There are also a few blockhouses standing from the days when Indians and whites were not always on best of terms: three are open to visitors (The John Alexander Blockhouse along Front Street, The Davis Blockhouse beside the cemetery, and Crockett Blockhouse just north of Crockett Lake). Anglers, divers, history buffs, and view seekers should visit Fort Casey State Park—a former army base built to guard the Sound. A boat launch near

Keystone Landing is a good spot to put in the waters for salmon fishing off Admiralty Head. These waters are also popular among scuba divers.

Finally, you should visit Langley, the island's most charming community. The town is built on a bluff overlooking Saratoga Passage, with the Cascade Mountains rising in the background. It is a good place to spend a day browsing and shopping galleries and shops or just walking the turn-of-the-century streets.

Bicyclists should take Maxwelton Road from Langley for a day at Maxwelton Beach. Hardier souls may wish to head out on Brooks Hill Road to Bayview Road. Turn right on State Route 525 to Double Bluff Road. At Double Bluff, you will find an isolated beach ideal for walking or clamming.

To reach Whidbey Island, you can take either the Mukilteo Ferry or the Keystone Ferry from Port Townsend. You can also drive to the northern tip by crossing Deception Pass Bridge.

THE SAN JUAN ISLANDS

Fourteen thousand years ago mile-thick glaciers ground the peaks of ancient mountains and carved deep valleys. When the climate warmed, the sea rushed in where ice had ruled. Once-proud mountains formed a granite-and-sandstone archipelago, known today as the San Juan Islands. Each day green-and-white ferries bridge four of the 172 named isles with Anacortes and the mainland.

About two-thirds of the islands' permanent residents live on either San Juan or Orcas islands. Because it sits at the end of the ferry line and boasts the only "real" town, San Juan Island makes a good place to begin tours.

The approach to Friday Harbor—a community of some twelve hundred residents—brings views of herons and gulls and a forest of bobbing masts within the marina. Once on land, storefront signs tell a story of small-town friendliness and familiarity. Greetings pour from Malloy's Hardware, Whitey's Food Center, Roman's Treasures, and Herb's Tavern.

Except for visiting the Whale Museum or dancing to the San Juan Island Dixieland Jazz Festival in July, nature is what this island advertises. With a map from the chamber in hand, take Argyle Road out of town and begin to explore.

San Juan Island's fifty-six square miles present a panoply of landscapes. Seldom-traveled country roads crisscross the island's heart. They cut through fields blushing with poppies and lupine and past pastures occupied by horses, cows, and sheep.

On the island's south side, from Cattle Point to False Bay, gnarled and wind-battered firs stand atop hills of wind-swept grasses. Below, rocky beaches littered with driftwood border the waters of Haro Strait. This is where the Americans garrisoned themselves from 1859 to 1872 during the Pig War.

Throughout this nonwar in which the only casualty was a wayward hog, the English took up residence at the opposite end of the island, where the environment is forested and hilly. About halfway between the two undeveloped sites stands Lime Kiln Lighthouse. This area features some excellent spots for picnics. With luck, you might even spot a whale.

Horseshoe-shaped Orcas Island is the most developed and the most popular destination point in the islands. Unlike San Juan Island, it boasts a rugged exterior: steep cliffs rim its shoreline and forested mountains make up its interior. The villages, particularly Eastsound and Olga, are worth a visit. Again, the best way to explore is to simply ride the roads: there are only a few, so it is impossible to get lost for very long.

The island's primary calling card is five thousand-acre Moran State Park. The park offers twenty-six miles of hiking trails, more than twenty-five picnic sites, swimming, fishing, and boating. (Rentals are available at both Cascade and Mountain lakes.) Ruling over the park, twenty-four hundred-foot Mount Constitution offers spectacular views of the San Juan Islands, Washington, and British Columbia. For the best scenes, walk to the top of the stone tower that rises above the summit.

Of the other two islands serviced by ferry, only Lopez is worth a visit. Its meadows and farmlands paint a pastoral portrait. Of special note, the island's relatively flat terrain and uncrowded byways create a haven for bicyclists.

A PRACTICAL GUIDE TO WASHINGTON'S ISLANDS

THE CLIMATE

Bainbridge and Whidbey islands feature much the same weather as Seattle, although rain is less frequent on Whidbey. The San Juan Islands lie at the north end of the Juan de Fuca banana belt and also receive fewer gray and rainy days than does Seattle.

YOUR CLOTHES

Your attire on any of the islands should always be comfortable and casual. Beach shoes, which are comfortable and will not be ruined by salt and sand, are a must. Light jackets and sweaters are necessary for ferry travel and cool evenings.

WASHINGTON STATE FERRIES

Ferries run on regular schedules, which change several times a year. They normally run on time, but long boarding lines can be a problem during summer months. If you must be on a particular ferry, line up early. The ferries are clean and comfortable. They provide amenities such as rest rooms and food service; however the food is overpriced. The Bainbridge Island ferry leaves from Seattle; Whidbey Island ferries depart from both Port Townsend and Mukilteo; trips to the San Juan Islands begin in Anacortes. For schedules call (206) 464-6400 (inside Seattle) or 800-542-7052 (inside Washington).

AIR TRANSPORTATION

Ferries are not the only way to reach Whidbey, San Juan, Orcas, and Lopez islands. Lake Union Air will deliver you to these destinations by floatplane. Call 206-284-0300 for more information. San Juan Airlines also serves the San Juan Islands (206-622-6077).

VISITOR INFORMATION

For more information, contact the following: Bainbridge Island Chamber of Commerce, 166 Winslow Way East, Bainbridge Island, WA 98110 (206-842-3700); Central Whidbey Chamber of Commerce, P.O. Box 152, Coupeville, WA 98239; Langley Chamber of Commerce, P.O. Box 403, Langley, WA 98260; San Juan Island Chamber of Commerce, P.O. Box 98, Friday Harbor, WA 98250; Orcas Island Chamber of Commerce, P.O. Box 252, Eastsound, WA 98245; or Tourism Development Division, 101 General Administration Building, AX-13, Olympia, WA 98504-0613 (800-562-4570, inside Washington, and 800-541-9274, outside Washington).

POINTS OF INTEREST

FAY BAINBRIDGE STATE PARK. Northeast corner of Bainbridge Island. Picnicking, boating, beach, and Seattle skyline views.

MAXWELTON BEACH. Southwest corner of Whidbey Island. Excellent Dungeness crabbing.

LANGLEY. Lower east side of Whidbey Island. Charming town perched on bluff overlooking Saratoga Passage. Good browsing. Views.

FORT CASEY STATE PARK. Just south of Coupeville, Whidbey Island. Fishing, diving, views, and small museum.

COUPEVILLE. North-central Whidbey Island. Historic preservation district. One of Washington's oldest towns.

FORT EBEY STATE PARK. West of Coupeville, Whidbey Island. Picnicking, beach walking, and views.

DECEPTION PASS STATE PARK. Northern tip of Whidbey Island. Said to be Washington's most popular park. Hiking, beach walking, picnicking, fishing, boating, and views.

THE WHALE MUSEUM. First and Court streets, Friday Harbor, San Juan Island. A small but interesting museum that looks into the lives of whales.

AMERICAN CAMP. Southern foot of San Juan Island. Little remains of the former garrison, but there are over one thousand acres of beaches and grasslands.

ENGLISH CAMP. Northwest side of San Juan Island on Garrison Bay. Historic display. Several restored buildings. Picnicking and hiking.

HOTEL DE HARO. Historic hotel on northern corner of San Juan Island. Teddy Roosevelt once stayed here. Part of Roche Harbor Resort.

MORAN STATE PARK. Makes up five thousand acres of eastern Orcas Island. Views from atop Mount Constitution. Hiking, fishing, swimming, boating, and picnicking.

RESTAURANTS OF NOTE

As you might expect, gourmet dining is a rare experience on the islands. However, the following restaurants can be relied upon to serve good food, although service may be more than a bit casual. The restaurants are listed by location, beginning with Bainbridge Island.

SALTWATER CAFE. 403 Madison Avenue, Winslow, Bainbridge Island (206-842-8339). Seafood prepared Cajun-style. Views of Eagle Harbor.

LE QUAI. 4813 Highway 525, Clinton, Whidbey Island (206-321-1071). Perhaps the best food on Whidbey Island. A small menu featuring French country-style cuisine.

NEW BAY CAFE. Lopez Village, Lopez Island (206-468-2204). A cozy, cheery atmosphere with good Mexican food.

CHRISTINA'S. Eastsound, Orcas Island (206-376-4904). Waterfront location. Professional service. Fresh local seafood. Excellent desserts.

DEER HARBOR INN. Deer Harbor, Orcas Island (206-376-4110). Rustic setting. Fresh seafood. Homemade ice cream.

DUCK SOUP INN. Roche Harbor Road, about four and a half miles north of Friday Harbor, San Juan Island (206-378-4878). Fresh seafood. Good pasta. Service can be curt.

WINSTON'S. 95 Nichols Street, Friday Harbor, San Juan Island (206-378-5093). Located in a restored Victorian house. Steaks and seafood.

All of these restaurants operate short and sometimes irregular hours. Call ahead to ensure they are open.

WHERE TO STAY

THE BOMBAY HOUSE

This turn-of-the-century home is tucked away on the southeast side of Bainbridge Island, just fifteen minutes from the ferry dock at Winslow. Its convenient location encourages guests to climb about the concrete canyons and mountains of Seattle during the day, top off their city adventure with a first-class dinner, then ferry to The Bombay House for a night in the country.

The home rises in three stories of classic Victorian, with a widow's walk crowning the pitched roof. The yards are made up of sloping lawns and flourishing flower gardens. In one corner, evergreens shade a cedar gazebo. The waters of Rich Passage ripple beyond the rooftops of West Blakely.

An eclectic blend of antique pieces appoint the home's interiors. But comfort is never sacrificed just for an old-fashioned look.

In the living room, plump furniture surrounds a large brick fireplace. Antique pieces include an 1850 square grand piano, an old loom, and four handcrafted violins.

A totally different environment exists in the modern kitchen/dining

The Bombay House (Kay Green)

room. This is a family style setting, where guests join innkeepers Bob Scott and Georgene Hagen for morning breakfast or perhaps afternoon coffee. On the other side of a sliding glass door, bird feeders alive with songbirds swing above the deck.

The country antique look dominates the five guest rooms. The largest accommodation, and the only one with views, sits upstairs. Among its antique pieces are a wood stove and a cradle filled with magazines and books.

Location brings The Bombay House to the forefront but there are other things to like about this bed and breakfast. At the top of the list stands a particularly good job of blending comfort and charm.

*   *   *

The Bombay House, 8490 Northeast Beck Road, Bainbridge Island, WA 98110 (206-842-3926). Five guest rooms, three with private baths. Rates range from $50 to $78 (subject to change). American Express. Children with prior approval; no pets; smoking permitted. From downtown Winslow, take a right on Madison to a left on Wyatt. From Wyatt, follow Blakely Avenue to West Blakely Avenue. Beck Road is the first street on the right.

CAROLINE'S

Frequent travelers to Whidbey Island will remember this remodeled turn-of-the-century farmhouse as Sally's. But, as so often happens in this business, an innkeeper has moved on. New owner Caroline Satterberg has moved in. The home is as charming and beautiful as ever.

The dormered, two-story exterior seems simple compared to many of the mansions that make up bed-and-breakfast real estate. But once inside, the home's country elegance sparkles like Tiffany.

The living room's walls are wrapped in sea green floral-print wallpaper and thick pile carpeting covers the floor. There is an emerald green Vermont castings wood stove standing before a custom fieldstone fireplace. Belgian drapes, a Louis XIV clock, and a mixture of classic French Provincial and Queen Anne furniture complete the scene.

The dining room is equally formal, whereas the sun-room is far more relaxed. It overlooks the backyard's gardens and outbuildings. Walls of glass and a ceiling of cedar create a rustic look. In the center of the room sits a large oak table. Plants and flowers add dabs of color. Adjacent to the sun-room, there is a spacious wooden deck. Both the sun-room and the deck host the homemade breakfast.

A potpourri of fragrances waft from all three guest rooms. The two upstairs accommodations feature wood floors, sloped ceilings, and Laura

Caroline's (Kay Green)

Ashley prints. Both boast water and mountain views. A more modern feeling pervades the downstairs Starlite Room, so named because of the skylight above the brass queen-size bed.

Since 1983, this home has been one of Washington's most popular bed and breakfasts. Its elegance is a primary reason. But its list of amenities, including exercise equipment and a hot tub, also contributes to its success.

*   *   *

Caroline's, 215 Sixth Street, P.O. Box 459, Langley, WA 98260 (206-221-8709). Three guest rooms, all with private baths. Rates are $65 (subject to change). VISA/MasterCard. No children; no pets; no smoking. From the Clinton ferry dock, take State Route 525 to Langley Road. This becomes Camano Avenue, which accesses Sixth Street.

LONE LAKE

Lone Lake on Whidbey Island is a two-cottage getaway that represents the efforts of Ward and Delores Meeks. They opened their arms to guests in 1984 after Ward retired and realized he was not the retiring type. From having been with the man on several separate occasions, I would have to say that is an understatement. His pace resembles a quarter horse, and his body is always racing to catch up with his mind. So it is not surprising that Lone Lake is designed around things to do.

Much of the activity takes advantage of the tiny lake that fronts the property. Sitting in a rural valley and as still as a country night, the lake is home to swans, ducks, and blue heron. In addition, it teems with thousands of rainbow trout.

With a fishing license in hand, guests are welcome to cast their lines into the waters. They can do it from the dock or they can troll from one of the rowboats or canoes. These vessels are also available just for sailing around the lake, as are a sailboat and a paddle-wheel boat.

There is also plenty for landlubbers to do. There are tables and a fire pit on the beach for picnicking, games such as croquet, horseshoes, and pickle ball, and bicycles for touring the island's back roads.

While Ward seems to be the recreation director, Delores is in charge of catering to guests' needs. The cottages, although modest in decor, boast more extras than a Cecil B. De Mille movie. The kitchens are completely stocked from staples to utensils; the bathrooms have everything from shampoo to curling irons; living rooms boast VCRs with a common film library, as well as books, magazines, and games.

*   *   *

Lone Lake, 5206 South Bayview Road, Langley, WA 98260 (206-321-5325). Two cottages. Rates range from $65 to $75 (subject to change). VISA/ MasterCard. Children and small pets with prior approval; smoking discouraged. Breakfast is delivered to the cottages on silver trays. From the Clinton ferry dock, take State Route 525 five and a half miles to Bayview Road. Turn right. Lone Lake will be on the left.

Lone Lake (Courtesy Lone Lake)

The Saratoga Inn

There is a theory floating around that proclaims a bed-and-breakfast inn must be old to have charm. If it is not Victorian or at least turn of the century, it is probably just another building. The Saratoga Inn, which was built in 1982, tears that theory to shreds.

Sitting on twenty-five acres of woods and meadows, the two-story, shingle-clad Cape Cod building looks out across Whidbey Island to Saratoga Passage and the Cascade Mountains. The large inn radiates country charm. There are sunburst gables, beveled-glass windows, wide verandas, English cottage gardens, and a picket fence that frames the entire picture. All of this represents the dream of Debbie and Ted Jones.

"We were living in southern California," Debbie says, "and wanted to start a business in a rural setting. My kids were grown and I needed something to do. But I wanted to do it at home."

Innkeeping seemed ideal. In a period of two weeks, Debbie flew to Whidbey Island, purchased this property and began making plans to build a new inn—one with modern conveniences and amenities—that looked old. The Saratoga Inn represents the results of those efforts. It welcomed its first guests in the spring of 1983.

The downstairs is open and airy. To one side sits a dining area, while the spacious living room occupies the remaining space. There are hardwood oak floors, hanging quilts, a used brick fireplace, and a blend of country antiques, Chippendale, and Queen Anne furniture. In the

The Saratoga Inn (Kay Green)

mornings, breakfast trays are left on a walnut Welch dresser in the dining area for guests to enjoy their morning meal in either this setting or out on the veranda.

All five guest rooms occupy the second floor. These quiet and crisp rooms make positive statements about new buildings: the walls are thick, the floors are solid, and the bathrooms are modern. Still, there is charm everywhere. There are Moreno wool blankets and down pillows on the beds, flannel sheets in the winter; English soaps in the bathrooms; Franklin stoves in Willow and Country Garden; a wicker rocker in Queen Anne's Lace and a willow rocker in Meadow; and a pine headboard distinguishing Hollyhock.

A place this large keeps Debbie busy, so if there is a drawback it exists in the absence of personal coddling—some might call that the presence of privacy. In any case, the inn provides enough pampering to satisfy just about anyone's needs.

*   *   *

The Saratoga Inn, 4850 South Coles Road, Langley, WA 98260 (206-221-7526). Five guest rooms, all with private baths. Rates range from $65 to $80 (subject to change). No credit cards. No children; no pets; no smoking. From the Clinton ferry dock, take State Route 525 to Coles Road. Turn right toward Langley. The inn will be marked by a gravel entranceway and sign on the left just before Brooks Hill Road.

GUEST HOUSE

The 1920s farmhouse sits on a tiny patch of rolling meadow, which tucks neatly into a forest of evergreens. State Route 525 passes in front of the house, while glimpses of Saratoga Passage and the Cascade Mountains peek through the roadside forest. Inside the farmhouse sits a single bed-and-breakfast accommodation called the Wildflower Suite. Tradition marks its features, which include a private entrance, sitting room, and private bath.

Guest House goes beyond tradition with its other facilities, however. Besides being remote from the main house, they are more spacious and private than most bed-and-breakfast accommodations.

Three cottages lie on the edge of the woods behind the farmhouse. Hansel & Gretel is a rustic log cabin, complete with a sleeping loft. The Carriage House boasts two skylights and a large picture window, knotty pine walls and an antique brass bed. The Farm Guest Cottage features a large deck. All of the cottages include televisions, airtight fireplaces, kitchens, electric heat, and baths.

The real star at Guest House, however, is a twenty-two hundred-

Guest House (Kay Green)

square-foot lodge that overlooks a wildlife pond. It was originally built as a
private home and includes air conditioning, a microwave oven, a
dishwasher, wall-to-wall carpeting, and two televisions. The lodge is
furnished in antiques, has a king-size bed and two large bathrooms. As
might be expected, booking the entire home is expensive; however, it is
possible to rent only the master bedroom suite.

   Although Guest House is a bed and breakfast, it feels more like a small
rustic resort with its variety of accommodations and amenities such as a
swimming pool and an exercise room. Travelers who embrace tradition
and a homey atmosphere may find this setting disconcerting. On the other
hand, those who enjoy privacy and extra amenities should find Guest

House very appealing.

*   *   *

Guest House, 835 East Christenson Road, Greenbank, WA 98253 (206-678-3115). One guest room, three cottages, and a log lodge, all with private baths. Rates range from $60 to $125 (subject to change). VISA/MasterCard. No children under fourteen; no pets; no smoking. Breakfast is done on a small scale (cereal, juice, etc.) and is optional. (Rates are $5 less without breakfast.) From the Clinton ferry dock, take State Route 525 sixteen miles to Christenson Road. Then take the first driveway on the right for Guest House.

HOME BY THE SEA

Sharon Fritts-Drew is the kind of person who makes you want to do something, to buy a ticket and go someplace, to quit your job and take a risk. She is an adventurer and a pioneer. How else would you describe a person who spent seven years teaching in Iran and three in Afghanistan? Neither are exactly the kinds of places you dream of spending peaceful days and quiet nights.

So when Sharon returned to the United States, you might think she would be happy just enjoying her beach home on Whidbey Island. There were the freighters steaming past and the geese, ducks, gulls, and

Home By The Sea (Kay Green)

sandpipers feeding and nesting nearby.

But something was missing. She was lonely. So she opened her home to travelers. She turned it into a bed and breakfast. In 1980, Sharon's home represented one of only three or four bed and breakfasts in the entire state. Most people did not even know what they were.

This is a homey place; it is traditional. Accommodations are spare upstairs bedrooms. They would serve as guest rooms even if this were not a bed and breakfast.

Smells tell you something about the place, too. They are vital to the ambience. They evoke thoughts of home. There is always coffee brewing or Norwegian bread baking.

The decor is inviting and natural. Sharon bought the furnishings and appointments herself, not to impress guests. Of course, you have to remember where she lived for ten years. The tribal Persian carpets and the brass Persian samovar, along with a number of other Middle Eastern treasures, are quite natural to Sharon, although they may seem a bit unusual in a two-story cedar beach house with a hot tub on the deck.

But that is part of the home's charm. It puts on no airs. Sharon is just herself, and guests can just kick off their shoes and be themselves. Home By The Sea promises casual hospitality in a natural, comfortable setting.

*   *   *

Home By The Sea, 2388 East Sunlight Beach Road, Clinton, WA 98236 (206-221-2964). Two guest rooms, both with private baths. Rates are $72 (subject to change). VISA/MasterCard. No children; no pets; no smoking. Full breakfast is served. From the Clinton ferry dock, take State Route 525 to a left on Bayview Road. (Look for Bayview Center.) Sunlight Beach Road will be on your right.

PILLARS BY THE SEA

Located on Whidbey Island, overlooking Holmes Harbor, this two-story gabled house was recently rescued from despair by Ellen and Walker Jordan. It was built in 1907 as a private residence but soon fell to other uses. Then in 1924 it returned to being a home; however, by 1979 the house drooped from neglect—its floors and walls sagged, its foundation seemed ready to crumble. That is when the Jordans purchased it for their retirement home and undertook extensive renovation. They restored its life and in the process added a front porch with cedar pillars, built back decks, put on cedar siding, and opened up the first floor to views of the harbor. In May of 1983, they decided the only thing missing was lots of company, so the Jordans began welcoming bed-and-breakfast guests.

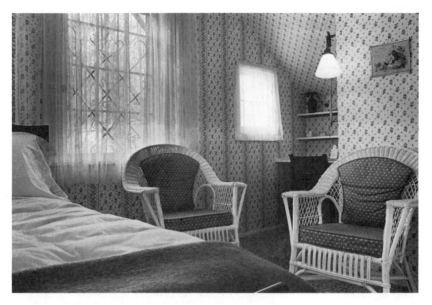

Pillars By The Sea (Kay Green)

Today, there are three guest rooms occupying the home—the Master Suite downstairs and the upstairs East and West rooms. The Master Suite conjures up visits to relatives' homes. There are portraits of the Jordan family gracing the walls and the atmosphere is much more homey than innlike. On the other hand, the upstairs rooms boast a traditional antique style. The East Room features an antique dresser and canopy bed, while the West Room has miniature rose-print wallpaper and hand-embroidered pillow cases. Both rooms offer tastes of elegant country living.

Like many bed and breakfasts, the morning meal is a special time. It is served in the dining room, which looks out on the water. Cranberry crystal and polished silver provide a very proper setting, while the menu features homemade items such as corn-apple hot cakes and freshly baked date muffins.

Of all the islands' bed and breakfasts, Pillars By The Sea is most like visiting with your very own grandparents. The credit for this atmosphere goes to Ellen and Walker Jordan.

*   *   *

Pillars By The Sea, 1367 East Bayview Avenue, Freeland, WA 98249 (206-221-7738). Three guest rooms, all with private baths. Rates are $60 (subject to change). VISA/MasterCard. Children with prior approval; no pets; no smoking. From the Clinton ferry dock, take State Route 525 eleven miles to Cameron Road, turn right and proceed to East Bayview in Freeland.

CHANNEL HOUSE

Anacortes is called "the gateway to the San Juan Islands." Ferries to the islands and to Victoria leave daily from this seaside town, which is just ten miles from Deception Pass State Park and Whidbey Island and only forty miles west of the Cascade Mountains. Travelers might find this a good starting point for exploring this corner of Washington.

Overlooking Guemes Channel, just five minutes from the ferry landing, Channel House represents one of Washington's finest bed and breakfasts. The house was built in 1902 for an Italian count; it still reflects gracious living.

The main floor is given over to the living room, library, and two guest rooms, where oak floors and Persian carpets weave a common thread. The library is warm and cozy, a good place to curl up and read. On the other hand, the living room commands an elegant rather than intimate atmosphere. It boasts a brick fireplace, French doors leading to a solarium, and a stained-glass window. It is better suited for admiration than conversation.

There are two main floor guest rooms. Canopy features a romantic canopy bed, fainting couch, and views of the channel. Wicker is cozy and boasts a touch of country.

The best upstairs room is Mahogany. It has views of green islands, blue waters, and white ferries. In addition, a lace bedspread adorns the

Channel House (Kay Green)

mahogany bed, an antique rocker and a wood stove surround a Persian carpet, and a brick chimney forms a pillar in the room's center.

All four guest rooms have floral-print wallpaper, large fluffy towels, fresh flowers, handcrafted dolls, music boxes, and turndown service. The innkeepers, Sam and Kathy Salzinger, serve a homemade breakfast in their ornate dining room, and they offer their hot tub for sunsets and wine.

*　　*　　*

Channel House, 2902 Oakes Avenue, Anacortes, WA 98221 (206-293-9382). Four guest rooms share two baths. Rates are $55 (subject to change). No credit cards. No children; no pets; no smoking. From downtown Anacortes, turn left onto 12th Street, which runs into Oakes Avenue. Look for Channel House on the right.

BLUE HERON

The Blue Heron is a two-story bungalow that sits hidden on a knoll planted with trees. The veranda and balcony look across a winding country lane to the gray waters and steep bluffs of West Sound. Except for a feeling of pastoral calm, the image gives little hint of what to expect inside.

The living room is cozy and has a brick fireplace. You walk through French doors to enter a spacious dining room, which has a fir floor, bay window, and dark wood trim. Furnishings include a large antique table, cabinets, and a buffet.

Polished fir floors maintain a rural sense upstairs, but the doors and trim have been painted turquoise, promoting an Art Deco look. Of the three accommodations, only Library lacks views. But its skylit antique bed and cozy setting make very pleasant surroundings. Both Balcony and the Suite are dormer rooms, providing those slopes and angles that always add charm. By far, the Suite is the grandest accommodation in the house. It features a large private bathroom, and it has a sitting area that looks through French doors, across the balcony, to the waters beyond. In each room guests find a basket full of goodies and complimentary sherry.

In the summer, breakfast is served buffet-style so guests can take theirs outside if they wish; the rest of the year it is served in the dining room. In both scenarios, it includes delicacies such as brioche, egg dishes, fruit crepes, and bacon and sausage.

Like all island bed and breakfasts, the Blue Heron is a quiet place. But it is also secure enough to make some bold statements.

*　　*　　*

Blue Heron, Route 1, Box 64, Eastsound, WA 98245 (206-376-2954). Three guest rooms, one with a private bath. Rates range from $35 to $90 (subject

Blue Heron (Courtesy Blue Heron)

to change). No credit cards. Children and pets with prior approval; smoking permitted. From the ferry dock, follow the signs three miles to West Sound. Blue Heron will be on the right.

KANGAROO HOUSE

"We try to keep things simple and comfortable," innkeeper Polly Nisbet says. "I think bed and breakfast should be homelike. That's what we strive for."

In many ways, Polly's philosophy dominates at Kangaroo House on Orcas Island. A guest here does feel more like he is staying in a home than in an inn. There are no pretensions. The guest rooms are cozy and avoid frills. Life is simple. And Polly and Ken's well-behaved children and pets

Kangaroo House (Courtesy Kangaroo House)

provide a family setting.

There also is a sense of whimsy at Kangaroo House. This fanciful feeling is rooted in history.

The house, a two-story bungalow, was built in 1907. The environment remained relatively staid until 1953. That is when Captain Harold "Cap" Ferris returned from a voyage to the south Australian coast with a new friend—a kangaroo named Josie. From then on, the house was a beehive of activity. Islanders, young and old alike, used to delight in Josie's bouncing antics. They also took to calling the private home Kangaroo House.

Cap and Josie are gone, but Polly and Ken retain the house's name and Josie's memory. They have planted kangaroo images all about the place.

Besides kangaroos, the house boasts comfort. Downstairs, the living room has a welcome atmosphere. The stone fireplace, fir floor, open beams, and wall quilts paint a pastoral scene, while Persian carpets and attractive stuffed furniture speak of understated elegance.

All of the accommodations sit upstairs. There are five guest rooms. They have painted board floors and country antiques. Comforters warm the beds, and soaps and lotions sit atop dressers. In the hallway, a bowl of fresh fruit invites snacking.

In the mornings, there are farm-fresh eggs, freshly baked berry muffins, and just-squeezed juice. The setting features oak tables, bright flowers, and rural views.

Although tranquil, rustic charms do have some drawbacks. At Kangaroo House it is the bathroom situation. While four of the rooms have sinks, there is but one full bath to accommodate the five rooms. Even this trade-off, however, may add to the simple and homey environment Polly wishes to inspire.

*   *   *

Kangaroo House, P.O. Box 334, North Beach Road, Eastsound, WA 98245 (206-376-2175). Five guest rooms share one and a half baths. Rates range from $45 to $55 (subject to change). VISA/MasterCard. Children with prior approval; no pets; smoking in living room only. From the ferry dock, follow the signs to Eastsound. Turn left at North Beach Road. The inn is on the left one mile.

TURTLEBACK FARM INN

The arrival of Turtleback Farm has taken too long. Despite its resorts and refurbished hotel, Orcas Island has had a void in its travelers' accommodations. In 1985, the hole was filled by a first-class country inn.

This is another story of mutual rebirth. Both the house and the innkeepers, Bill and Susan Fletcher, needed a change.

"We flew up from the Bay Area, saw this property and had an attack of insanity," Sue says.

Perhaps insanity is too kind a word. What they saw was a ramshackle pile of boards that framed a turn-of-the-century farmhouse. Of course, there were also the eighty acres of forest and farmland to consider, not to mention potential.

Turtleback Farm Inn (Lewis Green)

Today, following five months of intensive reconstruction and renovation, the farmhouse sparkles. Every detail honors craftsmanship.

The living room is elegant. A fir mantelpiece adorns the brick fireplace, which rises before overstuffed furniture. A Persian carpet adorns the fir floor. The nearby dining room looks out across a split-level deck to rolling pastures.

A feeling of openness and freedom dominates each of the seven guest rooms, except for The Bunk Room, which is surprisingly confining. More typical are Valley View in the north wing and Meadow View in the south wing. Both are spacious, open spaces that look out on the valley and the hills. Both have polished woods, walls of windows, American antiques, and private decks. The rooms upstairs share these same characteristics. Other than Bunk, only Garden View lacks scenes of the countryside.

In every sense of the word this place is an inn. It does not feature an air of homeyness. And except for its surroundings, it does not offer a sense of the Northwest. There is more of a California climate here. The rooms look and feel alike. Everything has been carefully laid out, spontaneity does not seem to have played a role. But as a bed-and-breakfast country inn, this place is a first-class role model.

*   *   *

Turtleback Farm Inn, Route 1, Box 650, Eastsound, WA 98245 (206-376-4914). Seven guest rooms, all with private baths. Rates range from $45 to $75 (subject to change). VISA/MasterCard. Children with prior approval; no pets; no smoking. From the ferry dock, follow the signs toward West Sound. Turn right on Crow Valley Road. The inn is on the right, about two miles from West Sound.

WOODSONG

One of my objectives in doing this book is to give you, the traveler, a wide variety of quality bed and breakfasts. Without a range of accommodations, a book such as this would end up looking like an elitist guide to gilded mansions and inns. If that had been my course, places such as Woodsong on Orcas Island could not be included.

Built as the West Sound School in the early 1900s, the sounds of school bells, children's laughter, and teachers' admonitions rang throughout its eaves until 1955. Then it became a hall of patriotism for the American Legion until 1978. That was its final year of public service.

The structure was then completely remodeled and transformed into a spacious home. In 1981, Carol and Alby Meyer bought the red barnlike building. At the time, they were living in San Francisco but were looking for a place to retire in the islands.

Woodsong (Kay Green)

"We just saw this place by chance," Carol says, "fell in love with it, and thought it would make a great guest house. Both of us enjoy staying in New England inns, and this place reminds us of New England."

Upon entering through large double Canadian spruce doors, guests step into an open combination living and dining room. It is furnished with a blend of antiques and features comfortable sitting areas. A ceiling fan circulates the dry, warm air pouring from the Vermont castings wood stove, and a wall of windows looks out on a sprawling meadow and a grove of fir trees.

Both upstairs guest rooms have sloped ceilings, patterned wallpapers, and country antiques. Fresh flowers and green plants add touches of homeyness.

Tradition dominates the setting at Woodsong, including the ideas of personal attention and low rates. While all inns appeal to different tastes, it is hard to imagine the bed-and-breakfast traveler who would not be comfortable at Woodsong.

*   *   *

Woodsong, P.O. Box 32, Orcas, WA 98280 (206-376-2340). Two guest rooms share one and a half baths. Rates are $50 (subject to change). No credit cards. Children with prior approval; no pets; no smoking in guest rooms. From the ferry dock, follow the signs to West Sound. Woodsong is on the left, about two miles from the landing.

SAN JUAN INN

The venerable San Juan Inn on San Juan Island has been a Friday Harbor landmark since 1873. Originally called the Bay View Hotel, it was built to serve the steamer trade out of Victoria and Seattle. In later years, the two-story building became known as the San Juan Hotel and began traveling down a path toward steady decline.

However, like so many Northwest hostelries, the hotel became a rescue project for Californians escaping the pace of their homeland. In 1979, Norm and Joan Schwinge left their corporate jobs in Los Angeles and took the innkeeping plunge.

"The hotel was in terrible shape," Norm says. "It looked like a good wind would carry it away. But being too ignorant to know better, we just thought we could bring it back."

Norm is being modest. If this refurbished inn is the result of ignorance, then we should immediately begin burning books and praising stupidity. The San Juan Inn represents a sparkling model of turn-of-the-century living, certainly not the work of ignorance.

When you enter the cozy foyer, you leave today on the doorstep. Clear

San Juan Inn (Lewis Green)

cedar paneling adorns the walls, while overstuffed furniture, large potted plants, and an 1873 marble-top sideboard make up the decor. A short flight of stairs leads upstairs to the parlor and ten guest rooms.

All of the accommodations are furnished in nineteenth-century American antiques—including brass or wicker beds—and boast polished woods, wallpaper, lace curtains, old-fashioned bedspreads, plants and flowers, and old black-and-white family portraits. Room four offers peaks of the harbor, while room eight features great water views. Rooms one, two, nine, and ten overlook a courtyard filled with lilacs, roses, and a one-hundred-year-old holly tree.

As well as hosting breakfast, the parlor is a comfortable room for reading or simply staring through the windows to the harbor. The oak floor, wainscoting, floral-print wallpaper, and an array of unique antiques make up the decor.

Location, setting, and ambience distinguish the San Juan Inn. Like all inns, there are some drawbacks: breakfast is continental and less elaborate than most served by bed and breakfasts, and bathrooms are limited to three in the hall. Despite these limitations, however, the inn boasts an island of charm and is a pleasant getaway.

*   *   *

San Juan Inn, 50 Spring Street, P.O. Box 776, Friday Harbor, WA 98250-0776 (206-378-2070). Ten guest rooms share three hall baths. Rates range from $40 to $42 (subject to change). VISA/MasterCard. No babies; no pets; smoking permitted. The inn is located one-half block from the ferry dock. Just follow the flow of traffic.

Wharfside Bed & Breakfast (Kay Green)

WHARFSIDE BED & BREAKFAST

Although the idea is beginning to catch on, the sixty-foot sailing vessel known as the *Jacquelyn* was the first floating bed and breakfast in the

Northwest. Her tall masts and rigging bob in the Friday Harbor Marina at San Juan Island.

Launched in 1972, this wooden beauty was built to fill its hold with fish. But Clyde and Bette Rice had other ideas when they first laid eyes on its sleek lines.

Clyde, who looks like he just stepped out of an Ernest Hemingway novel, has salt water flowing through his veins. He was sloshing around San Francisco Bay in his bassinet, when most of us were at the age of simply trying to overcome wet diapers. He grew up feeling more at home on the sea than on land. Bette, whose smile could launch a thousand ships, makes the perfect first mate.

The first things that popped into my mind when I made plans for staying on the *Jacquelyn* involved inconveniences. Would I feel like I was sleeping in a closet or might I succumb to motion sickness? Both fears were quickly allayed.

While you do have to watch your head in both accommodations—the aft state-room and the forward cabin—the berths are surprisingly roomy. In fact, the state-room has a queen-size bed and a private head. As for motion sickness, the gentle rocking is barely discernible and at night it is like falling asleep in the arms of your mother.

Besides the guest accommodations, the vessel holds a main salon and a cozy galley. A skylight brightens the salon, which is adorned with ash blue settees, pine paneling, an Oriental area rug, a captain's table, and a wood stove. A hearty (and I mean that seriously) seaman's breakfast is served daily in the galley or on the deck.

Normally, the *Jacquelyn* remains moored. But she can also be custom chartered for $100 per person a day for trips to Victoria or other points north. In addition, guided fishing trips and harbor tours are available aboard the Rice's Boston Whaler.

If there is a better way to experience the islands, I would be surprised. Wharfside brings island living into your bedroom and makes your stay here a personal San Juan Islands adventure rather than a vicarious experience.

*   *   *

Wharfside Bed & Breakfast, P.O. Box 1212, Friday Harbor, WA 98250 (206-378-5661). Two guest berths, one with a private bath. Rates range from $50 to $55 (subject to change). No credit cards. Children and pets with prior approval; smoking permitted. The *Jacquelyn* is moored at the end of K Dock at the Port of Friday Harbor Marina.

The Olympic Peninsula

W hen I think of a peninsula, I imagine a strip of land, often quite narrow, jutting into the sea. However, Washington's Olympic Peninsula is a great mass of land that makes up much of western Washington.

Bred in violence but imbued with tranquility, the peninsula thrusts its hulk into the Strait of Juan de Fuca to the north and creates a barricade to the sea on the west. It is mostly primeval wilderness, which draws its lifeblood from the very waters it holds at bay.

Forming the backbone of the peninsula, the Olympic Mountains rise above U-shaped valleys, alpine meadows, mountain woods, temperate rain forests, and tiny homespun villages. Much of the peninsula's landscape resides in the Olympic National Park.

Despite the peninsula's remoteness and untamed setting, the Olympic Loop Highway makes touring the area relatively easy (although the road makes few forays, and then only short ones, into the park). The loop is made up primarily of U.S. 101, which skirts the peninsula's length and breadth.

GETTING TO KNOW THE OLYMPIC PENINSULA

There are several ways to gain access to U.S. 101, but beginning at the southern end, several miles northwest of Olympia, seems a natural starting point.

From Potlatch to Quilcene, the highway channels between water and forest. Seaside villages—Hoodsport, Lilliwaup, Eldon, and Brinnon—edge the shore. In these little hamlets, everything seems connected to the sea. Docks reach out from beach houses; signs advertise oysters, clams, crab, shrimp, and salmon; and marinas bob with boats of every description.

Although the canal draws most visitors to this part of the peninsula, the wilderness also lures some to venture beyond the main highway.

Several roads, merely gray lines on a map, lead into the wild, traveling to parks such as Lake Cushman and Dosewallips and to the Mount Walker Lookout, whose turnoff is just north of Brinnon, past Dodie's Trading Post. From this viewpoint, much of Hood Canal and Puget Sound, framed within two mountain ranges, unfolds in a mural of glistening waters and rolling hills.

At Quilcene, famous for its oysters and commercial oyster farms, the highway turns its back on Hood Canal and travels toward Port Angeles, the peninsula's largest town and the gateway to both Victoria, British Columbia, and the Olympic National Park. Detours along the way lead to historic Port Townsend and a natural sand promontory called Dungeness Spit.

Port Townsend is a town of cafés and family restaurants, gift shops and craft stores. But its reputation endures on a bluff above downtown, where turn-of-the-century Victorian homes look through bay windows to views of Admiralty Inlet, the wooded hillsides of Whidbey Island, and the snowy slopes of the Cascade Mountains.

Many tourists come to see and tour these examples of Victorian architecture. However, Port Townsend is a community of culture, as well, so travelers should plan to visit during the Centrum Summer Arts Season (206-385-3102)—a cornucopia of music, dance, and theater—or the nationally famous Wooden Boat Festival (206-385-3628) in September.

Unlike the man-made wonders of Port Townsend, Dungeness Spit is a natural setting that helps you relax. Here, among the sun-bleached driftwood and tide flats, the shorebirds and sea creatures, the surf laps the shoreline, and the breezes fill with salty air.

Port Angeles represents the loop's midway point. This is a Northwest seaport whose livelihood sails on the Strait of Juan de Fuca. In recent years, however, tourists bound for Victoria, British Columbia, or the national park have helped to stabilize the town's economy.

Only seventeen miles from downtown, up good road, Hurricane Ridge climbs to five thousand feet and rises steeply above valleys. It looks out on mountain glaciers, the strait, and in the distance, the shores of Vancouver Island.

Leaving Port Angeles, U.S. 101 snakes southwest toward the Pacific. Just outside of town, State Route 112 leaves the highway for a narrow, winding trip along the north coast to Neah Bay and the Makah Indian Reservation, which is located in the northwest corner of the peninsula. This is a unique opportunity to experience a Northwest Indian culture and to explore the rugged terrain of Cape Flattery and Cape Alava.

Back on U.S. 101, just west of Sappho, the highway plunges south for its run along Washington's coast. Unlike Oregon's coast, the peninsula's Pacific mostly rolls beyond the sight of auto-tourists.

Except for tiny pockets of population, only the logging town of Forks bears any resemblance to organized civilization for the next 115 miles. It is also at Forks that travelers can take a detour to the ocean. Take the road to La Push, which leaves the highway 2 miles north of Forks. At this coastal village on the Quileute Indian Reservation, you will find sport fishing, sandy beaches, and ocean views.

The ocean nourishes Washington's temperate rain forests. Onshore breezes deliver some 140 inches of rain each year to the Hoh, Queets, and Quinault forests.

Thirteen miles south of Forks, a turnoff from U.S. 101 follows the Hoh River eighteen miles into the national park and the rain forest. A nearly constant deluge, which takes a brief vacation in the summer, has spawned a jungle. Only slivers of sunlight slant through a canopy of trees and morning fog. Moss hangs in fuzzy drapes, while the forest floor is a carpet of mosses, lichens, ferns, and rotting logs.

South of the Hoh rain forest, the highway briefly encounters the Pacific before darting inland once again toward Lake Quinault. This mountain lake also borders a rain forest, and the road leading to it makes an excellent scenic drive.

From Quinault to Aberdeen, U.S. 101 courses through rather ordinary country by Northwest standards. Aberdeen is a working-class community, which features few incentives for tourists. However, a final detour does offer rewards.

State Route 105 darts west from Aberdeen, twenty-two miles to the self-proclaimed salmon capitol of the world—Westport. Besides being a haven for deep-sea fishing, over eighteen miles of coastline lures travelers who enjoy crabbing, clamming, and beachcombing.

From here, you can continue south on State Route 105, which connects with U.S. 101 at Raymond and proceeds to the Long Beach Peninsula, or you can return to Aberdeen to complete the loop to Olympia.

A Practical Guide to the Olympic Peninsula

The Climate

While temperatures are mild year-round (60s and 70s in the summer, 40s and 50s in the winter), moisture levels vary from place to place. Along the Hood Canal, the weather is much like Seattle's. Between Port Townsend and Port Angeles, sunny days occur more frequently than in most parts of western Washington. The Olympics receive measurable snowfall during winter months. Gray skies, fog, and rain are not uncommon on the coast.

Your Clothes

Dress comfortably and always be prepared for cool and rainy weather, particularly on the coast. In the summer, it might be 80 degrees in Seattle while only 60 degrees near the ocean.

Visitor Information

For more information, write or call: Tourism Development Division, 101 General Administration Building, AX-13, Olympia, WA 98504-0613 (800-562-4570, inside Washington, or 800-541-9274, outside Washington). For information about Olympic National Park, write or call: Superintendent, Olympic National Park, 600 East Park Avenue, Port Angeles, WA 98362 (206-452-4501).

Points of Interest

LAKE CUSHMAN STATE PARK. Nine miles west of Hoodsport. Trout fishing. Excellent hiking trails into the high country.

MOUNT WALKER LOOKOUT. Just north of Brinnon. Views of Puget Sound.

PORT TOWNSEND. A Victorian seacoast town on the northeast tip of the peninsula. Home tours, shopping, views, and cultural events.

DUNGENESS SPIT. Located four and a half miles northwest of Sequim. National Wildlife Refuge. Hiking, horseback riding, boating, fishing, and clamming.

CLALLAM COUNTY MUSEUM. Lincoln and Fourth streets, Port Angeles (206-452-7831, ext. 364). Historical exhibits.

HURRICANE RIDGE. Seventeen miles south of Port Angeles. Hiking, picnicking, cross-country skiing, and views.

LAKE CRESCENT. Seventeen miles west of Port Angeles on U.S. 101. An eight-and-a-half-mile-long deep-water lake famous for its Beardslee Trout.

MARYMERE FALLS. Twenty miles west of Port Angeles on U.S. 101. An easy nature trail leads to the ninety-foot falls.

MAKAH MUSEUM AND CULTURAL CENTER. One hundred and twelve miles west of Port Angeles at the end of State Route 112 in Neah Bay (206-645-2711). A fine collection of Indian art and artifacts.

LA PUSH. Fifteen miles west of Forks. Sandy beaches and rocky shores. Fishing, hiking, and beachcombing.

HOH RAIN FOREST. Some thirty miles southeast of Forks. Road leaves U.S. 101 about thirteen miles south of Forks. Visitor center. Hiking.

LAKE QUINAULT. Some forty miles north of Aberdeen. Steelhead fishing, hiking, and scenic drives through rain forest.

WESTPORT. Twenty-two miles west of Aberdeen. Deep-sea charter fishing, beachcombing, and whale watching.

RESTAURANTS OF NOTE

Quality restaurants are rare commodities on the peninsula. The following are listed by community, beginning with the Port Townsend area.

THE AJAX CAFE. This funky restaurant is located in the tiny town of Port Hadlock south of Port Townsend (206-385-9821). Decor is so relaxed, it is nearly recumbent. But the service is friendly, and the seafood is good.

FOUNTAIN CAFE. 920 Washington Street, Port Townsend (206-385-1364). Expect good, fresh local seafood.

LANZA'S RISTORANTE. 1020 Lawrence Street, Port Townsend (206-385-6221). Italian food and seafood. Occasional live music.

WATER STREET DELI. 926 Water Street, Port Townsend (206-385-2422). Super clam bisque. Salads and sandwiches.

C'EST SI BON. 2300 Highway 101 East, Port Angeles (206-452-8888). An excellent French restaurant. Pleasant ambience.

THE COFFEE HOUSE RESTAURANT & GALLERY. 118 East First Street, Port Angeles (206-452-1459). Soups, salads, and sandwiches. Wonderful desserts. Weekend entertainment.

BILLY'S. Heron and G streets, Aberdeen (206-533-7144). Turn-of-the-century decor. Friendly service. Tall schooners of beer. Terrific burger.

WHERE TO STAY

ARCADIA COUNTRY INN

Bed and breakfast in Port Townsend has come to mean large doses of Victoriana. However, in 1983 the Arcadia Country Inn brought a different image to this seaside town—one steeped in country living.

Arcadia is a three-story brick-and-shingle farmhouse that sits outside of town on seventy acres of meadows and woods. A narrow country lane leads to a gravel driveway, which stretches between split-rail fences before circling in front of the wide porch. Inside the house, a feeling of tranquil openness dominates.

However, the ghosts of a not-so-quiet past still hang about the open beams. The house was originally built in 1908 to serve as a summer home for its wealthy owner. But this role was soon abandoned as Port Townsend's fortunes failed to prosper. By 1920, Arcadia was welcoming hungry travelers into its rooms, which were by then serving up restaurant

Arcadia Country Inn (Kay Green)

chicken.

After the smell of chicken faded in the late 1920s, travelers continued to motor up the long driveway. But they were not interested in food. Instead, they were coming to Arcadia to sample its bootleg whiskey and loose women. Federal raids discouraged this activity and eventually the house returned to more homely responsibilities.

Today, bed-and-breakfast travelers venture up the driveway. The home offers six guest rooms on the top two floors and two accommodations, a living room, parlor, and dining area on the main floor. All of the upstairs rooms feature rural views, some offer peeks of mountains. The environment is particularly inspiring to creative people, and the home has hosted several actors and writers.

Like most guest houses, antiques primarily make up the decor. There is a hot tub on the back deck. While soaking in the tub, it is not unusual to see a deer nibbling grass nearby.

Arcadia, which Webster's defines as any place of rural peace and simplicity, is a nice change of pace from Port Townsend's Victoriana.

        *   *   *

Arcadia Country Inn, 1891 South Jacob Miller Road, Port Townsend, WA 98368 (206-385-5245). Eight guest rooms, six with private baths. Rates range from $44 to $90 (subject to change). VISA/MasterCard. No children under twelve; no pets; no smoking. From State Route 20 heading into Port Townsend, turn left on Jacob Miller Road. The inn is on the right.

HASTINGS HOUSE INN

Hastings House represents the quintessential Port Townsend slice of Victoriana. Perched atop the bluff that overlooks Port Townsend Bay, the home demands reverence and respect. That has always been its purpose, even when it was originally built.

Hastings House Inn (Kay Green)

The house was constructed in 1890 as a temple for wealthy social climber Frank Hastings. Unfortunately, a depressed economy resulted in nothing more than a shell. While its three-story frame expressed the grandest elements of Queen Anne-style architecture, a lack of money prevented Hastings from installing even basic amenities, such as stairs and walls.

Eventually Hastings was forced to sell to a man named C. A. Olson, who finished the interior in a fashion that reflected turn-of-the-century wealth. Today, the house is a living museum of what Port Townsend had hoped to become.

All of the woodwork is hand-rubbed oak. There are curved windows, an octagonal cupola, and a rounded veranda. The house is furnished with antiques and draped in lace.

This opulence leads to results that are both positive and negative. The authentic environment inspires guests to lounge about their rooms; it also encourages nonguests to inquire about tours. These tours bring about the stringing of theater ropes across open doors to prevent visitors from tramping through the rooms. The technique may be functional for museums but it is not very homey for a bed and breakfast. Still, that may be a small drawback, especially since it only occurs during the day, when most guests will be out exploring.

There are seven guest rooms occupying the second and third floors. The Honeymoon Suite and the Ivory Tower Room are simply magnificent. Two antique double beds and a tower sitting room distinguish the suite, while grand views from the tower mark the Ivory Tower Room.

Now that it has been finished and kept in mint condition, the inn mirrors the grandeur that Frank Hastings could only dream of.

*   *   *

Hastings House Inn, 313 Walker Street, Port Townsend, WA 98368 (206-385-3553). Seven guest rooms—one with a full bath, four with half baths. Rates range from $45 to $75 (subject to change). VISA/MasterCard. Children with prior approval; no pets; no smoking. The inn sits on the edge of the bluff, overlooking the ferry dock and the marina.

THE JAMES HOUSE

In the late 1800s, movers and shakers predicted a golden future perched on Port Townsend's horizons. Unfortunately, it was a setting sun they saw rather than the dawn of a new day. But before reality brought the curtain down on the dream, wealthy citizens raised tributes to their successes. One such place was The James House, which today lays claim to being the Northwest's first guest house.

The James House (Kay Green)

The mansion was built in 1889 for the then exorbitant sum of ten thousand dollars, and boasted all the opulence of its time. Francis Wilcox James, the home's builder, installed parquet floors made of oak, walnut, and cherry and adorned the interior with woodwork of redwood and fir. Special attention was paid to the newel posts, and the spindles and bannisters carved from Virginia wild cherry. In addition, the mansion featured nine fireplaces, with ornate mantels and tile hearths.

Much of the home's early elegance remains, although the mansion is down to four fireplaces and there are some signs of wear. Still, because of its historical significance and grand proportions, the house remains a favorite among travelers.

Twelve guest rooms offer visitors a nice range of accommodations. All the rooms are adorned with period antiques, but each has its own personality. On the third floor, for example, rooms range from a cozy alcove with a fan-shaped window and angled ceiling, to a sunny room with splendid water and mountain views. The Bridal Suite, formerly the master bedroom, features a fireplace, morning room, and balcony, and distinguishes the second floor.

As well as offering unique accommodations for the leisure traveler, the spaciousness and Victorian elegance of the library, parlor, and dining room provide interesting facilities for meetings and weddings.

History dominates The James House. It is not as homey as some bed and breakfasts or as friendly as others. However, it does serve in bringing a luxurious yesterday closer to today.

*   *   *

The James House, 1238 Washington Street, Port Townsend, WA 98368 (206-385-1238). Twelve guest rooms plus a cottage. Three guest rooms and the cottage feature private baths. Rates range from $52 to $85 (subject to change). VISA/MasterCard. No children under twelve; no pets; smoking permitted. Breakfast is usually served in the country kitchen. The inn sits on the edge of the bluff, overlooking downtown and the bay.

LIZZIE'S

Few bed and breakfasts can match the charm and beauty of Lizzie's. This two-story Italianate villa with towering bay windows looks like the duchess of Port Townsend.

Inside, the mansion's parlor is distinguished by century-old French wallpaper and fir woodwork, while a hand-painted cast-iron fireplace crowned by a Louis XV rococo gilded mirror add to the rooms' stateliness.

The theme is continued in the adjacent music room. Again there is a hand-painted cast-iron fireplace. Surrounding it are a leather Chesterfield, claw-footed mahogany buffet, Chippendale love seat, and a 1925 grand piano.

In a more relaxed vein, the kitchen, where breakfast is taken, allows a breath of lighter air. Here a large oak table sits on pine flooring. Tall windows, purposefully drapeless, welcome showers of sunshine.

Like the parlor and the music room, all seven guest rooms sing the praises of wealth. Lizzie's is the most opulent, with its half-canopy high antique English bed, hand-painted fireplace, and Victorian wallpaper.

Lizzie's (Kay Green)

However, Georgia's Room, with 1840s furniture and painted rose walls, or Daisy's, boasting an Art Nouveau king-size bed, or Jessie's, featuring a high antique oak bed, are quite elegant as well.

Until 1985, Thelma Scudi welcomed guests to Lizzie's. In December of that year, Bill and Patti Wickline purchased the inn. Changes are imperceptible. There is still the fruit compote for breakfast, and there are lots of amenities, including down comforters on the beds and mints on the pillows.

Despite the home's elegance, Lizzie's remains a comfortable and inviting place. The fireplaces are meant for lighting, the furniture for relaxing, and the piano for playing.

*   *   *

Lizzie's, 731 Pierce Street, Port Townsend, WA 98368 (206-385-4168). Seven guest rooms, three with private baths. Rates range from $42 to $79 (subject to change). VISA/MasterCard. Children with prior approval; no pets; smoking permitted. Lizzie's sits atop the bluff, several blocks from Hastings House.

THE TUDOR INN

Staying alive in any business requries imagination. That is especially true in the bed-and-breakfast industry, where rooms outnumber guests.

The Tudor Inn (Kay Green)

Innkeepers Jane and Jerry Glass of The Tudor Inn understand the competition for travelers' attention, so in addition to having an architecturally significant inn furnished with antiques, they provide extras for their guests.

To begin with, the inn offers free pickup and delivery service to both the airport and the ferry dock. In addition, arrangements can be made for salmon charters or guided hiking and backpacking trips—convenient services considering the inn's nearness to both the strait and the national park.

The inn hits its stride in winter, when most bed and breakfasts go into hibernation. When there is snow on Hurricane Ridge, there are always eager skiers taking advantage of the inn's cross-country ski package. For a set price, guests receive two nights' lodging, two breakfasts, a packed trail lunch, and a home-cooked dinner on Saturday night. Equipment and basic ski instruction can also be included.

The inn takes its name from the Tudor style of its two-story frame. Inside, both the living room and the library boast fireplaces and stuffed furnishings. The dining room features an atmosphere of formal elegance.

European antiques and handcrafted adornments make up the five upstairs guest rooms. All of the rooms offer at least partial water and mountain views. Room number one takes advantage of its corner location to provide panoramas of both.

If I had to pick one thing that stands out here, it would be the inn's location. For exploring the peninsula, The Tudor Inn is perfectly located.

The hospitality, service, and comfort are all whipped cream.

*   *   *

The Tudor Inn, 1108 South Oak, Port Angeles, WA 98362 (206-452-3138). Five guest rooms share two baths. (There are plans to add two private baths.) Rates range from $43 to $53 (subject to change). VISA/MasterCard. No children under ten; no pets; no smoking. From U.S. 101 in downtown Port Angeles, go south on Lincoln. Then turn right on 11th to Oak. The inn is on the corner.

THE COONEY MANSION

Lee Esterbrook grew up in Cosmopolis. It is a tiny town with a couple of taverns, a gas station, and a once-thriving sawmill. It also boasts its very own mansion, and today Lee and his wife Jan live and work in it.

Built in 1908 as a private residence for mill manager Neil Cooney, this thirty-two-room, ten thousand-square-foot, three-story house always intrigued Lee. One day in 1978, Lee was playing golf on the course, which doglegs just past the mansion's back door, when, without reason or logic, he walked up and knocked. When the owner appeared, Lee asked him if he would like to sell. The next time Lee visited the mansion, he found himself moving Jan and their three daughters into their new home.

The Cooney Mansion (Courtesy The Cooney Mansion)

There have been no regrets, only lots of work. They spent the next seven years scraping, sanding, painting, and polishing. In March of 1985, the Esterbrooks decided the mansion was ready to share with guests. So they opened the downstairs and nine bedrooms to bed and breakfast.

The mansion has a look of strength about it. The hard lines and sturdy construction promote a masculine setting. All the rooms are large and boast an old-fashioned country air. There is almost a feeling of sternness. However, the Esterbrook family photos that adorn walls, the vases of flowers, and the dishes of candies help to soften the ambience.

The downstairs is made up of a spacious living room, dining room, and kitchen. A large brick fireplace and heavy wooden furnishings make up the living room. A collection of pewter blends with the dining room's solid look.

On the second and third floors, the guest rooms range from the large second-floor master bedroom, with a fireplace and large bath, to the third-floor rooms, which are made up of twin beds and feel dormlike.

Despite what at first glance seems to be a stern and spare environment, Cooney Mansion boasts charm. Surprisingly, the rooms are homey, and the furnishings are comfortable. There is also a lot of intrigue and history brewing here. And the Esterbrooks deserve "tens" for their innkeeping personalities and skills. Both are friendly and fun, which are the key ingredients to any guest house.

*   *   *

Cooney Mansion, 802 East 5th Street, P.O. Box 54, Cosmopolis, WA 98537 (206-533-0602). Nine guest rooms, five with private baths. Rates range from $50 to $65 (subject to change). No credit cards. Children with prior approval; no pets; smoking in kitchen only. Besides nearby golf and tennis, the home has a whirlpool and sauna. From downtown Cosmopolis, take C Street to a left on 5th Street. The mansion sits at the end of a dead-end street.

Inland Washington

Washington wears two faces. One has green eyes and a thick head of hair, while the other stares through brown orbs and boasts of its baldness. To Washingtonians, the two sides are known as the wet westside and the dry eastside.

In the west, ample amounts of moisture keep the landscape lush with forests, rivers, and lakes. In the east, a dry climate promises a desert golden with wheat and a big sky beaming blue. Keeping the two sides apart and guaranteeing their differences, the mighty Cascade Mountains form a jagged snow-capped wall that rambles through the state's midsection. These rugged monoliths and the communities that hug their slopes provide year-round recreational and sight-seeing opportunities. Beyond the desert, Spokane serves as the state's eastern gateway.

GETTING TO KNOW INLAND WASHINGTON

BEGINNING AT THE GORGE

The Columbia River forms Washington's southern border. Riding alongside and above its flow, State Route 14 connects Interstate 5 to central Washington. It bridges timber and agriculture. This is an area worth exploration but one often overlooked in favor of more famous destinations.

Beginning just outside Vancouver, Washington, the narrow highway twists and turns along basalt cliffs, through a gap in the Cascade Mountains. It passes the world's second-largest sheer-walled monolith, 848-foot Beacon Rock, and gazes out on steep forested cliffs, streaming with waterfalls cascading toward the river.

About twenty-five miles past Bonneville Dam, the road leads to the Rhineland communities of Bingen and White Salmon. Here there are good shopping opportunities, as well as views of Mount Hood.

Traveling farther east on State Route 14 brings visitors to one of this region's finest museums. Perched on a bluff overlooking the river, Maryhill Museum of Art features an excellent collection of Rodin sculptures, plus exhibits of nineteenth- and twentieth-century paintings, Cypriot pottery, American Indian artifacts, chess sets, weapons, and textiles. After touring the museum, drive three miles east to a replica of Stonehenge. From its bluff overlook, there are spectacular views of the river, Mount Hood, and Oregon's rolling plains.

At this point, U.S. 97 intersects State Route 14 and goes north to the vineyards, orchards, and farms of the Yakima Valley. Before leaving the area, however, you might wish to experience wind surfing at Maryhill Park, steelhead fishing in the Klickitat and White Salmon Rivers, or hiking near Mount Adams.

On the north side of 3,149-foot Satus Pass, beyond the dun-colored hills of the Toppenish Range, the Yakima Valley beckons fruit and wine lovers. From Yakima to the Tri-Cities, fruit orchards of nearly every kind—apples, cherries, peaches, pears, and apricots—fill the air and roadside stands with the sweet smells of fresh fruit.

In recent years, grapes have become one of Washington's most valued and famous crops. About a dozen valley wineries now produce some of North America's finest wines. For a brochure and map that details the industry and discusses tours, write the Yakima Valley Wine Growers Association, P.O. Box 39, Grandview, WA 98930.

MOUNT RAINIER NATIONAL PARK

I do not believe I will ever stop being in awe of The Mountain. On days when it is out, its glaciated mantle and 14,410-foot crest fill Washington's sky. The picture it paints is an artist's conception of strength and beauty. It is a masterpiece that never seems real. But real it is, and its hulk makes up Washington's most famous park.

There are several ways to explore The Mountain. The easiest is a loop tour by car, which is only possible between May and October when Chinook and Cayuse passes are open.

From Interstate 5 in Tacoma, take State Route 410 through the agriculturally rich valley communities of Puyallup and Sumner. The highway continues west to Greenwater, where Federation Forest boasts one of the few remaining stands of virgin timber in the Northwest. From here, the highway dips south past the ski resort at Crystal Mountain.

As you begin to climb the ascending highway, Emmons Glacier comes into view. Shortly thereafter you approach the road leading to the visitor center at Sunrise, which is open only in the summer. The center is at 6,400 feet and is but a short hike from the glacier.

From here, State Route 410 and Chinook Pass lead to Yakima. To continue the loop, take State Route 123 over Cayuse Pass and into the valley at Ohanapecosh, where there is another visitor center. A few miles beyond the valley, State Route 706 leads around the southern flank of The Mountain. On the way to the 5,400-foot level and Paradise (The Mountain's most popular visitor center), you will pass meadows beaming with wild flowers, lakes bluer than blue, and mountain views that stun the imagination.

On the return trip to the Interstate, State Highway 706 passes through the tiny town of Elbe. If you still have not tired of The Mountain, take a ride on the steam-powered Mount Rainier Scenic Railroad. The ride offers more good forest and mountain views.

In Elbe, you will pick up State Route 7. Within five miles, State Route 162 invites another side trip. Six miles north of Eatonville, on State Route 161, Northwest Trek represents one of the West's finest wildlife parks. Here you will see eagles, owls, wolves, bears, bison, moose, deer, and sheep roaming about in natural habitats.

One final note about the area: while a drive around The Mountain features lots of views, you cannot really experience Mount Rainier unless you hike or ski some of its three hundred miles of trails.

THE NORTH CASCADES HIGHWAY

Few scenic drives can live up to their press, but the North Cascades Highway (State Route 20) delivers everything promised and more. Open to traffic since 1972, this two-lane road crosses the Cascades in a blaze of lakes, rivers, valleys, and cliffs.

Between Concrete and Twisp there are several places worth exploration. The Skagit River, which parallels the highway, offers white-water rafting and fishing for Dolly Varden, steelhead, and salmon. Near Concrete, Baker Lake Road leads into the wilderness for hiking and fishing. East of Newhalem (Seattle City Light's company town), overlooks above Diablo Dam feature splendid views of Ross Lake and Ross Dam. Skagit Tours (206-625-3030) offers boat cruises across Diablo Lake and rides up the side of Sourdough Mountain on an incline railway. The next great views are at 5,447-foot Washington Pass. A granite perch looks out on towering peaks such as Silver Star and Liberty Bell.

From here, the highway descends rapidly. As the valley nears, the forests begin to thin, and the mountains start to roll. In the Old West town of Winthrop, the environment begins to give way to the parched landscape of Eastern Washington.

LAKE CHELAN

This fifty-five-mile-long stretch of blue is Washington's version of a split personality: one end likes being in Washington, the other has dreams of Florida. Both sides, however, get along just fine and together they welcome over 125,000 vacationers each year.

The northern end of this snakelike body of water strikes deep into the Cascades, where Washington's primeval wilderness reaches out to hug the lake. Thick forests of evergreens and sheer cliffs showered by waterfalls celebrate nature. The only ways in or out are by foot, boat (the *Lady of the Lake*, 509-682-2224), or floatplane (Chelan Airways, 509-682-5555).

While the northern end promises communes with the wild, the southern tip pledges contact with people—not just a few but crowds of them. Sunbathers, boaters, and gliders (the kind who leap off 3,900-foot Chelan Butte) swarm to Chelan to take advantage of its three hundred days of sunshine, particularly the sixty-two days falling between 1 July and 31 August. Surrounded by dun-colored hills planted with giant boulders and apple orchards, Chelan sparkles with enthusiasm.

If your desire is to get away, however, the crowds begin to disappear after Labor Day weekend, while the beauty and the sun remain.

LEAVENWORTH

In 1963, Leavenworth was desperate for an idea, one that would save this once-prosperous mill town from economic ruin. By 1965, a thought began to take shape. Working together in sixteen committees, the townspeople decided to give their town a new look, one that would attract tourists and their dollars. The sleepy town took advantage of its mountain location and transformed itself into a bright and lively Bavarian village. Today, tens of thousands of travelers visit Leavenworth each year.

There are shops, tourist attractions, and year-round recreation. During the summer, hikers, cyclists, and anglers find the area perfectly suited to their needs. Miles of trails wend through the high country; Icicle River and East Leavenworth roads are popular among bicyclists; and the Wenatchee River teems with game fish. In addition, from May to July the river boasts some of the best white-water rafting in the state.

Fall is the season for color. With streams of red, orange, and gold flowing through the Tumwater Canyon, Leavenworth celebrates its Autumn Leaf Festival, which begins the last weekend of September and lasts through the first weekend of October. Another festival—Christmas Lighting—opens the winter season. Throughout winter, powdery snow and miles of trails welcome cross-country skiers.

SPOKANE

From the east, Spokane is the gateway to the Northwest; from the west, it is a welcome oasis at the end of the desert. From either direction, Spokane is both a bridesmaid and a queen.

Despite the city's 1974 World's Fair, which left attractive Riverfront Park as its legacy, Spokane has never overcome its image of being Washington's second city. Travelers and tourists from the west side, who seldom venture over the mountains for reasons other than business or to visit the foothill communities, often look upon Spokane as sleepy and enervating.

While wetsiders may see only a napping Spokane, however, people who live in the Inland Empire—eastern Washington, Idaho, and Montana, and eastern British Columbia—look at the city as a thriving metropolis. It is their capital of commerce and trade.

Like most mirrors, neither reflection is completely accurate. Spokane is a city that requires no labels. It is secure in its looks and pleased with its economic progress. It is also a city that travelers from both directions should discover. It may not be a vacationer's paradise but Spokane is a pleasant diversion from the hectic pace of most cities.

The best times to visit are late spring or early fall, when you can avoid both the intense heat of summer and the snows of winter. Begin your tour at Riverfront Park.

Set within the cascading currents of the Spokane River, the park is one of footbridges, benches, rolling lawns, meandering pathways, and pleading marmots. It features an IMAX® Theater, a 1909 Looff carousel, the Great Northern Clock Tower, and a weekend farmers' market.

From the park, downtown stretches along the river's south bank. An enclosed skywalk system bridges several blocks of shops and department stores. Beginning a block north of J C Penney and the skywalk, at Lincoln Street, and extending three blocks to Jefferson, Riverside Avenue boasts several architecturally interesting buildings worth seeing. In the same area, do not miss Our Lady of Lourdes Cathedral on Sprague.

If historical homes intrigue you, continue west to Browne's Addition. Roughly bounded by West First and Second avenues, and Oak and Coeur d'Alene streets, Browne's Addition makes up some 126 acres of luxurious and prestigious homes. Most of the houses, which include Queen Anne, Colonial Revival, Tudor, and Georgian styles, were built between 1881 and 1905. Start your walking tour at the Campbell House and the Cheney Cowles Memorial Museum at 2316 West First. Here, the Eastern Washington Historical Society will get you off on the right foot.

Before leaving town you should also visit the following: the Museum of Native American Cultures on the campus of Gonzaga University, which boasts an excellent collection of Indian artifacts and art; the Crosby Library, also on campus, where you can view Bing's memorabilia; Manito Park, between 17th and 25th avenues along Grand Boulevard, where gardens flourish; and the Flour Mill, just north of Riverfront Park, which is a unique shopping center. Finally, treat yourself to a cherry cola and a dose of local color at the Elk Drug Store at 1931 West Pacific, where a 1940s soda fountain sets the pace.

A PRACTICAL GUIDE TO INLAND WASHINGTON

THE CLIMATE

While you are on the Cascade's west side, expect year-round mild temperatures, with the possibility of rain. The months of July, August, and September usually promise blue skies and temperatures in the 70s. In the passes, snow and ice can be a threat from November to April. You should carry chains. The east side features hot, dry weather (80s and 90s) from May to October and cold, possibly snowy weather in the heart of winter.

YOUR CLOTHES

While casual clothes are always advisable, dress according to the weather. Do not ever hike about the mountains without woolens—socks, sweaters, hats, gloves, etc. A bright sunny day can turn evil almost anytime at higher elevations. During the summer, wear cool, loose clothes on the east side. Bring sunglasses and sunscreen. Men should bring ties and women dresses to Spokane. Do not forget, winter is a reality east of the Cascades.

VISITOR INFORMATION

For more information, contact the following: National Park Service, U.S. Department of the Interior, Pacific Northwest Regional Office, 1018 First Avenue, Seattle, WA 98104 (206-442-0170); Spokane Regional Convention and Visitors Bureau, West 301 Main, Spokane, WA 99201 (509-624-1341); or Tourism Development Division, 101 General Administration Building, AX-13, Olympia, WA 98504-0613 (800-562-4570, inside Washington, and 800-541-9274, outside Washington).

POINTS OF INTEREST

MARYHILL MUSEUM OF ART. Located on State Route 14 just west of U.S. 97 (509-773-4792). A fine collection of Rodin sculptures and drawings, plus other world-class exhibits. Open 15 March through 15 November.

STONEHENGE. Located three miles east of Maryhill on State Route 14. A conjectural model of the Salisbury Plain original. Good views.

GOLDENDALE OBSERVATORY STATE PARK. Located one mile north of Goldendale (509-773-3141). Good views of the Cascades, plus a twenty-four and a half-inch reflecting telescope.

FORT SIMCOE STATE PARK. Take State Route 220 West out of Toppenish to its end in the heart of the Yakima Indian Reservation (509-874-2372). Several old army buildings remain, as well as a museum.

SUNRISE VISITORS CENTER. Located on the east face of Mount Rainier at sixty-four hundred feet. Open only in summer. Peaceful. Good views. Hiking.

PARADISE VISITORS CENTER. Mount Rainier's most popular center. Information auditorium. Views. Hiking. Can be crowded.

MOUNT RAINIER SCENIC RAILROAD. Trips aboard a steam-driven train begin in Elbe (L-bee) and end in Mineral. Good views of the countryside and Mount Rainier.

NORTHWEST TREK. Located six miles north of Eatonville on State Route 161 (206-832-6116). A natural wildlife park.

SKAGIT TOURS. Tours of the Skagit Project in the upper Skagit Valley (206-625-3030). Includes a boat cruise across Diablo Lake and a ride on an incline railway.

ALTA LAKE STATE PARK. Several miles outside of Pateros off of State Route 153. Fishing, swimming, wind surfing, and horseback riding.

ROCKY REACH DAM. Located seven miles north of Wenatchee on U.S. 97. Picnicking, fish-viewing area, and historical exhibits.

OHME GARDENS. Located on a rocky bluff three miles north of Wenatchee. Valley views. Spectacular gardens. Open April to October.

LAKE WENATCHEE. Located north of Leavenworth off State Route 207. Fishing, boating, and swimming.

TUMWATER CANYON. North of Leavenworth off U.S. 2. Splendid views, particularly in the fall.

DRYDEN PINNACLES. Just west of Cashmere, north of U.S. 2. Rock climbing.

COULEE DAM NATIONAL RECREATION AREA. Stretches from the Grand Coulee Dam to Evans and Barstow. This section of the Columbia River is also called Roosevelt Lake. Besides viewing the dam, water activities dominate: waterskiing, boating, swimming, and fishing. There are visitor centers at the dam, Fort Spokane, and Kettle Falls.

RIVERFRONT PARK. Downtown Spokane. IMAX® Theater, carousel, walking, jogging, and weekend public market.

MUSEUM OF NATIVE AMERICAN CULTURES. Gonzaga University, Spokane (509-326-4550). Indian artifacts and art.

RESTAURANTS OF NOTE

The following eateries are listed by location, beginning in the southern part of the state.

THE GRAND OLD HOUSE. On State Route 14 in Bingen (509-493-2838). An 1860 farmhouse that is also a country inn. Good seafood and home-baked desserts. The mocha torte is superb.

THREE CREEKS LODGE. 2120 Highway 97, five miles north of Satus Pass (509-773-4026). A small resort just north of Goldendale. Professional service. Fresh seafood. Excellent specialties. Try the Tournedos Rossini.

DEL CONTE'S TIMBERLINE RESTAURANT. 4286 Highway 20, Concrete (206-853-8771). Your basic steaks, chops, and chicken.

MOUNTAIN SONG RESTAURANT. 5860 Highway 20, Marblemount (206-873-2461). Good country cooking. Fresh Skagit Valley vegetables. Home-made pies.

THE CAMPBELL HOUSE. 104 West Woodin, Chelan (509-682-2561). Fresh ingredients go into wholesome and unpretentious entrées. The food here is always good.

KATZENJAMMERS. 221 8th Street, Leavenworth (509-548-5826). Quality steaks and seafood.

RATSSTUBE. 216 8th Street, Leavenworth (509-548-4673). Continental cuisine. Menu changes frequently.

REINER'S GASTHAUS. 829 Front Street, Leavenworth (509-548-5111). Authentic Bavarian food.

THE JOHN HORAN HOUSE. 2 Horan Road, Wenatchee (509-663-0018). Located in a fine old turn-of-the-century home. Fresh seasonal foods. Excellent soups. Fine service and presentation.

THE WINDMILL. 1501 North Wenatchee Avenue, Wenatchee (509-663-3478). You go here for the steaks. Do not even bother looking at the other entrées. Desserts are also quite good.

MILFORD'S. North 719 Monroe, Spokane (509-326-7251). Fresh fish. Menu changes daily. Good service. If it is seafood you want, this is the place.

MORELAND'S. North 216 Howard, Spokane (509-747-9830). Intimate dining. French cuisine. Menu changes frequently. For dessert, try the Killer Pie.

PATSY CLARK'S. West 2208 Second Avenue, Spokane (509-838-8300). Located in Browne's Addition in a great old mansion. Elegant dining. Entrées include veal, duck, lamb, steaks, and seafood.

WHERE TO STAY

INN OF THE WHITE SALMON

Calling Loretta Hopper's morning feast a breakfast is like referring to nearby Mount Hood as a mole hill. Though it began as a modest affair of coffee and rolls served on a Sears card table, today the inn's presentation mirrors a gustatory extravaganza.

With linen tablecloths and heirloom china gracing several cozy dining room tables, and four-color scenes of Washington's wilderness projecting on a screen, guests waft toward breakfast on the smells of fresh-baked pastries and savory seasonings. An expansive buffet featuring some thirty-five to forty baked goods, from Hungarian love letters to Alsatian apple tarts, spreads across the front of the dining room. In addition, there are six to eight egg dishes offered, as well as juice and fresh fruit.

Loretta's breakfasts have been frequent subjects of media attention. Nevertheless, breakfast, while important, is but one part of the bed-and-breakfast experience. There are other equally important sides to an inn.

In size, the inn has no Washington equal. The two-story rectangular brick building, which was built in 1937 and served the area as the Hood View Hotel, houses twenty guest rooms. While they are not nearly as elaborate as breakfast, all are attractive and comfortable. Most boast portraits and paintings of flowers and landscapes, floral-print wallpapers,

Inn of the White Salmon (Kay Green)

antique dressers, and queen-size beds. Amenities include color televisions, room telephones, and large soft towels. There is also a Jacuzzi on the back deck.

The inn's location has much to offer, as well. Portland is just an hour's drive away, the Gorge flows nearly within walking distance, Mount Hood looms just outside some of the second-floor guest room windows, and White Salmon is a quiet and charming theme town.

So while the architecture is motellike and nondescript, and the rooms are not luxurious, the Inn of the White Salmon always proves to be a comfortable and pleasant experience. And nowhere will travelers be treated to a better breakfast.

*   *   *

Inn of the White Salmon, 172 Jewett, White Salmon, WA 98672 (509-493-2335). Twenty guest rooms—203 is the only room lacking a private bath. Rates range from $60 to $130 (subject to change). VISA/MasterCard/American Express. Children with prior approval; no pets; no smoking in dining room. From State Route 14, take State Route 141 through White Salmon. The inn is on the right.

WHALEY MANSION

A trip back in time. That phrase is constantly flowing from the lips of bed-and-breakfast innkeepers. It is how Mary Kay, owner of Whaley mansion, likes to describe her place.

"We give people a romantic place to go," Mary Kay says, "by exposing them to the wonderful way of living that my grandparents experienced—a slower pace, satin sheets, and sterling silver."

Whaley Mansion may be romantic and nearby Lake Chelan does encourage a slower pace; however, none of the grandparents I have ever known experienced the kind of opulence that radiates from this house. Satin sheets and sterling silver were the kinds of things found only in the motion pictures during my grandparents' lives.

Upon entering the two-story, turn-of-the-century house (at which time guests are asked to remove their shoes), elegance, luxury, and a touch of ornate clutter embrace you. Teal blue carpets cover the dining and living room floors, with handmade French wallpaper adorning several walls. China, crystal, sterling silver, linen, and lace grace the dining room, while silk flowers, a silvered mirror, and slab tiger oak distinguish the living room.

Two additional downstairs rooms—the music room and the Indian room—also display rich tastes. An 1867 rosewood square grand piano fills the music room, and a museumful of artifacts garnish the Indian room.

Whaley Mansion (Kay Green)

True to Mary Kay's recollections of her grandparents' time, silk and satin shimmer in the upstairs guest rooms. Cozying up to the silk flowers and satiny sheets are iron beds, plush carpets, delicate wallpapers, warm colors, brass fixtures, ruffled fabrics, polished woods, antique appointments, and walls of mirrors.

Realizing that some people prefer a simpler getaway, Mary Kay opened the Judge Long House next door to guests in 1986. Its five rooms (expected to expand to seven) promote comfort and peace rather than romance and luxury.

*   *   *

Whaley Mansion, 415 Third Street, Route 1, Box 693, Chelan, WA 98816 (509-682-5735). Six guest rooms, all with private baths. Rates range from $75 to $95; $50 to $65 at Judge Long (subject to change). VISA/MasterCard. No children; no pets; no smoking. From Wenatchee on U.S. 97, turn left on Third Street. The inn is on the right.

FRENCH HOUSE

At the confluence of the Columbia and Methow rivers glistens a swath of sapphire called Lake Pateros. A fiery eastern Washington sun plants rows of crystals on its surface, while the rolling hills that rise from its rocky banks take on a golden hue.

French House (Kay Green)

Sitting on the lake's western shores, the tiny gas stop of Pateros goes about its business. Children on bicycles race about otherwise empty streets, and women sit on front stoops carrying on animated conversations, while their male counterparts hover over outboard motors. The picture is one of apple pie and peace.

In the midst of this setting stands a two-story, white Dutch Colonial house. Its red shutters and red roof draw attention to its clean lines. The shadows from evergreens make the close-cropped lawn seem greener than green. Since 1982, this middle-class home has been a bed and breakfast. Formerly called Lake Pateros Bed & Breakfast, it is now named French House in honor of its builders in 1922.

Charlene and Bob Knoop are the owners and proprietors of this establishment. They are friendly and interesting folks who were drawn to Pateros by their love of the surrounding countryside. Their two boys, both well-behaved and bright, have grown up with the business. Their presence creates a family environment that is rarely experienced in West Coast bed and breakfasts.

The atmosphere reflects close harmony. There are but two guest rooms, but the Knoops promote a professional guest house environment. Both accommodations boast antiques and amenities such as ruffled curtains, down pillows, handmade quilts, fresh flowers, and bowls of seasonal fruit. In addition, guests do not share the one and a half bathrooms with the Knoops, as might be the case in other small operations.

Still, homeyness dominates. There is nothing innlike about the pale green walls and overstuffed furniture in the living room, the wicker settee and porch swing in the sun-room, or the large aquarium in the dining room. This is a country home, and travelers will never confuse it with anything else.

*   *   *

French House, 206 West Warren, Pateros, WA 98846 (509-923-2626). Two guest rooms share one and a half baths. Rates are $42 (subject to change). VISA/MasterCard. Children with prior approval; no pets; no smoking. Breakfast is full and homemade. Steelhead fishing and cross-country skiing are excellent in the area. From Chelan on U.S. 97, take the first left beyond the intersection with State Route 153. Then bear right. The home is on the left.

HAUS ROHRBACH PENSION

They are a perfect match. Looking like a large Alpine chalet—its balconies garnished with flowers and its roof pitched against a mountain backdrop—Haus Rohrbach overlooks the Bavarian village of Leavenworth.

In some ways it marches out of step with most bed-and-breakfast inns, which start out as private homes and metamorphose into guest houses. Haus Rohrbach was never meant to be anything other than a pension. This explains the long hallways and the relatively large number of guest rooms.

However, a more important difference relates to the owners. Kathryn and Bob Harrild have been the innkeepers here since 1978. This is a millennium in innkeeping. Most proprietors have been running their inns for perhaps half that time.

The Harrilds continue to enjoy their business and their guests. In addition, their knowledge of innkeeping, plus their awareness of the area, result in benefits to travelers; stays are made comfortable and activities are readily planned and easily accommodated.

Simple homelike pleasures rather than luxury and elegance dominate the twelve guest rooms. Each has a spare, rustic look with lots of wood paneling and trim. Fresh flowers and complimentary candies add welcome touches, while windows that open let in both mountain air and country views. There are also some good views, especially from rooms 10 and 11.

Breakfast is served in the spacious common room, where pine wainscoting and a wood stove carry out the inn's country mission. Large windows and sliding glass doors look out on the upper Wenatchee Valley, Leavenworth, and the foothills beyond. The balcony, where breakfast is

Haus Rohrbach Pension (Kay Green)

offered in good weather, overlooks the swimming pool and hot tub.

* * *

Haus Rohrbach Pension, 12882 Ranger Road, Leavenworth, WA 98826 (509-548-7024). Twelve guest rooms—nine share three baths, while three have private baths. Rates range from $60 to $70 (subject to change). VISA/MasterCard. Children with prior approval; no pets; smoking in common rooms only. From U.S. 2, just west of downtown, turn left on Ski Hill Drive (at Kristall's Restaurant). Drive one mile, then turn left on Ranger Road. The inn sits straight ahead on the rise.

BROWN'S FARM

Brown's Farm is not for everyone and it certainly is not for anyone in search of gilded finery. However, if you enjoy the smells of fresh hay and tall pines, the sounds of horses neighing, chickens clucking, and the sights of a country farm, this rustic getaway will warm the cockles of your heart.

Located deep in the woods, just outside of Leavenworth, Brown's Farm is as close to a Northwest backwood's experience as you can find and still stay within the grasp of civilization. The home is a two-story, cedar structure with three gables and a wide wrap-around porch. The location, design, and ambience are the result of dreams.

Both Steve and Wendi wanted to live in the country. In 1979, they found this property, moved a mobile home onto it, and began the process of fulfilling their fantasy. Using pine, fir, hemlock, and cedar, Steve—a carpenter and furniture maker—built the house from the ground up with the help of his family. Then, on the suggestion of a friend, they opened up two bedrooms for bed and breakfast in the spring of 1983.

The key to their operation is its gentle, family environment. There is the farm, its animals and its chores, and there are the Brown's three children. A life that is both natural and honest revolves around this setting. There is no time or room for pretension.

Guests and hosts share the rustic living room. The furnishings are fat and comfortable, not suitable for showrooms but ideal for reading or conversation. The rock fireplace wears its singed smudges proudly. In the adjacent kitchen, a long table looks at open cupboards and a wood cook stove. Farm-fresh eggs and home-canned fruit spell a country breakfast.

The two guest rooms offer more of the same. There are exposed log beams, plank ceilings, antique quilts, and fresh flowers. The one object of decadence, a claw-footed tub, adorns the shared bathroom.

While it may sound corny, the Browns and their farm are a slice of Americana that is all-too-quickly fading from the American landscape. The environment here is real and homey.

*   *   *

Brown's Farm, 11150 Highway 209, Leavenworth, WA 98826 (509-548-7863). Two guest rooms share a bath. Rates range from $55 to $65 (subject to change). VISA/MasterCard. Children with prior approval; no pets; no smoking. Take State Route 209 just east of downtown. Drive one and a half miles to a gravel road on the left. Keep to the left and drive a short distance to the farm. (The gravel road is marked by a sign that hugs the right side of the highway.)

Brown's Farm (Kay Green)

FOTHERINGHAM HOUSE

Spokane's Fotheringham House has an ideal setting in the heart of historic Browne's Addition and across the street from Patsy Clark's—one of the city's finest restaurants.

For reasons that avoid pinpointing, bed and breakfasts have been slow developing in Spokane. Although a few mom-and-pop homes have been operating for several years, the city has not had a quality guest-house inn to call its own. Fortheringham House changes that.

The building itself has been around since 1891, when it was built to accommodate David B. Fotheringham—incorporated Spokane's first mayor. Its design is referred to as eclectic stick style; the interior spaces reflect the Victorian period. Original to the house are tin ceilings, wood floors, hand-carved woodwork, an open staircase, and ball and spindle fretwork.

The living room is particularly old-fashioned and elegant. Filtered light passes through high bay windows and settles on a vintage rug. A tile fireplace, which features a hand-carved oak mantle, stands on one wall, while floral-print wallpaper distinguishes the other partitions. Furnishings are antique yet still comfortable.

A walk up the stairway leads guests to the accommodations. Named Mayor's, Pink, and Mansion, each boasts an antique look. A four-poster bed and antique armoire highlight the Mayor's Room, which has its own close-quartered bath, while the Mansion Room is made up with a hand-

Fotheringham House (Peter Hall)

carved oak bed. The Pink Room features a white iron bed, pedestal sink, and rose-print wallpaper.

Current owners, Jay and Sue Moynahan, did not come into inn-keeping by accident. They bought this house and moved to Spokane in 1984 specifically to do bed and breakfast.

"We knew exactly what we wanted," Jay says.

"We got three steps into this house and knew this was the right place," Sue adds.

Now they have added the 1904 Hoover House next door to their fledgling bed-and-breakfast empire.

*   *   *

Fotheringham House, 2128 West 2nd Avenue, Spokane, WA 99204 (509-838-4363). Three guest rooms, one with a private bath. Rates range from $37 to $45 (subject to change). VISA/MasterCard/American Express. Children with prior approval; no pets; no smoking. From downtown Spokane, take West 2nd Avenue to Browne's Addition. The inn is on the corner of 2nd and Hemlock.

BLAKELY ESTATES

John and Kathy Smith are the kind of people who you wish would move in next door. Their personalities bubble over with enthusiasm. John would drive or fly all day and night if fun waited at the end of the road, and Kathy would be alongside him all the way. It is this indomitable spirit that gave birth to Blakely Estates—their own mom-and-pop bed and breakfast.

The accommodations are traditional—a home within a home—and the Smiths want to keep it that way, especially Kathy. They reject the idea that this is a business. Kathy is looking to keep her home cozy and fun.

Located in a subdivision, which was once the estate of a Spokane businessman, this contemporary ranch-style home overlooks the Spokane River. Ducks waddle across the backyard and water laps the tiny dock. Every time a boat passes, the Smith's canoe and rowboat dance to the water's rhythm.

Inside the house, guests eat breakfast in the family dining room and are welcome to join the Smiths in their living room. However, the entire downstairs, including a sitting room, is for the exclusive use of guests.

The sitting room is comfortable. Stuffed swivel rockers sit on either side of a stone fireplace offering both the artificial stimulation of color television and the natural refreshment of views of the river.

A short hallway leads to both guest rooms. Lagoon is very cozy but, while fine for getting a good night's sleep, offers little in the way of extras. Riverview, on the other hand, boasts a light and airy feeling, fat rockers,

Blakely Estates (Lewis Green)

and views of the water. Snacks are usually waiting in both rooms for arriving guests.

While there are amenities—the use of the canoe and rowboat, a hot tub, the homemade breakfast—and the rooms are comfortable, those should not be the reasons for booking a reservation here. Most bed and breakfasts feature similar attributes. What separates Blakely Estates from run-of-the-mill homes is hospitality. It is in great abundance here.

*   *   *

Blakely Estates, East 7710 Hodin Drive, Spokane, WA 99212 (509-926-9426). Two guest rooms share one bath. Rates range from $40 to $45 (subject to change). No credit cards. Children with prior approval; no pets; no smoking. About five miles east of downtown, take Exit 287 off Interstate 90. Drive 1.7 miles to Upriver Drive. Head west one mile to a left on Hodin Drive. The house sits over the crest at the bottom of the hill.

CASCADE MOUNTAIN INN

Wedding anniversaries are indeed special events, especially when they celebrate three decades of marriage. On June 4, 1984, Ingrid and Gerhard Meyer popped corks on their thirtieth.

For most of us, thirty years of marriage means a routine, a settling in has taken place. However, that was not true for the Meyers. Instead, they celebrated a birth, a new beginning, and a new life. For on that day, the

Meyers welcomed their first guests to the Cascade Mountain Inn.

The Meyers, who are from Germany, moved to the United States in 1971. One year later, they began taking family vacations to the Skagit Valley and the North Cascades. They fell in love with the countryside and decided they would move there upon retirement.

When the time came to stop punching the clock, however, the Meyers wanted more from life than just a place to relax.

"We had to have something to do," Ingrid says. "We had traveled all over the world, enjoyed staying in hotels and inns, so thought running an inn would be the ideal way to keep us going."

In March of 1984, the Meyers began building their inn on ten acres of farmland, surrounded by the forested foothills of the North Cascades. When the hammering stopped, a two-story, cedar-frame building stood. Its gambrel roof, characteristic of New England barns, infuses the inn with the essence of country.

Inside, the open spaces promote a sense of freedom. A brick fireplace dominates the living room, which is garnished with bric-a-brac from around the world. A wall of windows looks out on sheep and horses grazing in the meadow, with rolling hills forming a backdrop. The living room opens into a country dining room. To the right, there is a sunken breakfast area, which accesses a terrace.

Five of the six guest rooms are upstairs. Each is named for a country the Meyers have spent time in—America, Peru, Germany, Scotland, and the Philippines. They are appropriately appointed to reflect those settings.

Cascade Mountain Inn (Lewis Green)

The sixth, called Bremen for Gerhard's hometown, is a studio above the garage.

*   *   *

Cascade Mountain Inn, 3840 Pioneer Lane, Concrete-Birdsview, WA 98237 (206-826-4333). Six guest rooms, all with private baths. Rates range from $62 to $68 (subject to change). VISA/MasterCard. Children with prior approval; no pets; no smoking. As well as a full breakfast, guests may also request dinner for an additional charge. From Interstate 5, take State Route 20 east exactly twenty-four miles, then turn right onto Wild Road to another right at Pioneer Lane. Watch your odometer. Wild Road is not clearly marked.

British Columbia

Victoria

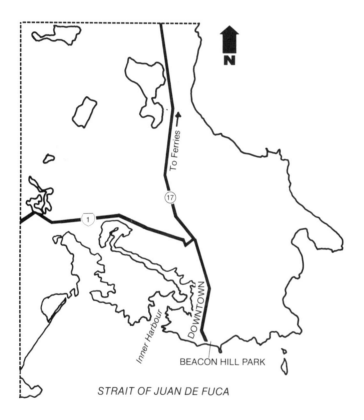

Abigail's
The Beaconsfield Inn
Heritage House
Prior House

Vancouver

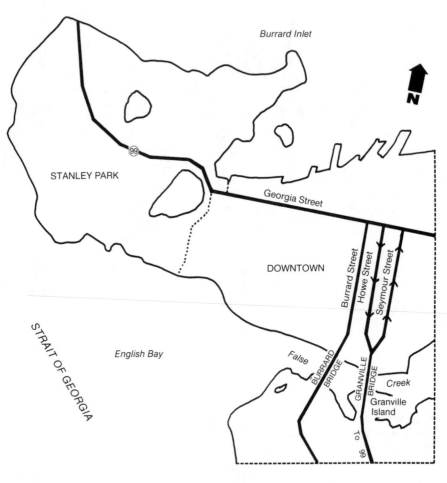

Burrard Inlet

STANLEY PARK

Georgia Street

DOWNTOWN

Burrard Street

Howe Street

Seymour Street

STRAIT OF GEORGIA

English Bay

False

BURRARD

BRIDGE

GRANVILLE

BRIDGE

Creek

Granville
Island

To 99

Gables Guest House
West End Guest House

Victoria

A sense of calm, dignity, and prosperity prevails. Dozens of schooners and sloops, their sails full, cover the water of Victoria's Inner Harbour like whitecaps tossed up by a fresh breeze. Alongshore, the crowded marina tucks its curved shoulder into a city reflecting the faces of several generations. There are the modern high rises symbolizing hope for the future, and standing alongside this younger generation two ornate turn-of-the-century palaces that recall the images of a propitious past.

The ivy-covererd walls of The Empress Hotel rise above the harbor to meet peaked gables, copper cupolas—now oxidized and splashed with turquoise—and steeply pitched slate roofs. Kitty-corner from The Empress, the twenty-three-karat-gilded statue of Captain George Vancouver, who surrounds himself with an army of thirty-three weathered domes, stands atop the neo-Gothic Parliament Buildings.

Both of these grand dames watch over Victoria's wide central boulevard—Government Street. Here, hanging flower baskets drape old-fashioned lampposts. Horses drawing Tally-Ho carriages clip-clop slowly up the street, mindless of automobiles competing for space. Nearby, middle-aged men and women spend their days bowling on the green, while more youthful sports compete in a game of cricket.

GETTING TO KNOW VICTORIA

Victoria is a city that takes its English heritage seriously; the Union Jack flies as high as the maple leaf. It is an island metropolis of some 230,000 citizens, sitting on the southeastern tip of 282-mile-long Vancouver Island.

Across the Strait of Juan de Fuca rise the snow-capped crests of Washington's Olympic Mountains. This nearness to America represents more than mere geography, it is also a symbol of the city's lifeblood—tourism. Each day ferries ply these waters bringing tourists both from Canada's southern neighbor but also from the homeland itself. Every year travelers numbering in the hundreds of thousands board ferries in Port

Angeles, Seattle, and Anacortes in the United States, or Tsawwassen and Horseshoe Bay on the Canadian mainland, for the relatively short trip to Vancouver Island and Victoria.

Now that mining and forestry have fallen on hard times, Victoria depends upon tourist dollars for its very survival. Unfortunately, there is a negative side to this. Entrepreneurs seeking their piece of the action have constructed the inevitable tourist traps, whose gaudy fronts scream for attention in an environment where natural beauty speaks louder than neon. But the blight is slight, and there is no evidence of uncontrolled growth. It is doubtful that Victoria's heritage would permit the rampant spread of honky-tonk capitalism.

Victoria's reputation as a peaceful and dignified town germinated in 1843 on a quadrangular plot of grassland measuring 330 feet by 300 feet. It was originally labeled Fort Victoria and despite its wilderness setting always had a gentle air. In 1858, author Alfred Waddington described the developing colony as a place where there is "No noise, no bustle, no gamblers ... a few quiet gentlemanly behaved inhabitants ... secluded as it were from the whole world."

As Victoria's reputation spread, as Europeans learned of the mild climate, unspoiled coastline, and rolling hills, British expatriates sailed to the city in search of a new life. Refinement, culture, and money arrived as part of their baggage. By its sixtieth birthday, Victoria had become both British and sophisticated. Bowling on the green, cricket, and afternoon tea were parts of daily life.

Today, tradition continues to play a role. Bowlers still dress in white; the crack of a cricket bat resounds across Beacon Hill Park. But it is afternoon tea that most captures the imaginations of tourists.

Victoria tearooms dot the city's sidewalks. My favorite is the Bantley House Tearoom, several blocks from downtown on Fort Street, away from the ringing cash registers of commercialism. Here you can enjoy your Earl Grey tea, freshly baked scones, tea sandwiches, and Devon cream, with only classical music and fresh flowers to distract you.

High tea arrived in Victoria aboard a ship from England and has become an important attraction, as well as tradition. However, Victoria is not without home-grown charms. The city's landscape pulses with life. Salmon, whales, sea lions, and seabirds teem along the coastline. Rambling hills sprout oak, maple, beech, linden, and fir. And gardens abound. Flowers blossom nearly year-round in plots as tiny as window boxes and as sprawling as the world-famous Butchart Gardens.

Realizing a limestone quarry produces two things, wealth and scarred land, Jennie Butchart, whose husband owned a properous pit, decided to enjoy the money but to heal the scars. In 1904, she ordered tons of topsoil spread on the floor of the quarry and sowed the seeds for a sunken garden. By 1929, the grounds were blooming with rose, Japanese, and Italian gardens.

Victoria is also blessed with an urban oasis that is a natural masterpiece. Winding paths thread through Beacon Hill Park's gardens and forests, wooden bridges cross tiny lakes, and park benches sit alongside lily ponds. From the top of Beacon Hill, the view captures blue-gray waters and the forests and mountains of Washington.

Victoria's pace is slow. It is a place to walk, to see, and to smell the flowers.

Other than the gardens and the park, most of what there is to see and do exists downtown near the harbor. For that reason, and because this is a compact city, good walking shoes are more valuable than an automobile.

There are a number of touristy attractions, some worth a visit. The Undersea Gardens and the Wax Museum beckon from their perches in front of the Parliament Buildings, and the exotic plants and birds at The Crystal Garden, located behind The Empress, are interesting. However, these sights fail to put travelers in touch with the city, whereas a walking/shopping tour, with stops at Victoria's museums, provide a better understanding of this town.

The first stop should be the Parliament Buildings. Stand outside the main entrance to join one of the regularly scheduled tours. The guides offer insight into the history of these magnificent structures. In the evening, return with your camera to take pictures of the buildings, which are brilliantly outlined in hundreds of lights.

Kitty-corner to the buildings sits the British Columbia Provincial Museum. It is one of the world's finest galleries of natural and human history. After touring the exhibits, walk down Government Street, where boutiques, bakeries, and specialty shops line the sidewalks.

At Fort Street, a turn in either direction is worthwhile. A walk toward the water to Wharf Street brings you to the Emily Carr Gallery, a tribute to one of the province's most respected artists. Continuing north, Wharf leads to several other galleries, as well as Bastion Square—a favorite center for shopping. Fort is also known as Antique Row. Walking east brings travelers past a number of antique shops and eventually to the Art Gallery of Greater Victoria and Craigdarroch Castle.

Victoria's double-decker buses, which depart from in front of The Empress, are the best way to see the neighborhoods and the shoreline. If you have an automobile and wish to tour on your own, begin by taking Douglas Street past the park to Dallas Road. Stay on Dallas Road, which changes names several times before it becomes Beach Drive. This route (also called Marine Drive) offers water and mountain vistas from atop steep bluffs. You might also wish to follow the marked route that leads to the very English neighborhood of Oak Bay.

Whatever your plans, you should relax and feel comfortable in Victoria, and be willing to explore. There is nothing about the city that is intimidating, and it has lots of experience with out-of-towners. No one is a stranger here.

A Practical Guide to the City

The Climate

Victoria lies in the rain shadow of the Olympic Mountains so it receives less rain than either Vancouver or Seattle. Temperatures are mild year-round: expect daytime temperatures in the 70s during the summer and in the 50s during spring and fall. December is the rainiest month.

Customs and Driving

Americans will pass through customs upon entering Canada. Aboard ferries, custom checks are handled upon disembarkation. It is prohibited to carry firearms into the country; pets must have certificates of rabies vaccination.

United States' citizens can drive within Canada on their state driver's license. All distances and speed limits are posted in kilometers. British Columbia has a seat belt law.

Currency

While most commercial outlets will take American money, it is wise and convenient to exchange at banks.

Your Clothes

While casual clothes are de rigueur, it is best to ask about the appropriate dress for specific restaurants and the theater.

Transportation

Victoria may be reached aboard the following ferries: Princess Marguerite (206-441-5560)—Seattle, Washington to Victoria, British Columbia, from May to October, four hours; Black Ball Transport (206-457-4491)—Port Angeles, Washington to Victoria, British Columbia, one and a half hours; Washington State Ferries (206-464-6400)—Anacortes, Washington, to Sidney, British Columbia, three hours; British Columbia Ferries (604-669-1211)—Tsawwassen, British Columbia, to Swartz Bay, British Columbia, one hour and thirty-five mintues, or Horseshoe Bay, British Columbia, to Nanaimo, British Columbia, one hour and thirty minutes.

VISITOR INFORMATION

For more information, write or call: Greater Victoria Visitor Information Centre, 812 Wharf Street, Victoria, B.C., Canada V8W 1T3 (604-382-2127).

POINTS OF INTEREST

ART GALLERY OF GREATER VICTORIA. 1040 Moss Street (604-384-4101). Canadian and European prints and drawings. An excellent collection of Japanese art.

BEACON HILL PARK. Located several blocks east of the Parliament Buildings and bounded on the west by Douglas Street. A sprawling urban oasis.

BRITISH COLUMBIA PROVINCIAL MUSEUM. Kitty-corner to the Parliament Buildings on the corner of Belleville and Government streets (604-387-3701). Vast collections depicting the natural and human history of British Columbia.

THE BUTCHART GARDENS. Located thirteen miles north of downtown Victoria (604-652-4422). Thirty-five acres of gardens. From May through September, the gardens are illuminated at night.

CRAIGDARROCH CASTLE. 1050 Joan Crescent. A large stone mansion built in the late 1880s.

CRYSTAL GARDEN. 713 Douglas Street (604-381-1213). An exotic environment of birds and plants.

EMILY CARR GALLERY. 1107 Wharf Street (604-387-3080). A collection of Emily Carr's works and memorabilia.

THE EMPRESS HOTEL. 721 Government Street. A majestic turn-of-the-century structure.

FORT RODD HILL. Some five miles northwest of downtown. Take 1A out of town. A tranquil park that looks out on Esquimalt Harbour and the Strait of Juan de Fuca. Gun emplacements. The oldest operational lighthouse on the west coast of Canada.

GOVERNMENT HOUSE. On Rockland Avenue, three blocks south of Craigdarroch Castle. Home of the provincial Lieutenant Governor. Lovely grounds and gardens.

HELMCKEN HOUSE. Just east of the Provincial Museum, behind Thunderbird Park (604-387-3440). Considered to be the oldest remaining residence in British Columbia.

THE MARITIME MUSEUM. 28 Bastion Square (604-385-4222). A collection of artifacts, ship models, and photographs depicting British Columbia's maritime heritage.

REGENTS PARK HOUSE. 1501 Fort Street. An 1885 Victorian Italianate home open for viewing from May through October.

SEALAND. Located at the Oak Bay Marina on Marine (Beach) Drive (604-598-3373). An interesting aquarium. Underwater exhibits, shows featuring sea lions, harbor seals, and killer whales.

RESTAURANTS OF NOTE

Victoria is not a haven for great restaurants, but the following represent good choices.

ARMADILLO DDINER. 1150 Cook Street (604-386-2166). This is a converted gas station, which has a funky 1950s look. Booth seating. Excellent burgers and soups. Homemade desserts.

CHEZ DANIEL. 2522 Estevan (604-592-7424). An intimate ambience. Modest decor. Out of the tourist way. French cuisine is very good. Wine list is commendable.

HERALD STREET CAFFE. 546 Herald Street (604-381-1441). Located in an old warehouse. Very popular with the locals. No reservations accepted. Long lines sometimes form outside the door. Noisy after 8 P.M. Fresh, consistently good foods.

METROPOLITAN DINER. 1715 Government Street (604-381-1512). Another restaurant that is popular with the locals. The food, from the pasta to the rabbit, is quite good.

PABLO'S. 225 Quebec Street (604-388-4255). Located in an old home. Elegant dining. The food is consistently good, particularly the rack of lamb. Good wine list.

PAGLIACCI'S. 1011 Broad Street (604-386-1662). While the pasta dishes are fresh and good, the ambience is the main attraction here. Victoria's hip young and trendy adorn this intimate spot. Live music is regularly scheduled. Tables are at a premium after 6 P.M.

WHERE TO STAY

ABIGAIL'S

It wears the fashions of Europe: half-timbers, window boxes, paned windows, symmetrical dormers, and colorful gardens. It is quite possibly the most elegant bed and breakfast north of San Francisco.

Abigail's represents the combined genius of Bill McKechnie and Stuart Lloyd. This is the same duo that developed The Beaconsfield Inn several years ago. At that time, The Beaconsfield was the class of the field in the Northwest and British Columbia. However, Abigail's upstages her bigger brother just slightly.

The Tudor-style building was first raised in 1930 to serve as an

Abigail's (Courtesy Abigail's)

apartment complex. Through the years the structure fell into disrepair. McKechnie and Lloyd, who have a keen sense of style and understand the essence of renovation, recognized the potential behind these stuccoed walls and purchased the structure in 1985. They gutted and stripped, installed new heating and plumbing, and created a classic sixteen-room bed-and-breakfast hotel.

The main floor creates an environment not often found in bed and breakfasts. Granite fireplaces and polished hardwood floors highlight the lobby and library, while burgundy leather furniture, vintage rugs, and a piano give the library additional touches of class. The breakfast room also has hardwood floors and, as is true of the entire inn, a lot of windows welcome natural light.

A curved, solid oak stairway winds up three floors to the guest rooms. All of the rooms have access to hallways but still there exists intimacy. Many of the accommodations have working fireplaces; all are furnished in antique oak and mahogany pieces. Smaller rooms have showers, while the larger ones have soaking tubs. In every instance, comfort is stressed.

"When you come right down to it," McKechnie says, "we are still selling a night's sleep. We try to make it a very pleasant one."

Inns such as Abigail's, with their expensive looks and professional staffs, bring a new level of excellence to bed and breakfasts. Abigail's deserves praise for her contribution.

*   *   *

Abigail's, 906 McClure Street, Victoria, B.C., Canada V8V 3E7 (604-388-5363). Sixteen guest rooms, all with private baths. Rates range from $75 to $155 Canadian (subject to change). VISA/MasterCard. Children with prior approval; no pets; smoking discouraged. Closed in January. Full breakfast served. Off-street parking. The inn is located just a few blocks from the Inner Harbour. From downtown, take Fort Street east to Vancouver Street. Turn right four blocks to another right on McClure Street. Abigail's is on the right at the end of a cul-de-sac.

THE BEACONSFIELD INN

She is the queen of Humboldt Street: a three-story mansion trimmed in burgundy, green, and cream. Well-tended gardens embellish her skirt; a wrought-iron fence marks her corner lot.

The Beaconsfield Inn is a picture of elegance and luxury. A peacock's flowing plummage graces the glass double doors, which welcome new arrivals into the sun-room. Sunlight splashes through stained-glass windows, washing the black-and-white checkerboard floor and wicker chairs in prisms of color.

The library is down a short hall, past one of the inn's fireplaces. Its black leather couches, pressed back oak chairs, hardwood floors, and red tile fireplace reflect the air of an English gentlemen's club. More than any other, this room conjures up the inn's fabled past.

The home was originally built in 1905 by millionaire R. P. Rithet as a wedding gift for his only daughter, Gertrude. The mansion became a gathering place for Victoria's socialites and gentry. In recent decades, however, the home suffered from neglect. Today, following complete restoration, the house again displays its original Edwardian luster.

Besides the plush common rooms, there are twelve guest accommodations. They radiate soft and subtle emotions, appealing to feminine tastes, which historically distinguish Edwardian decor. The rooms range in size from cozy—Willie's—to spacious—the Attic. All are furnished with antiques and some have fireplaces.

There are few inns outside San Francisco that equal The Beaconsfield in accommodations or style. In most ways, the inn is run like a first-class small hotel. This is particularly evident in the professionalism of the staff.

Still, there is a sense of family and togetherness here. This is best experienced at breakfast, when guests gather family style around a large table in the kitchen.

The Beaconsfield Inn (Kay Green)

Without overstating the case, The Beaconsfield is a class act. While those looking for a cozy, homey atmosphere may prefer less sophisticated surroundings, those seeking elegance, luxury, and service will be hard pressed to find a better inn.

*   *   *

The Beaconsfield Inn, 998 Humboldt Street, Victoria, B.C., Canada V8V 2Z8 (604-384-4044). Twelve guest rooms, all with private baths. Rates range from $75 to $150 Canadian (subject to change). VISA/MasterCard. Children with prior approval; no pets; smoking discouraged. The inn is located on a tree-lined residential street, just a few blocks from the Inner Harbour. There is private off-street parking. From Government or Douglas streets, take Humboldt Street away from downtown. The inn is on the left, at the corner of Humboldt and Vancouver.

HERITAGE HOUSE

No matter how civilized the city, there are travelers who just do not enjoy staying in town. Heritage House is just right for them. It is perfect for exploring Victoria by day, tasting its fruits in the evening, and getting away from its high rises at night.

The home is actually located in the bedroom community of Saanich, about ten miles from downtown. Its craftsman frame is dressed in brown

Heritage House (Lewis Green)

shake shingles and is embraced by flower gardens and tall evergreens. A broad veranda looks across the front yard as it sweeps downward towards a residential street.

A sea captain originally built the house in 1910, but in later years the home stopped being a home and eventually fell into disrepair. In 1980, Irvin and Doreen Stang purchased the derelict structure. They spent six months scraping, sanding, peeling, and painting before the house smiled again. Then in 1982, they put out the bed-and-breakfast welcome mat.

There are four upstairs guest rooms, which line a wide hallway. All boast a different atmosphere. Number one is modestly furnished but opens onto a balcony that overlooks the front yard. Number two is warm and rich, with a double brass bed and a wicker sitting area; number three has two twin beds and a stuffed sofa. The coziest room, and a great bargain, is number four, which was once a sleeping porch.

The most unusual aspect of Heritage House is its lack of a common sitting room for guests. The Stangs are talking about sharing their parlor, but as of this writing there is little opportunity for guests to socialize except at breakfast time. Of course, in good weather they can gather on the front porch or in the gardens, which boast lawn furniture.

This is a quiet and peaceful setting, ideally suited for home-style vacations. While not as luxurious as some bed and breakfasts, friendliness, comfort, and hospitality are in ample supply.

*   *   *

Heritage House, 1100 Burnside Road West, Victoria, B.C., Canada V8Z 1N3 (604-479-0892). Four guest rooms share two hall baths. Rates range from $50 to $54 Canadian (subject to change). No credit cards. No children under six; no pets; no smoking in the dining room. The inn is three miles north of downtown. From Victoria, take Douglas Street (Trans Canada Highway 1) to a right on McKenzie. Then turn left on Burnside. The inn is on the right, at the end of a hidden driveway.

PRIOR HOUSE

Since Victoria's first bed and breakfast opened its doors in the late 1970s, the scales of guest house accommodations have tipped heavily toward homeyness and away from elegance. But in recent years, several young and innovative entrepreneurs have brought a balance of comfort and luxury to Victoria's bed and breakfasts. Marianne Middleton took early membership in this group.

Her entrance into the hospitality business came in 1980 when she purchased a derelict mansion. Sitting behind a hedge, surrounded by lush grounds, the two-story Rockland residence was a shell of its former self. It was built in 1912 for Lieutenant Governor Edward Gawling Prior. However, multi-usage in the 1950s and the 1960s made Prior House unfit for even ghosts. Then Marianne began her rescue mission.

She restored the patina to the hardwood floors, oak paneling, and dark ceiling beams. Marble and tile fireplaces received cleanings, stained-glass windows came out from behind false walls, beveled-glass doors were shined and walls covered with fresh paint. Finally, she added vintage rugs, period antiques, stylish bric-a-brac, and silk flowers.

Today, Prior House boasts three upstairs guest rooms, with a fourth, The Gardener's Suite, scheduled to make its debut in late 1986 or early 1987. Each room features queen-size canopy beds and working fireplaces. The Blue Lace offers panoramas of the Strait of Georgia, with the white-capped Olympic Mountains rising in the distance, while the Chintz offers a large private bath.

While the Victoriana furnishing the parlor creates a luxurious setting, the dining room deserves special praise. Sunlight pours through stained-glass windows, adding layers of gold to a sideboard gleaming with silver trays and dishes. And potted ficas raise towers of green in front of the bay window, which curves before an antique table set with silver service, etched glasses, and hand-painted bone china.

Places such as Prior House help to balance Victoria's scales of hospitality. They provide travelers with elegant alternatives.

* * *

Prior House, 620 St. Charles, Victoria, B.C., Canada V8S 3N7 (604-592-9328). Four guest accommodations, two with private baths. Rates range

Prior House (Lewis Green)

from $95 to $145 Canadian (subject to change). No credit cards. No children; no pets; no smoking. The house is available for catered parties. From downtown, take Fort Street east to St. Charles. Turn right. The house is on the right.

Vancouver

Vancouver sits in a setting reserved for portraits and postcards. Its glass-and-steel temples overlook parks and gardens, beaches and marinas. A bevy of bridges reach out across bays and inlets. Mountains roll across the northern horizon, sacrificing their peaks to cold arctic fronts so the city may bathe in mild marine air.

It has been called "Canada's Playground" and the "Gem of the Pacific." Vancouverites are accused of working only so they can afford skiing in the nearby mountains, sailing in the waters of English Bay, and dining in the more than two thousand restaurants that dot the city.

Stamped on a peninsula and virtually surrounded by water and wilderness, it is not surprising that Vancouver enjoys the outdoors. Locals and visitors alike revel in nature's bounty when the snow flies or the sun comes out.

Do not get the idea, however, that Vancouver is a city more comfortable in hiking boots than high heels. This is a cosmopolitan and sophisticated metropolis, with world-class hotels, first-rate restaurants, and top-notch nightspots. Vancouver's 1.3 million citizens are multiracial and multicultural. As well as a strong British influence, the city boasts the second-largest Chinatown in North America and a dynamic Italian community. Every sidewalk sings with the accents of immigrants from India, France, Germany, and Greece.

This man-about-town image paints an unfamiliar face to most first-time visitors, though, and vacationers continue to flock here for beauty rather than substance. Fortunately, there is plenty of both. And with the coming and going of Expo 86, there are going to be more and more visitors wanting to sample the fruits and savor the wine.

GETTING TO KNOW VANCOUVER

DOWNTOWN

The city center underwent cosmetic surgery in 1979. That was the year urban landscape artist Arthur Erickson designed Robson Square—a three-block area that gave Vancouver a heart. Stretching from the Vancouver Art Gallery to the futuristic pyramid of the British Columbia Law Courts, the complex provides a haven for people to gather in. Within its terraced gardens, pools, and waterfalls, street performers entertain crowds of shoppers enjoying lunch, while gaily clad skaters glide across the ice rink and sightseers rest their feet.

Vancouver's main boulevards reach out from the Square like tentacles of a giant squid, connecting the complex with the city's major shopping and tourist attractions. The pace is slow and relaxed, more like San Francisco than New York, but the air is definitely one of sophistication.

Georgia Street bounds the Square on its northern edge. This wide, crowded thoroughfare is a gateway to several underground malls that offer shopping opportunities within the protective arms of concrete. In a city that receives more than its share of rain, these shopping playgrounds are well received. The malls are all within a few blocks of each other, beginning with the largest—the Pacific Centre Mall—which starts beneath the Four Seasons Hotel. Pacific Centre connects with the Vancouver Centre Mall; both sprawl below the Granville Mall.

While the malls offer the city's most convenient shopping, Robson-strasse features its most exciting. The aromas of imported cheeses and meats waft down Robson Street. Their source is a three-block area between Hornby and Bute. Here, delis, restaurants, bakeries, gift shops, and European boutiques cater to the senses and pocketbooks.

There is no doubt that Vancouver is a paradise lush with shops and eateries; however, travelers must always think views, which are the desserts of this city. As in Seattle, some of the best scenes can be captured from the water.

Walk north on Granville Street to the waterfront and the SeaBus ferry terminal (604-324-3211). The ferry ride across Burrard Inlet to North Vancouver presents panoramas of mountains, marinas, skyscrapers, and residential hillsides. Avoid rush hours, when queues are unending. If you are a romantic, make the ten-minute crossing in the evening. With the city turning pink in the setting sun and the moon beaming across the inlet, set sail for North Vancouver and dinner at Corsi Trattoria, an intimate slice of Italy just blocks from the North Vancouver terminal.

But if you prefer to meld views with more shopping, forget the SeaBus and turn right on Cordova Street before reaching the waterfront. The saucerlike observation deck of the Harbour Centre looms forty floors overhead. Here you can shop at the mall, take the skylift elevator to the deck, then dine at the Harbour House Revolving Restaurant.

GASTOWN

Both the Harbour Centre and the SeaBus terminal lie at the edge of Gastown, the place where Vancouver began in the 1860s. As the city moved eastward and the suburbs grew, this neighborhood fell on hard times. Today, however, urban renewal, with an eye on preserving historical heritage, has turned Gastown into a trendy tourist lure. Except for the restored buildings, the area has little to do with today's Vancouver, but it is fun and worth seeing once. There are a number of eateries, shops, and boutiques; many of them open on Sundays.

CHINATOWN

A far more interesting and human neighborhood is Chinatown, which sprawls about a half-dozen blocks southeast of Gastown along Pender Street. This is the shopping and cultural center for Vancouver's one hundred thousand Chinese.

The streets are lined with restaurants, markets hawking barbecued meats, and gift shops. The air is full of sing-song banter and the smells of herbs and exotic teas. Colorful Chinese lampposts and street signs lend an authentic mood. This is Vancouver's Oriental bazaar. Before leaving Chinatown, walk east from the shopping district into the residential section, a quiet neighborhood of old frame houses.

STANLEY PARK

In 1889, this one thousand-acre thumb of land, which divides the waters of English Bay and Burrard Inlet, was dedicated "To the use and enjoyment of people's of all colors, creeds and customs for all time." Lord Stanley would be pleased to learn that the park has served his wishes well. Besides being a symbol of Vancouver's marriage to nature, the park enjoys immense popularity.

The park is located on the western edge of downtown and is cradled by water on three sides. The main entrance lies at the foot of Georgia Street.

This urban wilderness is home to a forest of Douglas firs and western cedars, to the ducks at Lost Lagoon, and to swimmers and sunbathers enjoying the beaches. It is crisscrossed by roads and trails with enchanting names such as Lovers Walk and Cathedral Trail. And it is looped by the six-mile Seawall Promenade, which features views of the inlet and bay. On weekends the loop is crowded with strollers, joggers, and bicyclists.

There is a touch of Portland's Washington Park here because of the pristine environment, which surrounds a number of attractions. The Vancouver Public Aquarium features a killer whale and dolphin show. Plays are presented under the stars at Malkin Bowl. The zoo, the children's zoo, and a miniature railway are here. There are also tennis courts, swimming pools, and an eighteen-hole, pitch-and-putt course. Finally, for those who like a view with lunch or dinner, there is the Teahouse on Ferguson Point.

Stanley Park is no place for high heels or fancy shoes. The grounds are meant for walking, not human sacrifice. Groans of pain interrupt the tranquility. However, wheels can be appropriate. Bicycles and roller skates may be rented at Stanley Park Rentals, 676 Chilco Street.

GRANVILLE ISLAND

Granville Island is really a peninsula, located south of downtown across False Creek and beneath the Granville Bridge. It is a trendy version of Seattle's Pike Place Market.

A few years ago the warehouses that dot this triangular-shaped landscape buzzed with industry. Today, the blue collars of the working class have been replaced by Hawaiian shirts. Instead of the sounds of manufacturing, there are the sights and smells of hip restaurants, specialty shops, galleries, and the Granville Island Public Market.

The island is also a good place for leisurely walks along the boardwalk. The city rises across the waters of the inlet, and shopping or eating always beckons visitors to take breaks.

Parking here is like trying to squeeze King Kong's feet into Cinderella's slippers. A better alternative to driving is to take either the Number 20 bus from the Granville Mall downtown, and transfer to the Number 51, or the twelve-passenger False Creek Ferry from the Vancouver Aquatic Center at the eastern edge of Sunset Beach Park, which docks near Bridges, a popular restaurant on the Island.

SOUTH OF DOWNTOWN

The cosmopolitan flavor of downtown gives way to scenic drives, greenbelts, cultural centers, and quiet neighborhoods on the south side of False Creek and English Bay. A good way to explore the area is to begin at Vanier Park. The seaside park is located near the Burrard Street Bridge. Inside its boundaries are the MacMillan Planetarium, Vancouver Museum, and Maritime Museum.

After visiting the park, wind around its edges, past Hastings Mill Store—Vancouver's first store and post office—to Marine Drive. English Bay sparkles to the north, while downtown rises in the northeast.

Marine Drive is also known as Scenic Drive: it is a picture of tree-lined shores, blue-gray waters, and distant mountains. The drive leads to the University of British Columbia, known for the Nitobe Japanese Memorial Gardens, the Rose Garden, the Museum of Anthropology, and the Fine Arts Gallery.

Leave Marine Drive at 41st Avenue and drive to Oak Street. Van Dusen Botanical Gardens await some four blocks north. This fifty-five acre greenbelt flourishes with ornamental plants, flowering trees, and fragrant shrubs. Another flowery delight beckons east on 33rd Avenue. Queen Elizabeth Park boasts views, as well as the exotic plants in the Bloedel Conservatory.

NORTH OF VANCOUVER

Mountains, canyons, views, and mansions roam the hills of North and West Vancouver. Cross the Lions Gate Bridge at the northern tip of Stanley Park and take Marine Drive east to Capilano Road. Going north, the first stop is the 450-foot-long Capilano Suspension Bridge—one of the world's longest—which sways 230 feet above the Capilano River and Canyon below.

Then drive north to Cleveland Dam, a good place to hike and picnic. Continue on to Grouse Mountain. In winter there is good skiing here but there does not have to be snow on the slopes to take the Superskyride—an aerial tramway that climbs to the mountain's summit. Be sure to ride facing the city for the best views. There are tourist facilities on the mountaintop.

A PRACTICAL GUIDE TO THE CITY

THE CLIMATE

Vancouver's weather is much like Seattle's except on the average the Canadian city receives more precipitation and more cloudy days.

CUSTOMS AND DRIVING

Border customs is mainly quick and easy—usually just a few questions about place of birth, residence, and nature of business. (This applies to United States citizens entering Canada.) As for driving, seat belts are compulsory in British Columbia. In Vancouver, private vehicles are banned from the Granville Mall, from Nelson to Hastings on Granville Street.

CURRENCY

To guarantee current rates, it is best to exchange foreign currency at banks.

YOUR CLOTHES

Casual clothes are acceptable during the day but more formal attire is appropriate for restaurants and nightclubs. Vancouver is the one place north of San Francisco, except for rare instances in Seattle, where you can strut your stuff in designer fashions and feel part of the crowd. It is always practical to pack sweaters, light jackets, and an umbrella.

PUBLIC TRANSPORTATION

Buses provide a convenient and inexpensive means of transportation. (A new rapid transit system that combines bus and rail began in 1986.) Call 604-324-3211. The Hustle Bus, 604-273-0071, transports arrivals from the airport to downtown.

VISITOR INFORMATION

For more information, write or call: Greater Vancouver Convention & Visitors Bureau, #1625-1055 West Georgia Street, P.O. Box 11142, Royal Centre, Vancouver, B.C., Canada V6E 4C8 (604-682-2222).

POINTS OF INTEREST

THE ARTS, SCIENCES & TECHNOLOGY CENTRE. 600 Granville Street (604-687-8414). A hands-on museum that melds art, science, and technology.

CAPILANO SUSPENSION BRIDGE. Capilano Road, North Vancouver (604-985-7474). One of the world's longest suspension bridges. Spectacular views of the gorge below.

CHINATOWN. The Oriental bazaar is located on West Pender, between Carrall and Gore.

CLEVELAND DAM. Capilano Road, North Vancouver. Good views. Hiking and picnicking.

EXHIBITION PARK. Hastings and Renfrew streets. Home to a giant fair in August called the Pacific National Exhibition. There is also a race track on site, which runs from late spring until early fall.

GASTOWN. Bounded by Carrall and Richards along Water Street. The birthplace of Vancouver. Shopping and dining.

GRANVILLE ISLAND PUBLIC MARKET. Located under Granville Street Bridge on the south side of False Creek. Fresh produce, seafood, and meat.

GRANVILLE MALL. Granville Street between Nelson and Hastings. A pedestrian mall ideal for shopping.

GROUSE MOUNTAIN. Capilano Road, North Vancouver. Downhill skiing, horseback riding, hiking, and views. Aerial tramway to the top.

HARBOUR CENTRE. Located at the west end of Gastown between Cordova, Seymour, and Richards streets. Shopping. Views from the observation deck.

H. R. MACMILLAN PLANETARIUM. 1100 Chestnut Street, Vanier Park (604-736-4431). Frequently changing programs.

LIGHTHOUSE PARK. Located five miles west of Lions Gate Bridge. Hiking through wooded trails. A lighthouse. Views from rocky bluffs of the Strait of Georgia.

LYNN CANYON SUSPENSION BRIDGE. Lynn Canyon Park, North Vancouver. (Take Lynn Valley Road from Trans-Canada 1.) The bridge stretches some 270 feet above Lynn Creek.

MARITIME MUSEUM. 1905 Ogden Street, Vanier Park (604-736-7736). A collection of model ships, marine relics, and artifacts.

MUSEUM OF ANTHROPOLOGY. 6393 Northwest Marine Drive, University of British Columbia (604-228-3825). A collection of Northwest Coast Indian Art and artifacts, including totem poles.

NITOBE MEMORIAL GARDENS. Tip of Point Grey, University of British Columbia (604-228-3928). Japanese gardens.

QUEEN ELIZABETH PARK. 33rd Avenue and Cambie Street (604-872-5513). Highest point in the city. Views, rose garden, arboretum, Bloedel Conservatory, tennis, and pitch-and-putt golf.

ROBSONSTRASSE. On Robson between Hornby and Bute. Shopping European-style.

STANLEY PARK. Located at the northwest tip of downtown (604-681-1141). Hiking, bicycling, picnicking, swimming, tennis, and golf. Also visit the zoo, miniature train, summer theater, and aquarium.

VAN DUSEN BOTANICAL GARDENS. 37th Avenue and Oak Street (604-266-7194). Ornamental plants, sculptures, and man-made lakes. A forest interpretive center.

VANCOUVER ART GALLERY. 800 West Georgia Street (604-682-8621). Works of Emily Carr. Contemporary exhibitions.

VANCOUVER MUSEUM. 1150 Chestnut Street, Vanier Park (604-736-7736). Historical exhibits.

VANCOUVER PUBLIC AQUARIUM. Stanley Park (604-682-1118). Performances by killer whales and dolphins. Some eight thousand species of sea life on exhibit.

WHYTECLIFFE PARK. Marine Drive, West Vancouver. Scuba diving, swimming, and picnicking. Views. Marina.

RESTAURANTS OF NOTE

The following restaurants are suggested on the basis of recommendations by Vancouverites and fellow travel writers.

CAFE DE MEDICI. 1025 Robson Street (604-669-9322). Elegant and comfortable setting. The veal and the pasta highlight the menu.

CEDARS OF LEBANON. 1190 Robson Street (604-684-0821). Intimate. A family operation. Personable service. Good food.

CORSI TRATTORIA. 1 Lonsdale, North Vancouver (604-987-9910). An intimate and romantic environment. Simple decor. Fresh seafood. Excellent veal. If you are really hungry, try the feast or the L'Abbuffata.

HY'S MANSION. 1523 Davie Street (604-689-1111). Located in a heritage mansion. Elegant dining. Steak and seafood. Good service. Expensive.

JINYA. 567 West Broadway (604-873-5040). Cozy and simple with excellent Japanese food.

A KETTLE OF FISH. 900 Pacific Street (604-682-6661). Good fresh fish.

LE CROCODILE. 818 Thurlow Street (604-669-4298). Excellent French fare. Very good soups and desserts.

THE ONLY. 20 East Hastings Street (604-681-6546). A tiny Chinese operation with just two counters for seating. Fresh fish and low prices.

WILLIAM TELL. 773 Beatty Street (604-688-3504). Elegant and expensive. May be Vancouver's finest restaurant. Service and food superb.

YANGTZE. 1542 Robson Street (604-687-7142). Pleasant surroundings. Good Mandarin food.

WHERE TO STAY

GABLES GUEST HOUSE

Bed and breakfasts are rare in Vancouver. Strict zoning codes prevent them from multiplying. So when you find one that is located only a few blocks from the city's shopping, financial, and hotel district, it is akin to uncovering buried treasure.

Gables Guest House sits just ten minutes from Vancouver's best. It is located on a wide and busy boulevard, in a contemporary-looking, two-story house, which was actually built at the turn of the century. Since October 1985, the business has been operated by two women who recently moved to Vancouver from Calgary.

Gables Guest House (Lewis Green)

The house is surprisingly large and features five guest rooms in addition to a living room, dining room, and large kitchen. The living room is an intimate setting with overstuffed furniture and a home entertainment center, while the adjacent dining room is bright and cheery.

One of the five guest rooms sits off the kitchen. It boasts lots of natural light and is well furnished, including a sitting area, color television, and two beds. However, since it offers a hall bath beyond the kitchen, its location is not for travelers who cherish their privacy.

The remaining four guest rooms are upstairs. Numbers one and two are both sunny, and open onto private balconies. In addition, number two is large and features an antique look. Number three has a kitchenette, while number four is a quiet and private abode. All of the rooms have queen-size beds, which are covered with comforters.

Despite its street-side setting, Gables is quiet inside. But even if street noise invaded the premises, this location makes the house ideal for exploring the city.

*   *   *

Gables Guest House, 1101 Thurlow Street, Vancouver, B.C., Canada V6E 1W9 (604-684-4141). Five guest rooms share two hall baths (one on each floor). Rates are $50 Canadian (subject to change). VISA/MasterCard/JCB. Children with prior approval; no pets; smoking in living room only. Off-street parking available. From Highway 99 entering downtown from the Granville Bridge, take Seymour to a left on Smithe. Take another left on Thurlow, which is one way. The house is on the right.

WEST END GUEST HOUSE

What a surprise! Usually I can tell quite a lot about an inn by the quality of its brochure and the rates for its rooms. Thin-papered, hand-

West End Guest House (Lewis Green)

folded commercials and low charges usually indicate a double whammy. That is not the case here. Despite its modest pamphlet and extremely reasonable rates, West End is a classic home with first-class accommodations.

The three-story 1906 frame house sits on a tree-lined street that once boasted dozens of charming homes just like this one. Today, however, apartment buildings surround West End. Still, the neighborhood radiates a residential calm.

The current owners of West End, George Christie and Charles Weigum, purchased the building in 1985. Prior to buying this house, they were the innkeepers at nearby Gables. Once they moved here, George and Charles undertook extensive refurbishing, including the development of the home's third floor. They opened the house to guests in October 1985.

A dining room and adjacent living room make up much of the main floor. Plants fill a bay window and roses dot beige wallpaper. The rattan chairs and cedar trim combine to create an exotic setting.

There are four guest rooms occupying the second floor and two on the third. The second-floor rooms have a homey air, with floral-print wallpaper and comfortable furnishings. A more urban, contemporary look dominates the spacious third-floor rooms. In every room, robes and hand-knit slippers (made by Charles' mom) are provided for the guests.

The breakfast menu changes daily and always features a special entrée. And at this writing, the innkeepers are making plans to offer guests who make advanced arrangements five-course gourmet dinners. (Reservations will be necessary nightly.)

In addition to its comfort and charm, West End is located within walking distance of downtown and Stanley Park.

*   *   *

West End Guest House, 1362 Haro Street, Vancouver, B.C., Canada V6E 1G2 (604-681-2889 or 681-5979). Six guest rooms share three and a half baths. Rates are $50 Canadian (subject to change). VISA/MasterCard/American Express/JCB. Children with prior approval; no pets; smoking in designated areas only. Off-street parking available. From Highway 99 after crossing the Granville Bridge, take Seymour to a left on Smithe, which runs into Haro. Cross Thurlow Street. The house is on the left between Jervis and Broughton.

Index to Places

CALIFORNIA

Calistoga   43
Chico   92
Eureka   104–5
Ferndale   104
Fort Bragg   104
Georgetown   75–76
Geyserville   44–45
Grass Valley   76
Healdsburg   44
Ione   75
Jackson   75
Mendocino   104
Murphys   74–75
Napa   43
Nevada City   76
Point Reyes Station   103
Red Bluff   92
Sacramento   91
St. Helena   43
San Francisco   10–40
Santa Rosa   44
Sonora   74
Sutter Creek   75

OREGON

Ashland   155–56
Astoria   137–38
Bandon   134–35
Brookings   133–34
Eugene   157
Florence   136

Gold Beach   134
Grants Pass   156–57
Jacksonville   156
Newport   136
Portland   124–32
Seaside   137
The Dalles   157–58

WASHINGTON

Bainbridge Island   198–99
Columbia River Gorge   239–40
Coupeville   199
Lake Chelan   241–42
Langley   200
Leavenworth   242
Lopez Island   201
Mount Rainier National
    Park   240–41
Olympic National Park   225
Orcas Island   201
Port Angeles   226
Port Townsend   226
San Juan Island   200–201
Seattle   178–97
Spokane   242–44
Whidbey Island   199–200

BRITISH COLUMBIA

Victoria   260–72
Vancouver   273–83

Index to
Bed-and-Breakfast Inns

CALIFORNIA

San Francisco   10-40
  The Archbishops
    Mansion   23-25
  The Bed and Breakfast
    Inn   25-26
  Casa Arguello   26-28
  Hermitage House   28-29
  Inn on Castro   29-31
  The Inn San
    Francisco   31-33
  The Monte Cristo   33-35
  The Spreckels
    Mansion   35-37
  Union Street Inn   37-39
  Victorian Inn on the
    Park   39-40
Wine Country   41-72
  The Ambrose Bierce House (St.
    Helena)   52-53
  Bartels Ranch (St.
    Helena)   54-55
  Beazley House (Napa)   48-49
  Camellia Inn
    (Healdsburg)   66-68
  Chestelson House (St.
    Helena)   55-56
  Cinnamon Bear (St.
    Helena)   57-58
  Coombs Residence
    (Napa)   49-50
  Foothill House
    (Calistoga)   63-64

Forest Manor
  (Angwin)   61-63
Grape Leaf Inn
  (Healdsburg)   68-69
Haydon House
  (Healdsburg)   69-71
Hope-Merrill House
  (Geyserville)   71-72
The Ink House (St.
  Helena)   58-59
Melitta Station Inn (Santa
  Rosa)   64-66
The Old World Inn
  (Napa)   51-52
Villa St. Helena (St.
  Helena)   59-61
Gold Country   73-90
  American River Inn
    (Georgetown)   79-80
  Dunbar House
    (Murphys)   81-82
  The Foxes (Sutter
    Creek)   82-84
  Gate House Inn
    (Jackson)   84-85
  The Heirloom (Ione)   86-87
  Murphy's Inn (Grass
    Valley)   87-88
  Red Castle Inn (Nevada
    City)   89-90
The Interstate 5
  Corridor   91-102

Amber House
  (Sacramento)   95–96
The Briggs House
  (Sacramento)   96–98
Bullard House
  (Chico)   98–100
The Faulkner House (Red
  Bluff)   100–101
The North Coast   102–22
  Carter House
    (Eureka)   121–22
  The Gingerbread Mansion
    (Ferndale)   119–21
  Glendeven (Little
    River)   110–11
  The Grey Whale Inn (Fort
    Bragg)   118–19
  The Headlands Inn
    (Mendocino)   113–14
  Holly Tree Inn (Point Reyes
    Station)   109–10
  Joshua Grindle Inn
    (Mendocino)   114–16
  The Victorian Farmhouse
    (Little River)   111–13
  Whitegate Inn
    (Mendocino)   116–18

OREGON

Portland   124–32
  Allenhouse   129–31
  Corbett House   131–32
The Oregon Coast   133–54
  The Boarding House
    (Seaside)   151–52
  Cliff Harbor Guest House
    (Bandon)   144–45
  Endicott Gardens (Gold
    Beach)   142–44
  Guest House at Gardiner by the
    Sea (Gardiner)   147–48
  Ocean House
    (Newport)   148–49

Rosebriar Inn
  (Astoria)   152–54
Sea Dreamer Inn
  (Brookings)   141–42
Spindrift (Bandon)   145–47
Three Capes
  (Oceanside)   149–51
Oregon's Heartland   155–76
  Campus Cottage
    (Eugene)   170–72
  Chanticleer Inn
    (Ashland)   161–63
  Griswold Bed & Breakfast
    (Eugene)   172–73
  The Handmaidens' Inn (Grants
    Pass)   169–70
  Mattey House
    (McMinnville)   173–75
  McCully House Inn
    (Jacksonville)   168–69
  The Miners Addition
    (Ashland)   163–64
  The Morical House
    (Ashland)   164–66
  Romeo Inn
    (Ashland)   166–67
  Williams House (The
    Dalles)   175–76

WASHINGTON

Seattle   178–97
  Chambered Nautilus   191–92
  Chelsea Station   192–94
  Galer Place   194–95
  Gaslight Inn   188–89
  Roberta's   189–91
  The Williams House   195–97
Washington's Islands   198–224
  Blue Heron (West Sound, Orcas
    Island)   215–16
  The Bombay House (Bainbridge
    Island)   204–5
  Caroline's (Langley, Whidbey

Island) 205-6
Channel House
  (Anacortes) 214-15
Guest House (Greenbank,
  Whidbey Island) 209-11
Home By The Sea (Clinton,
  Whidbey Island) 211-12
Kangaroo House (Eastsound,
  Orcas Island) 216-18
Lone Lake (Langley, Whidbey
  Island) 206-7
Pillars By The Sea (Freeland,
  Whidbey Island) 212-13
San Juan Inn (Friday Harbor,
  San Juan Island) 221-22
The Saratoga Inn (Langley,
  Whidbey Island) 208-9
Turtleback Farm Inn (Orcas
  Island) 218-19
Wharfside Bed & Breakfast
  (Friday Harbor, San Juan
  Island) 223-24
Woodsong (Orcas
  Island) 219-21
The Olympic Peninsula 225-38
  Arcadia Country Inn (Port
    Townsend) 229-30
  The Cooney Mansion
    (Cosmopolis) 237-38
  Hastings House Inn (Port
    Townsend) 231-32
  The James House (Port
    Townsend) 232-34
  Lizzie's (Port
    Townsend) 234-35
  The Tudor Inn (Port
    Angeles) 235-37
Inland Washington 239-58
  Blakely Estates (Spokane)
    255-56
  Brown's Farm
    (Leavenworth) 252-53
  Cascade Mountain Inn
    (Concrete-Birdsview) 256-58

French House
  (Pateros) 249-51
Fotheringham House
  (Spokane) 254-55
Haus Rohrbach Pension
  (Leavenworth) 251-52
Inn of the White Salmon (White
  Salmon) 247-48
Whaley Mansion
  (Chelan) 248-49

BRITISH COLUMBIA

Victoria
  Abigail's 266-68
  The Beaconsfield
    Inn 268-69
  Heritage House 269-71
  Prior House 271-72
Vancouver 273-83
  Gables Guest House 280-81
  West End Guest
    House 282-83

Also of interest from The Globe Pequot Press:

"Guide to the Recommended Country Inns" series:
West Coast • Rocky Mountain Region • Arizona, New Mexico, and
Texas • South • Midwest • Mid-Atlantic States and Chesapeake
Region • New England

The Seattle Guidebook

Alaska's Southeast: Touring the Inside Passage

Camping Alaska and Canada's Yukon:
The Motorist's Handbook to North Country Campgrounds and Road-
ways

Journey to the High Southwest: A Traveler's Guide

Guide to the National Park Areas: Western States

Guide to the National Park Areas: Eastern States

Bed and Breakfast in California

Bed and Breakfast in New England

Bed and Breakfast in the Mid-Atlantic States

Bed and Breakfast in the Caribbean

Rocky Mountain National Park Hiking Trails

Parks of the Pacific Coast

Colorado: Off the Beaten Path

How to Open and Operate a Bed & Breakfast Home

Available at your bookstore or direct from the publisher. For a free
catalogue or to place an order, call 1-800-243-0495 (in Connecticut,
call 1-800-962-0973) or write to The Globe Pequot Press, 138 West
Main Street, Chester, Connecticut 06412.